SAINT THERESA

THE
HISTORY OF HER FOUNDATIONS

Reproduced by kind permission of Mr E. Nash

PORTRAIT OF SAINT THERESA

From the portrait in the possession of the Discalced Carmelite Nuns of Valladolid

Father Jerome Gracian, being her Superior, caused the original to be made, as he says, "to mortify her and because otherwise there would have been no portrait of her at all," by a lay Brother, Juan de la Miseria, who was but a poor artist. It is said that when the Saint saw it, she said laughingly to the artist, "God forgive you, Brother John; after making me go through no one knows what, you have turned me out ugly and blear eyed."

SAINT THERESA

THE

HISTORY OF HER FOUNDATIONS

Translated from the Spanish

by

SISTER AGNES MASON, C.H.F.

with a Preface by

The Rt. Hon. SIR E. M. SATOW, G.C.M.G.

Cambridge
at the University Press
1909

CAMBRIDGE UNIVERSITY PRESS
Cambridge, New York, Melbourne, Madrid, Cape Town,
Singapore, São Paulo, Delhi, Tokyo, Mexico City

Cambridge University Press
The Edinburgh Building, Cambridge CB2 8RU, UK

Published in the United States of America by
Cambridge University Press, New York

www.cambridge.org
Information on this title: www.cambridge.org/9781107655454

First published 1909
First paperback edition 2011

A catalogue record for this publication is available from the British Library

ISBN 978-1-107-65545-4 Paperback

PREFACE

IN the first volume of the works of Saint Teresa de Jesus, published by the pious care of D. Vicente de la Fuente, are contained the autobiography of this wonderful woman and the series of chapters in which she narrates the incidents that accompanied her successful efforts to establish convents and monasteries of the reformed rule of the Carmelite order. The juxtaposition is significant. In the one we have the history of a soul, in its growth towards maturity, in the other that of the practical work accomplished by the personality in which that soul was enshrined, after it had emerged from the chrysalis stage into that of the perfect saint. Taken together they teach the invaluable lesson that holiness of character on this earth finds its aim and object realized in practical work for the good of others.

Teresa de Ahumada as she was called in the world was born, the daughter of pious parents, at Avila in the year 1515. Her father, she tells us, was of great charity to the poor and pitifulness for the sick and for servants. No one had ever been able to persuade him to own a slave, for he pitied them too much; one belonging to a brother of his being in the house, he was as good to her as if she had been one of his children. He said that her not being free overwhelmed him with pity. He was most truthful; no one ever heard him swear or grumble; and most honourable. Her mother a woman of many virtues, and a great invalid. Though of great beauty it was never heard that she made account of it; sweet-tempered and highly intelligent. She took great care to teach her children to pray, and to be devoted to Our Lady and to certain saints. Teresa was one of twelve children, all of whom, she says, except herself, resembled their parents in virtue. One of her brothers, nearest herself in age, was the dearest, though she loved them all and they her. They used to read together the lives of the saints, and when she saw what sufferings they underwent for God, she thought they bought very cheaply the privilege of going to enjoy Him, and wished greatly to die like them, not because she loved Him, but in order so speedily to enjoy the great happiness that she read there was in heaven. She consulted with her brother about the means of obtaining it. They agreed to go to the land of the Moors, begging their way thither, in order that there they might be beheaded. They were frightened when they found in what they read that punishment and glory lasted for ever; they used to talk much of this, and took pleasure in repeating 'for ever, for ever, for ever.' "When I saw it was impossible to go where they would kill me for God's sake, we arranged to become hermits, and in a garden attached to the house we tried, as well as we could, to build us hermitages of little stones, which immediately tumbled down, and so we found no way of attaining our desires. I gave alms as well as I could, but it was little. I sought to be alone in order to say my prayers, which were many, especially the rosary, to which my mother was much attached, and she made us so also. I was very fond of playing at convents with other little girls and of pretending to be nuns, and it seems to me that I wished to be one, though I did not wish it as much as the other things of which I have spoken." The simplicity and sincerity of the saint are transparent in these stories of her childhood.

Her mother died when she was twelve years of age. The saint records how after this she fell under the influence of a relation, and fell away from her early religious inclinations. Then she contracted a friendship with a wise and holy nun, and was gradually attracted towards a conventual life. At the age of eighteen she entered the noviciate at the monastery of the Incarnation close to Avila, and took the veil a year later. Then she fell ill, and had to be taken home. Her life was despaired of, and she returned to the Convent, where for three years she lay helpless, till at last her health was restored to something like what it had been before. There she remained for another eighteen years, becoming more and more dissatisfied with the semi-worldly life of a nun under the relaxed rule, till at last she was inspired with the will to issue forth and live a life of poverty and self-denial in the first convent founded by herself in accordance with the ancient strict rule of the Carmelites, dedicated to Saint Joseph of Avila. The following pages relate the history of the other foundations she carried out in the sequel, up to that of Saint Joseph of Saint Anne at Burgos, whence she started to return to Avila, but died at Alba de Tormes, literally, so say the pious chroniclers, in the odour of sanctity, on the 4th October 1582.

The most famous of books of devotion was written by a monk for the use of monks, but it has nevertheless for centuries past been the favourite spiritual reading and inseparable companion of innumerable lay people, both men and women. Saint Teresa, in the course of her narrative, turns aside to instruct the prioresses how to govern those whom they have to guide in the path of perfection. She dwells on the necessity of endeavouring to conform the will to the Divine Will, of sacrificing self-love and self-satisfaction, of complete detachment from all worldly things, on the danger of sentimentalism and exaggeration in religion, to which she thinks women are especially prone. She does not shun the use of homely language, as where in speaking of obedience, she says "if you have to be employed in domestic duties, as for instance in the kitchen, remember that the Lord goes about among the pots and pans, helping you in all things."

The counsels of Saint Teresa are of practical value, not only for nuns, but also for those who live in the world, not only for Roman Catholics, but also for ourselves.

E. M. SATOW.

JULY 1909.

TRANSLATOR'S NOTE

THE History of the Foundations is a sequel to Saint Theresa's *Life*, written by herself in obedience to her confessor. The *Life* brings the story up to the completion of the first foundation, that of St Joseph's Convent at Avila; and here the History of the Foundations takes it up.

While the *Life* is the more important work as regards instruction in the spiritual life, the Saint's great treatise on Prayer being intercalated between two narrative chapters, the Foundations is the more interesting from the point of view of secular history. The same qualities which make St Theresa's teaching priceless to those who desire instruction in spiritual things give also a very high value to her accounts of ordinary matters. She not only loved truth for its own sake and spoke it readily against herself; but she also was able to see it as few people can, in both inner and outer matters. She had a quite extraordinary insight : an absolute accuracy in noting detail, together with a keen logical faculty for appreciating the bearings of the facts she noted. And she also possessed in a high degree the power of putting her thoughts into words clear and vigorous, if not always concise. She was determined that her readers should understand exactly what she meant, in matters of any importance, and she cared little what might be thought of her style.   If need be, she would write parenthesis within parenthesis to guard against misunderstanding.   If there are passages which are really obscure, this is, no doubt, because, as she says, she wrote in odd scraps of time and never read over her MS.   Hampered though she was by the psychology of the time, which she obediently and humbly accepted, although her own was far in advance of it, she yet describes (e.g.) the difference between one state of trance and another just as a modern observer describes the behaviour of plant tissues under different stimuli.   And what she could accomplish in matters so exceedingly difficult to speak of at all, she effected with ease in the ordinary matters of life.   So that her accounts of events and people and things are of quite first-rate interest, both directly and indirectly.   Directly, for the reasons given above ; indirectly, from the light they throw on her own character and on what Dr Sidgwick would have called the Common Sense of the time : its moral judgements and ways of looking at things.

Spain, too, in her time—the time of Mary and Elizabeth, which in England is so familiar to us—is not known to us ordinary English people as it deserves to be.   And among contemporary writings there can be none, I think, which give more vivid pictures, more interesting or more amusing glimpses of Spanish life, not only in the cloister, but in all sorts of society: for the Saint, in her journeys and negotiations, came across all sorts, from the king to the peasant.

For the following translation a better text has been available than could be had before 1881 ; for in 1880 Don Vicente de la Fuente, who had already been working at Saint Theresa's writings for twenty years or more, brought out a facsimile reprint of the original : and of this he made most careful use for his edition published in 1881. Of the considerable number of restored readings in this edition, a good many are of real and substantial interest; and taken together, they shew clearly that the Saint's writings had, from early times, been "edited" with a view to the edification of the faithful. It is from this 1881 edition, with la Fuente's notes, that the present translation has been made.

My thanks are due first of all to the Bishop of Gibraltar for much help and encouragement without which I should probably not have attempted the work : to Mr Cunninghame Graham for help in shewing each Foundation on the map, and for other information : to Major Martin Hume for two valuable notes : to Miss Ellen Conant, for photographs which she made on purpose for this book: to Messrs Garzon for permission to reproduce their photograph of Granada : to Señor Arteaga for his translations of a few obscure passages : but above all to Sir Ernest Satow, who has allowed me to consult him on all sorts of difficulties, especially in the translation, sparing no time or pains to get the smallest point right. I know that there are clumsinesses, and I cannot hope that there are no slips in the translation : but that there are not more is owing to his knowledge and care.

✠ AGNES MASON.

Community of the Holy Family.

July 1909.

CONTENTS

Contents

Contents

LIST OF ILLUSTRATIONS

The Foundation at Granada was made in January 1582, under St Theresa's direction, by Sister Anne of Jesus.

BOOK OF THE FOUNDATION
OF HOUSES OF REFORMED CARMELITES
MADE BY SAINT THERESA

The original MS. in the Escorial bears in a clear hand-writing the following inscription: ORIGINAL BOOK OF THE HOUSES FOUNDED IN SPAIN BY THE GLORIOUS VIRGIN SAINT THERESA DE JESUS ACCORDING TO HER REFORMED RULE, *written with her own hand : Library of the Escorial, for a perpetual memorial.* The original is, however, not kept in the library, but in the relic chamber.

PROLOGUE

Besides what I have read in many places, I have seen by experience the great blessing which it is for a soul to continue in the practice of obedience. In this, I believe, lies the secret of continually making progress in virtue and covering the progress with humility: in this lies our security from the doubt, which it is well for us mortals to be exposed to during this life, whether we are wandering from the path to heaven. In this is to be found that peace so highly prized by souls who desire to please God. Because if they have really given themselves up to this holy obedience, and yielded their judgement to it, seeking to have no other opinion than that of their confessor, or, if they are in Community, that of their Superior, the devil ceases to assail them with his incessant disquietudes, because he finds that he comes off loser rather than gainer thereby. Likewise our own restless motions, so eager to get their own way and even to overmaster our good sense in matters of liking,—even these cease when they remember that the will is definitely surrendered to God's will, through being subjected to one whom they have chosen as God's representative.

Since His Majesty, in His goodness, has given me light to recognize the great treasure contained in this precious virtue, I have sought, however weakly and imperfectly, to possess

myself of it. Often, however, I am hindered by the scant
virtue which I find in myself: for I see that it does not suffice
for some things which are commanded me. May the Divine
Majesty supply what is lacking for this present task !

While I was at St Joseph's at Avila, in 1562, the same
year in which this Convent was founded, I was ordered by
Father Fray Garcia de Toledo, a Dominican, who was then my
confessor, to write an account of its foundation[1], together with
a good many other matters, which, if it should ever see the
light, whoever reads it will read there. Now, eleven years
later, in 1573, at Salamanca, my present confessor, Maestro
Ripalda, Father Rector of the Company of Jesus, having seen
the book about the first foundation, thought it would be to our
Lord's service if I wrote the story of the seven other convents
which, by our Lord's goodness, have since then been founded,
and also the beginning of the monasteries of Barefoot Fathers
of the primitive Rule : so he ordered me to do it.

It seemed to me an impossibility, because of the many
things I had to do, letters and other works which I was bound
to go on with because my Superiors had laid them upon me.
I was commending the matter to God, feeling it press rather
hardly, because I am good for so little, and have such poor
health that even without this additional burden I often felt
hardly able to endure my labours, poor creature that I am. Then
our Lord said to me, "My child, obedience gives strength[2]."
May it please His Majesty that so it may prove, and may He
give me grace enabling me to write, to His glory, the great
things He has done for our Order in these foundations !

[1] [This book was her *Life*. Tr.]
[2] In the original MS. these words are underlined and enclosed between
vertical lines.

CARMELITE MONASTERY AT AVILA

It may be held for certain that they will be related with absolute truthfulness, without the least exaggeration—to the best of my knowledge—but exactly as they took place. For even in the most trifling matters I would not tell an untruth for anything in the world. And in this which I am writing to the praise and glory of God, it would be altogether against my conscience; and I should feel that I was not only wasting time but deceitfully handling the things of God ; and it would be a grave treason that He should be offended thereby instead of being honoured. May it please His Majesty, lest I do so, to hold me in His hand !

Each foundation shall have its separate story ; and I will try to be brief, if I can : but my style is so heavy, that, with all my good will, I am afraid I shall both weary myself and be wearisome. My daughters, however, to whom this writing will belong after my death, will be able to put up with this for the love they bear me. In nowise herein do I nor have I any reason to seek my own profit, but His praise and glory alone ; for there will be found herein many things for which to praise Him. May it, then, please our Lord that anyone who reads this may be very far from attributing any of these things to me ; for that would be against truth : but let them pray to His Majesty to forgive me for having profited so little by all these gracious acts. My daughters have much more cause to complain of me for this than to thank me for what has been done in the foundations. Let us all, my daughters, give thanks to the Divine goodness for all the great things He has done for us. For the love of Him, I beg of everyone who may read this, one Hail Mary to help me to come out of purgatory and to attain to the vision of Jesus Christ our Lord, who liveth and reigneth with the Father and the Holy Ghost, world without end. Amen.

My memory being very poor, I have no doubt that I shall leave out a good many really important things, and mention others which might well be left out: indeed, it will all be what could be expected from my stupidity and clumsiness, together with my scanty leisure for writing.

I am bidden also, if opportunity presents itself, to treat of some matters concerning prayer, and of the delusions about it which sometimes keep Sisters who practise it from making progress. I submit myself without reserve to what is held by our Mother the Holy Roman[1] Church, and I intend that learned and spiritual men shall see this writing before it comes into your hands, my sisters and daughters. I begin in the name of the Lord, invoking the aid of His glorious mother, whose habit I wear, though unworthy, and of my glorious father and lord St Joseph, in whose house I am: for to him is dedicated this convent of Barefoot nuns, by whose prayers I have been continually aided. In the year 1573, on the 24th of August, which is the Day of St Louis, King of France.

To God be praise.

---

[1] The word *Romana* appears to be written over the *y* (*and*); and both *y* and *Romana* appear to be written by a different hand, in a writing thicker and of later date.

JESUS MARY

CHAPTER I

How this and the other Foundations came to be made.

For five years after the foundation of St Joseph's at Avila,
I lived there : and I think, as I now see, that they were
the most peaceful in my life ; for my soul often greatly misses
the tranquillity and repose I then enjoyed.

During that time there came in to be nuns several girls,
young in years, whom the world, as it seemed, held already as
its own, to judge from their style of dressing and living: but
the Lord drew them away quickly from those vanities and
brought them to His house, endowing them with such perfection that it covered me with confusion. They made up the
number of thirteen, the number which it had been determined
not to exceed. I delighted to be among souls so holy and
pure, who had no other care but how to serve and praise our
Lord. His Majesty sent us there, without our begging, all
that we needed: and whenever we were in want, which was very

seldom, their joy was the greater. It made me praise our Lord to see such high virtues, especially their disregard of everything but His service.

I, who was Superior there, never remember troubling my head about our necessities, for I held it for certain that the Lord would not fail those who had no other care but to please Him. And if sometimes, when there was not enough for us all, I said that those must have it who most needed it, each thought that she was not one, and so it went on until God sent enough for us all. As regards the virtue of obedience—which I prize most highly, although I did not know how to practise it until these servants of God taught me so that I could not fail to learn if I had any goodness in me, —I could tell of a great many things which I saw them do. Here is one which presents itself to me at this moment. One day when we were in the refectory, we were helped to cucumbers, and to me was given a very poor one, all rotten inside. To test her obedience, and without really intending it to be done, I called one of the cleverest and most sensible Sisters there, and told her to go and plant the cucumber in a little garden we had. She asked me, Was she to plant it upright or sideways? I said, Sideways. She went and planted it without its ever coming into her head that the cucumber could only decay; for doing it in obedience blinded her natural understanding so that she thought it a very reasonable thing to do. Another time I happened to give one of them six or seven incompatible pieces of work, and she accepted them in silence, esteeming it possible to do them all.

We had a well of very bad water, according to those who had tried it; and it seemed impossible to get it to flow, because it was very deep. When I sent for workmen to attempt it, they laughed at me, saying that I should be throwing away money for nothing. I asked the Sisters what they thought. One of them said, "Let us try: our Lord has to provide us with someone to bring us water and with something with which to provide him food: it would cost His Majesty less to give us water in the house, and therefore He will not fail to do so." I, considering the great confidence and boldness with which she said this, could not doubt; and I ordered the work to be done, contrary to the wish of the man who understood springs and had experience of water. And it pleased the Lord that we should lead a pipe from the well which brought us quite sufficient water, and fit to drink: and they have it still. I do not relate this as a miracle—for I could tell other things of that sort—but to shew what faith those Sisters had; for all took place just as I have told it: nor is it my first intention to praise the nuns of those monasteries; for by the Lord's goodness, they all continue like this up to the present day. And of these things and many others I could write at great length, and indeed not unprofitably, for it might sometimes animate those who come after to imitate them: but if this should be to the Lord's service, the Superiors might order the Prioresses to write it.

So I[1] *miserrima* was living among these angelic souls—for indeed they seemed to me nothing less—and they hid from me no fault, even of thought. The graces and great aspirations and detachment which the Lord gave them were very great. Their joy was to be in solitude, and they assured me that they never had enough of being alone; and so they disliked visits, even from their relations. The one who was

[1] In the original, the words *esta miserable* are scratched out and *yo* substituted in an apparently different hand.

able to spend most time in a hermitage thought herself the most lucky.

When I considered the strength and excellence of these souls, and the courageous spirit, certainly passing that of women, which God gave them to suffer and to serve Him, I often thought that it must be for some great purpose that the Lord committed to them such treasures. But what has since come of it never entered my mind; for there was no beginning which could have suggested the idea, and it would have seemed an impossible thing. However, as time went on, my desires to be of some good to some soul somewhere went on increasing; and I often felt like someone who is in charge of a great treasure and desires that all should benefit by it, but his hands are tied so that he cannot give it out. So it appeared to me my soul was bound; for the favours which the Lord gave it during those years were very great, and it all seemed ill bestowed upon me. With my own poor prayers I continually served the Lord, and I took pains to get the Sisters to do the same and to care for the good of souls and the increase of the Church. Everyone who had to do with them was always edified; and in this my great desires found their satisfaction.

After about four years, or I think rather more, there came to see me a Franciscan Friar, Fray Alonso Maldonado, a great servant of God. He had the same desires as I for the good of souls, and he was able to put them in practice, which made me envy him greatly. He had lately come from the Indies: and he began to tell me of the many millions of souls who were perishing there for lack of teaching, and he gave us a sermon and address exhorting us to do penance, and he went away. He left me so sorely distressed at the perdition of so many souls that I could not contain myself; I betook myself with many tears to a hermitage, and cried to our Lord, beseeching Him to grant me the means of doing something to gain some soul for His service, since the devil was carrying off so many; and that my prayer might avail something, since that was all I could give. I greatly envied those who for the love of our Lord could employ themselves in this work, even if they suffered a thousand deaths. And so it is that when we read in the lives of the saints how they converted souls, it raises in me more ardour, more emotion, and more emulation than all the martyrdoms which they suffered: for this is the disposition which the Lord has given me. And it seems to me that He values one soul which, through His mercy, we might gain for Him by our labours and prayers, more than all other services we could render Him.

Well, while I was going on in this great distress, one night when I was in prayer, our Lord appeared to me in His accustomed manner, and shewing me much affection, as though He wished to comfort me, He said, "Wait a little, my daughter, and you shall see great things." These words remained so deeply imprinted on my heart that I could not put them from me: and though for all my thinking over them I could not guess what this might be, nor see any way in which to imagine it, yet they left me greatly comforted and with full assurance that those words would come true. But in what way never entered my imagination. Another half-year, I think, went by in this way; and then came to pass what I will now relate.

CHAPTER II

How our Father General came to Avila, and what came of his Visit.

Our Generals always live at Rome, and none of them had ever come to Spain[1], so it seemed impossible that one should come now : but as nothing which our Lord wills is impossible, His Majesty appointed that what had never yet been done should be done now. When I knew of it, I was sorry, I think; because as I have already said in the history of the foundation of St Joseph's, that house, for the reason I there gave, is not subject to the Carmelite Friars. I feared two things : first, that he would be angry with me, and reasonably so, not knowing how everything had come about ; next, that he might order me to return to the monastery of the Incarnation, which keeps the mitigated Rule. This would have been a distress to me, for several reasons which I need not give. One will suffice, which is that there I could not keep the strictness of the primitive Rule, and that there are more than a hundred and fifty Sisters there ; and certainly when there are fewer, there is more order and quiet.

Our Lord ordered these things for me better than I thought : for the General is so great a servant of God and so wise and learned that he considered it a good work, and in no respect did he shew himself displeased with me. His[2] name is Fray

[1] Two Generals had been to Spain and held Chapters there : Fray Juan Alerio at Barcelona in 1324, and Fray Raimundo de Grasa at Perpignan in 1354. But these Chapters were only for the Kingdom of Aragon, where the Order of Carmelites was widely extended.

[2] The surname *Rubeo* is latinised from *Rossi*, after the fashion of the time. He came to Spain in 1566, at the instance of Philip II., and with a Bull of St Pius VI., who had recently come to the Papacy. He held a

AVILA

from photograph by Messrs Laurent & Co.

Juan Bautista Rubeo de Ravenna, and he is a person very highly thought of in the Order, and justly so.

Well, when he arrived at Avila, I got him to come to St Joseph's; and the Bishop thought good that all honour should be shewn to him, as if it had been to himself. I gave him an account of everything with all sincerity and simplicity; for it is natural to me to deal thus with Superiors, come what may, since they stand in the place of God, and with confessors too; and I should not feel my soul safe, if not. And so I gave him an account of my soul, and almost of my whole life, very bad though that is. He comforted me much, and assured me that he would not order me to leave St Joseph's. It gave him pleasure to see our way of living, a copy, however imperfect, of the early days of our Order; and to see that the primitive Rule was kept in all its strictness. (For in the whole Order there was not another house where they kept this and not the mitigated Rule.) He desired that this beginning should go forward; and so he gave me complete licences to found more monasteries, with penalties to prevent any Provincial from hindering me. I did not ask for these; but he understood from what I told him of my manner of praying how great were my desires of doing what I could that some soul might draw nearer to God.

I did not seek for myself these means of service; rather it would have seemed to me absurd: for I saw very well that a poor woman with so little influence as I had could do nothing. But when such desires come to the soul, it is not in its power to put them away. The ardent desire to serve God and the Faith make possible that which according to natural

Provincial Chapter in Andalusia, and then went on to Castile. Fray Alonso Gonzalez was appointed Provincial, Fray Angel de Salazar remaining Prior at Avila.

reasoning is impossible. And so when I saw our Reverend General's great wish that more convents should be founded, I seemed to see them already established; for, remembering the words which our Lord had said to me, I saw now some beginning of what up till then I could not understand.

I felt it very much when I saw our General returning to Rome. I had conceived a great affection for him, and I seemed to be left very desolate. He shewed me the greatest affection, and much kindness; and when he could get leisure, he used to come to St Joseph's to treat of spiritual matters, for he was a person to whom the Lord must have given great graces. It was a great comfort to us to listen to him on these subjects.

The Lord Bishop, Don Alvaro de Mendoza, who is always thinking how he can help those whom he sees to be desirous of serving God more perfectly, tried, even before the General's departure, to get his leave to have some monasteries of Barefoot Friars of the primitive Rule founded in his diocese. Other people also asked for this. He would have wished to do it; but he met with opposition in the Order, and so, not to stir up strife in the province, he let it drop for the time.

When some days had passed, I reflected how necessary it was, if there were to be convents of nuns, to have Friars also of the same Rule; and seeing how few there were in the province, it seemed as if they were dying out. Commending the matter greatly to our Lord, I wrote to our Father General a letter begging this of him in the best way I could. I gave him reasons why it would be greatly to the service of God, and said that any difficulties which might arise were not serious enough to be a reason for leaving undone so good a work; and I set before him the service he would do to our Lady, to whom he had a great devotion. It must have been she who brought this to pass. He was at Valencia when my letter came into his hands, and thence—as one who desired the stricter observance of the Rule of the Order—he sent me licences to found two monasteries. In order that there might be no opposition, he stipulated for the consent of the present and the late Provincial, which was very difficult to obtain: but now that I saw the chief thing done, I hoped that the Lord would do the rest; and so it was, for by the aid of the Lord Bishop, who made our cause his own, both of them agreed to it.

Well, now that I was encouraged by having the licence, my anxieties increased; for there was no Friar that I knew of in the province who would take up the task, and no secular person willing to make such a beginning. I did nothing but pray to our Lord that at least one person might be stirred up to it. Neither had I a house, nor means to get one. Behold a poor Barefoot nun with no help on any side, except from the Lord, furnished with licences and with good desires, but with no possibility of putting them in practice! But my spirit did not fail, nor my confidence that since the Lord had given the one He would also give the other: indeed all seemed possible to me; and so I began to set to work.

Oh greatness of God! And how Thou shewest Thy power in giving boldness to an ant! And how, O my Lord, it is not Thy fault, but the fault of our cowardice and pusillanimity that those who love Thee do not carry out great works! Because we never make resolutions without being full of a thousand fears and human cautiousness, therefore Thou, O my God, dost not work Thy wonders and great deeds. Who is more desirous to give, if Thou dost find anyone willing to receive, or who more ready to accept services at Thine own cost! May it please Thy Majesty that I may have done Thee some service, and may I not have a greater account to give for all that I have received. Amen.

CHAPTER III

How the Convent of St Joseph at Medina del Campo
came to be planned.

WELL, when I was thinking anxiously over all these things, it occurred to me to seek the help of the Fathers of the Company of Jesus, who were in high esteem at Medina. As I have said in the account of the first foundation, these Fathers had guided my soul many years: and I always hold them in special reverence for the great good which they did me. I wrote what our Father General had enjoined on me to the Rector there, who happened to be the one who had heard my confessions for many years; as I said, although I did not give his name: it was Baltasar Alvarez, who is now Provincial. He and the others said they would do what they could in the matter: and they made great efforts to obtain the leave of the townspeople and of the Bishop—for it is always difficult to get leave to establish a house founded without endowment: and so the business took some days to arrange.

To see to this there went a priest, Julian of Avila, a great servant of God, singularly detached from the world and much given to prayer. He was chaplain of the convent in which I was living, and God had given him the same desires that He had given me; and so he has been a great help to me, as will presently be seen. Well, though I now possessed the licence, I had no house nor a penny to buy one, nor any securities on which to get credit. If the Lord did not give it, how could a pilgrim like me possess it? The Lord ordained that a very excellent girl for whom there had not been room at St Joseph's, hearing that another house was to be established,

MEDINA DEL CAMPO

from photograph by Messrs Laurent & Co.

came and asked me to take her in there. She had some money, very little, not enough to buy a house, but enough to rent one, and to help with the expenses of the journey. So we looked out for a hired house. With no more than this to depend upon, we set out from Avila, two nuns from St Joseph's and I, and four from the Incarnation, the convent of the mitigated Rule where I lived before St Joseph's was founded. Our chaplain, Father Julian of Avila, was with us.

When it was known in the town, there was a great deal of talk. Some said I was mad; others would wait to see the end of this nonsense. To the Bishop, as I was afterwards told, it seemed great folly, although at the time he did not let me know this, because, having a great affection for me, he did not like to hamper me or cause me pain. My friends gave me their opinion roundly : but I attached little weight to it ; because to me that which they thought hazardous seemed so easy that I could not persuade myself that it could fail to turn out well.

When we left Avila I had already written to a Father of our Order, Fray Antonio de Heredia, to buy me a house. He was at that time Prior of St Anne's, a monastery of monks of our Order at Medina. He opened negotiations with a lady who was much attached to him, who had a house. Its walls were in a ruinous state, all but those of one apartment ; but it was in a very good situation. She was so kind as to promise to sell it without demanding security for the payment, on the strength of his word alone : for we could not have given any security. The Lord ordered all this for us : and so they made the agreement. The walls of the house were in such a ruinous state that we had to hire another until it was repaired, for there was a great deal to be done to it.

Then at the end of our first day's journey, it was already
dark, and we were tired because of our bad equipage. As we
were nearing the town by way of Arévalo, there came out to
meet us a friend of ours, an ecclesiastic, who had got rooms
for us in the house of some devout women : and he told me
privately that we should not get our house, because it was
near a monastery of Augustinians, and they would resist our
taking possession, and there would certainly have to be a law
suit. O, válame Dios ! when Thou, O Lord, art pleased to
give courage, how little does any opposition avail ! Rather
it seemed to encourage me, because I felt that if the devil
was already beginning to make a disturbance, it must be
because this convent would be to the Lord's service. Anyhow I asked him to say nothing, in order not to disturb my
companions, especially the two[1] from the Incarnation ; for the
others would have gone through any troubles for my sake.
One of those two was sub-prioress there, and the Sisters did
all they could to stop her. Both of them were of good family;
and they came against their relations' wish, for all the Sisters
thought it absurd ; with ample reason, as I afterwards saw.
For when it is the Lord's will that I should found one of these
houses, nothing seems able to get into my head which seems
to me sufficient to make me give it up, until I have actually
done it. Afterwards the difficulties present themselves to me
all at once, as will presently be seen.

When we got to the lodging, I found that there was in the
place a very great servant of God, a Dominican friar, who had

---

[1] The Saint had said above that she took four from the Incarnation.
Doubtless two of these were less to be trusted than the other two. [Or,
more probably, the explanation is that, according to a limitation imposed
by the General, she took only two, technically speaking : but two more
had gone from the Incarnation to St Joseph's a few days before her departure. *Ribera*, bk. ii. ch. vii. Tr.]

heard my confessions while I was at St Joseph's. As in my account of that foundation I have spoken much of his goodness, I will here only say his name, the Master Fray Domingo Bañez. He is very learned and wise, and I always took his advice. And to his thinking this was not so difficult a work as others that I had had to do : for the more anyone knows of God, the more easily he does God's work : and because he knew how gracious God had been to me in certain matters, and from what he had seen in the foundation of St Joseph's, it all seemed to him quite possible. It gave me great encouragement when I saw him ; for I felt sure that with the help of his advice all would go well. Well, when he came, I told him in great secrecy what was going on : and he thougth we could speedily come to terms with the Augustinians. But to me any delay was distressing because I did not know what to do with so many nuns. All who were in our lodging soon heard everything : and so we all spent an anxious night.

Early in the morning the Prior of our Order, Fray Antonio, arrived, and said that the house which he had agreed to purchase would do for us, and had an entrance which we could turn into a little chapel with the help of some hangings. We determined to go there: to me at least it seemed the best thing : for the shorter the time the better, as we were out of our own convents ; also, having learned my lesson in the first foundation, I feared some opposition. So my plan was that before any one got wind of it we should already have taken possession ; so we determined to do it at once. The Master Father Fray Domingo agreed with us.

We arrived at Medina del Campo on the Vigil of the Assumption at midnight. We alighted at St Anne's, so as not to make any noise, and went on foot to the house. It

was just the time when the bulls which were to fight next
day were being driven to the enclosure, and it was a great
mercy that some of them did not toss us. As for us, our
minds were so taken up that I never thought of such a
thing; but the Lord, Who is always mindful of those
who are desiring—as I certainly was—to serve Him, kept us
safe.

We arrived at the house and went into the *patio*[1]. The
walls looked to me very ruinous, but not so bad as by day-
light I afterwards saw them to be. The Lord seems to have
been pleased to blind that good Father so that he should
not see how unfit it was to place the Blessed Sacrament
there.

I went to see the entrance. There was a good deal of
earth to be shovelled out, it had an open roof, and the walls
were unplastered. The night was short; and we had only
brought with us a few hangings, I think three, which were not
nearly enough to cover the length of the entrance: and I
did not know what to do, for I saw it was not fit to set an altar
there. It pleased the Lord—for He desired that it should be
done at once—that the lady's steward had in his house a
great deal of tapestry of hers, and some blue damask bed-
hangings: and she had told him to give us anything we
wanted; for she was very good. When I saw such good
garniture, I gave praise to the Lord, and so did the others.
We did not know what to do for nails, nor could we buy them
at that hour; but we hunted in the walls, and at last with a
good deal of trouble we found plenty. Some put up the
hangings; we nuns cleaned the floor: and we worked with

---

[1] [The house was built as an ordinary Spanish house, round a square
court-yard or *patio*, into which all the windows looked. The entrance
was something like that of an old English inn.   Tr.]

such a will that when morning dawned the altar was set up, and the little bell in a passage; and mass was said at once. This sufficed to take possession : but as at the time we did not know this, we also had the Blessed Sacrament reserved. We nuns saw mass through the chinks of a door opposite; for there was nowhere else for us to be.

Up to this time I was very happy : for it is my greatest pleasure to see one more church where the Blessed Sacrament is reserved. But my joy was shortlived; for when mass was over, I went to look at the patio through a little window, and I saw that all the walls were fallen to the ground in places, so that it would take many days to repair them.

Oh válame Dios ! what anguish filled my heart when I saw His Majesty set in the street in a time of so much danger from these Lutherans[1] ! And together with this arose in my mind all the difficulties which those who disapproved of our venture had spoken of, and I saw clearly that they were right. It seemed impossible to go forward with what I had begun : because, just as up till now all had appeared easy, since it was for God that it was done, so now I was tempted to think so little of His power that it seemed as if I had never received any grace from Him : my own littleness and impotence was all that was present to my mind ; and when success depended on such a wretched creature, what could be hoped for ? I think I could have borne it better had I been alone ; but what was so dreadful was to think of my companions having to go home after the opposition which their departure had raised. It seemed to me too, that now this beginning had gone wrong, there was no possibility of all that I

[1] [Especially at Medina del Campo, in which, being one of the greatest foreign marts in Spain, there would always be merchants from the countries which had broken with Rome. Tr.]

had understood our Lord meant to do further. And an
added fear at once arose that what I had understood in
my prayer was a delusion. This was not my least distress,
but my greatest ; because it made me exceedingly afraid that
the devil had deceived me. Oh my God ! what a thing it is
to see a soul whom Thou art pleased to leave to suffer !
Certainly, when I remember this misery and some others
which I have suffered in these foundations, it seems to me
that the bodily sufferings, severe though these have been,
were nothing to be compared to them.

Of all this burden of distress which weighed me down
I said nothing to my companions, because I did not want to
give them any more distress than they already had. I went
on in this unhappiness until the evening, when the Rector of
the Jesuits sent a Father to see me, who greatly comforted
and encouraged me. I did not tell him all my troubles, but
only the distress which it was to find ourselves in the street.
I began to see about finding a hired house, at whatever cost,
to go into while this one was being repaired. Then I began
to take comfort from seeing how many people came to the
house, and that none of them found fault with our folly ;
which was a mercy : for I felt certain they would take away
from us the Blessed Sacrament. Now I see that I was foolish
and others were thoughtless in not consuming the Host : but
at that time I thought that all would be undone if we did so.

For all we could do, we could not find a house in all the
place : so I spent very troubled days and nights ; for although
I always had men to watch over the Blessed Sacrament, I was
always anxious lest they should go to sleep ; so I kept getting
up in the night to look through the window, and I could see
well because there was very bright moonlight. During all
those days a great many people came ; and not only were

they not offended, but it moved their devotion to see our Lord again in an outhouse: and His Majesty, never tired of humbling Himself for our sake, did not seem to desire to leave it. It was not until after a week that a merchant who lived in a very good house, seeing our necessity, asked us to move to the upper part of it, to dwell there as in our own house. There was a great gilded hall there which he gave us for a chapel; and Doña Elena de Quiroga, a lady who lived close to the house which we had bought, a great servant of God, said she would help me to begin at once to make a chapel for the Blessed Sacrament to be reserved, and would also fit up the house for our enclosure. Other people gave us plenty of money for our food: but it was this lady who helped me most.

This being arranged, I began to be in peace, because where we were, we could be completely enclosed; and we began to say the office. And the good Prior made great haste about the house, taking a great deal of trouble. For all that, the work took two months, but it was done so well that we were able to live there fairly comfortably for some years; after that our Lord provided something better for us.

While I was there, I was always thinking over the monasteries of friars; and since, as I said, I had not one friar, I did not know what to do. So I determined to talk to the Prior about it in strict confidence, to see what he would advise; and so I did. When he heard of it he was very glad, and promised to be the first himself. I took this for a jest, and so I told him: for although he was a very good Brother, recollected and very studious and a lover of his cell, and was learned, I thought he would not have the energy, nor be able to endure the necessary hardships; for he was delicate, and not used to them. He earnestly assured me that he

could : and he declared that, for some time, the Lord had
been calling him to a stricter life ; and so he had determined
to join the Carthusians, and they had already promised to
receive him. For all this, I was not quite satisfied, although
I was glad to hear it ; and I asked him to let us put it off for
some time, during which he should practise the things which
he would have to promise : and so he did. A year passed,
during which he had to endure so many troubles and the persecutions of so many false accusations that it seemed our Lord
desired to prove him : and he bore it all so well and made
such progress that I gave praise to our Lord, and I thought
His Majesty was preparing him for this.

A little later, there happened to come a young Father who
had been studying at Salamanca. Another priest accompanied him, who told me great things of the life which this
Father lived. His name was Brother John of the Cross.
I gave thanks to our Lord. When I talked to the Father,
I was much pleased with him. He told me that he also
meant to become a Carthusian. I told him my projects, and
earnestly begged him to wait until the Lord should give us
a monastery, pointing out that if he meant to better himself,
it would be a great gain to do so within his own Order, and
much more to the Lord's service. He gave me his word that
he would, if he had not to wait too long.

When I saw that I already had two friars [1] to begin with,
I thought the thing already done. However, as I was not
altogether satisfied with the Prior, and also we had nowhere
to commence in, I waited some time.

The Sisters kept growing in favour with the people, and
gaining their affection ; and, as I felt, justly : for they

[1] "A friar and a half" St Theresa used to call them, because of the
diminutive stature and youth of St John of the Cross.

thought of nothing but how each could best serve our Lord. They went on exactly as at St Joseph's at Avila; for they had the same Rule and Constitutions. The Lord began to call some in the neighbourhood to take the habit; and He bestowed on them such great graces that it amazed me. May He be blessed for ever. Amen. For He seems to require nothing but to be loved, to love.

CHAPTER IV

Which treats of certain graces which the Lord bestows on the nuns in these convents, and gives counsel to the prioresses in dealing with them.

As I do not know how long a life the Lord may give me, nor what time for writing, and now I seem to have a little, it seems a good thing, before going any further, to set down some instructions so that Prioresses may understand their office, and may guide their nuns to the greater profit of their souls, although less to their own satisfaction.

It must be remembered that, when I was ordered to write the history of these foundations, there were—besides the first, that of St Joseph's at Avila, whose story was written immediately—seven monasteries founded, by the help of our Lord, including that of Alba de Tormes, which was the last of them. The reason why more were not founded was that my superiors set me to another work, as will be seen later.

It is from considering the course of spiritual affairs in those monasteries during these years that I have seen the need of saying what I am going to say. May it please the

Lord that it may succeed in meeting that need! And since the things which have taken place are not delusions, people's minds must not be alarmed: for, as I have said elsewhere in certain little writings[1] I have made for the Sisters, if we proceed in obedience and with a clear conscience, the Lord never allows Satan so free a hand that he can injure our soul by deceiving us. On the contrary, it is he who finds himself deceived; and, as he is aware of this, I do not believe he does us so much harm as our own imaginings and evil tempers, especially melancholic tempers. Women are weak by nature, and the self-love which prevails in us is very subtle. Thus many people have come to me, both men and many women, as well as the nuns of these houses, in whom I could plainly see that, without intending it, they often deceived themselves. I quite believe that the devil may take part in this to mock us: but of the many of these women whom, as I say, I have myself seen, there are none that I know of who, by the Lord's goodness, have not been kept safe. May be He is pleased to try them with these failures that they may come out wiser. Prayer and perfection, through our sins, are so decayed in the world that it is necessary to make this plain statement. For if people are afraid to walk in this way even when they do not see its dangers, how will it be if we should shew them some? Although indeed there is really danger everywhere; and so long as we live we shall always have to walk in fear, and to entreat the Lord to teach us and not to forsake us. But, as I think I have said before, if there is one way which is less dangerous than another, it is the way of those who attain most nearly to keeping God in mind and to seeking to live in perfection.

O my Lord, when I see that Thou dost often deliver us even from the dangers into which we run by going against Thy

[1] [*The Way of Perfection*, ch. LXX.   Tr.]

will, how can I believe that Thou wilt not deliver us when we are caring for nothing but to please Thee and find our joy in Thee? I can never believe this. It may be that God for some other hidden ends may permit certain things to fall out thus and thus. But good has never brought evil. So that such falls may serve to make us walk on our way better, to please our Spouse the better and find Him the sooner, but not to make us give up the journey; to animate us to walk bravely through the rugged passes of this life, but not to make us cowards for the rest of it. For if we walk humbly, in the end, through God's mercy, we shall arrive at that city of Jerusalem where all that we have endured will appear little or nothing in comparison with our joy there.

Well, when these little dovecotes of our Lady the Virgin began to be filled, His Divine Majesty began to shew His greatness in these poor women, weak in themselves, but strong in their desires and in their detachment from all created things. And this must be what most closely unites a soul with its Creator, given a conscience void of offence. This condition I need hardly mention: because if the detachment is sincere, I think it is not possible for a soul that has it to offend the Lord: and as the soul in all its sayings and doings is unchangeably centred in God, so His Majesty seems to be unwilling to withdraw His presence from it. This is what I see at the present time, and I can say it with all truth. Let those who come hereafter and read this be in fear: and if they do not see what may be seen now, let them not put it down to the times; for it is always a time when God will give great graces to anyone who serves Him truly. And let them try to see whether there is any failure in this, and amend it.

I have sometimes heard it said about the early days of Orders that, because those our Saints of old were the foundations of the edifice, the Lord gave them more abundant graces. So it is. But it must be remembered that they were the foundation for those who should come after. And if we who are now living did not fall away from the holiness of the past, and those who shall come after us likewise, the building would always stand firm. What good is it to me that the Saints of old were such as they were, if I, coming after, am so bad that I leave the building ruined with my evil ways? For it is plain that new comers do not think so much about those who lived a long time ago as about those whom they actually see. A fine thing indeed to put down my badness to my not being one of the first; and not to lay to heart the difference there is between my life and virtues and that of the founders to whom God granted such great graces! Alas, my God! how crooked are these excuses, how glaring these delusions!

I am not speaking of the founders of Orders: for, as God chose them for a great work, He gave them greater grace. It is a distress to me, O my God, to be so bad, and of so little use in Thy service; but well do I know that it is my own fault that Thou givest me not the graces which Thou gavest to those who have gone before me. It grieves me, O Lord, when I compare my life with theirs; and I cannot say it without tears. I see that I have wasted what they laboured for; but in no wise can I complain of Thee. Nor is it right that any of us should complain; but that if we should see our Order in any way decaying, we should each try to become a stone such that it may serve for building up the edifice again: for the Lord will give His aid in this.

Then to return to what I was saying—for I have made a long digression—the graces which the Lord gives in these houses are so great that, though there may be one of the Sisters whom the Lord is leading by the way of meditation only,

all the rest are arriving at perfect contemplation, and some
advanced as far as raptures. To some the Lord gives grace in
a different manner, together with revelations and visions
which can clearly be known to have come from God. At
the present time there is not one house where there are not
one or two or three such nuns. I know very well that this is
not what sanctity consists in: nor is it my object only to praise
them, but rather to shew that the instructions which I intend
to write down are not beside the mark.

CHAPTER V

In which certain cautions are given concerning prayer and revela-
    tions. It is profitable reading for those who are occupied in
    active work.

I DO not intend or suppose that what I am now going to
say will be so precise as to afford an infallible rule: that
would be folly in matters so difficult. But, as there are
many ways in the way of the Spirit, it may be that I shall
succeed in explaining some points of some of them. If those
who are not walking by that way do not understand me, that
will be because they are going by another way. And if I do no
good to anybody, the Lord will accept my good will; for He
knows that if I have not experienced it all myself, yet I have
observed it in other souls.

In the first place I want to shew, according to my poor
understanding, what is the essence of perfect prayer: for I
have met with some people who suppose that the whole
matter consists in thoughts; and if, even though by doing

themselves great violence, they can for the most part keep their thoughts on God, they at once think themselves spiritually minded. And if they cannot help being distracted, even though it may be on account of right things, they are at once dreadfully unhappy and think themselves lost. Learned men do not suffer from these mistakes and ignorances—though indeed I have met with one who did so—but we women need to be warned of all such ignorances. I do not deny that it is a gift from the Lord to be able to meditate continually on His works, and it is good to make the attempt. But it must be borne in mind that not all minds are able by nature to do this, but all souls are able to love Him; and that perfection consists in loving Him rather than in thinking. I have elsewhere spoken of the causes of this wandering of the mind—of some, at least; not of all, for that would be impossible—so I will not speak of it here: but I want it to be understood that the soul is not thoughts; nor ought the will to be controlled by them, for it would be in evil case, as I have said above: because the soul's good does not consist in thinking much, but in loving much. And if you ask, How is this love to be gained? I answer, By a soul's resolving to work and suffer for God, and doing so when it gets an opportunity.

It is quite true that reflecting on what we owe to the Lord, what He is, and what we are, is efficacious in fixing the soul's determination; and that this is an excellent practice, and very helpful in the beginnings. But with this proviso—that this exercise does not interfere with matters of obedience or of the good of our neighbour which charity requires of us. For in such cases, either of these two things has the first claim on our time, and we must give up what we crave to give to God; that is to say, the meditating on Him in solitude and rejoicing in the joys which He gives us. To give up this for either of those two things is to give joy to the Lord; and it is done for Him, as He said with His own mouth, Inasmuch as ye have done it unto one of these little ones, ye have done it unto Me. And as to matters of obedience, He would not have us walk in any other way than the way in which He Himself was well pleased to walk. Follow Him, for He was *obediens usque ad mortem*[1].

Then if this is really true, whence comes that vexation which we mostly feel when we have not spent a great part of the day quite alone and absorbed in God, although we were all the time occupied in works of obedience and charity? From two sources, I think. The first and chief, from a self-love which is here so very subtly mingled that we do not perceive that it is ourselves we are wanting to please rather than God. For it is clear that when a soul is beginning "to taste and see how gracious the Lord is," it must be more to its taste to be enjoying this communion, and the body not toiling but at rest.

Oh the charity of those who sincerely love our Lord and know their own state! How little rest can they take if they see that they can ever so little help a single soul to advance and love God more, or can in any way comfort it or liberate it from any danger! How little rest could such an one take in any selfish repose! And when he cannot help by deeds, he will by prayers, pleading with the Lord for the many souls which he grieves to see being lost. Such a soul loses its own enjoyment and counts it well lost, because it does not think about its own happiness but about how best to do the Lord's will.

So it is also in matters of obedience. It would be unseemly behaviour if God plainly told us to go and do

[1] [Phil. ii. 8. Tr.]

something which He wanted done; and we would not, but
remained gazing upon Him because that was more to our
pleasure. A fine advance in the love of God, to bind His
hands by believing that He can do us good in only one way!
Besides what I myself, as I have said, have experienced,
I know several people with whom I have conversed, who
taught me this truth, when I was troubled at having so little
time myself, and so was sorry for them when I saw them
continually occupied in business and many affairs laid upon
them in obedience. And I thought within myself, and even
said so to them, that in such a racket it was not possible to
grow in spirituality—for at that time they had no large measure
of it. O Lord, how different are Thy ways from what we
imagine! When a soul is simply set upon loving Thee and
is left in Thy hands, Thou requirest of it nothing but to obey,
and carefully to learn what is most to Thy service, and to
desire this. It has no need to seek out its own paths or
choose them : for its will is simply Thine. Thou, O my Lord,
takest upon Thyself the charge of guiding it in the way that
is best for it. And even if the Superior does not concern
himself about our soul's good, but only about getting the
business done which he thinks is for the Community's good,
Thou, O my God, dost keep our soul, and dost continually
dispose it and its doings in such wise that, without our
knowing how, but only faithfully obeying our orders for God's
sake, we presently find ourselves so much better and more
spiritually minded that we are filled with wonder.

So it was in the case of someone to whom I was talking
a few days ago. For about fifteen years his obedience had
laid upon him such hard work in offices and the oversight of
others that in the whole of that time he could not remember
that he had had one day to himself; although he secured

some time in the day, as best he might, for prayer and to keep his conscience clear. He is one of the most obediently disposed souls that I ever saw, and so he communicates that virtue to all whom he has to do with. The Lord has well rewarded him: for, without knowing how, he finds himself to have gained that liberty of spirit, so greatly prized and desired, which is possessed by the perfect, wherein lies all the felicity that can be desired in this life; because, seeking nothing, he possesses all things. Such souls neither fear nor desire anything upon earth; troubles do not perturb them, nor do pleasures excite them: whatever may happen, no one can take away their peace, for it rests on God alone; and as no one can take away God from them, nothing can cause them anxiety but the fear of losing Him: for everything else in the world is to them as though it were not, for it can neither make nor mar their happiness. Oh blessed obedience, and blessed distraction for obedience's sake, which can win so great a good! That person is not the only one I have known : for there have been others like him, whom I had not seen for many years; and when I asked them how these years had been spent, it was all in works of obedience and charity, and on the other hand I could see that they had made most marvellous progress in spiritual things.

Well then, my daughters, let there be no repining, but when obedience keeps you employed in exterior works, remember that even if it is in the kitchen, the Lord walks among the pitchers, aiding us both in body and soul.

I remember a monk's telling me that he had resolved and firmly made up his mind that he would never refuse anything which the Superior might require of him, whatever trouble it gave him. And one day he had been working so hard that he was quite done up and could hardly stand, and he was going to

sit down and rest a little. It was already late. The Superior
met him and told him to take the spade and go and dig in the
garden. He kept silence, although it seemed hard to the flesh,
because he did not know how he should get through it. He
took the spade and was going into the garden by a path which
I saw many years after he told me this ; for I happened to be
founding a house in that town. There our Lord appeared to
him with the cross on His shoulders, so wearied and worn out
that he very well could see his own fatigue was nothing in
comparison of that.

I believe that it is because the devil sees there is no way
which leads more quickly to the highest perfection than that
of obedience, that he sets up in it so many distastes and difficulties under the colour of good. Let this be carefully thought
over, and it will be seen clearly that what I say is true. As to
what constitutes the highest perfection; it is clear that it is
not interior satisfaction, nor great raptures, nor visions, nor
the spirit of prophecy, but it is the entire conformity of our
will to the will of God, so that there is nothing which we see
He desires which we do not also desire with our whole will,
and we accept the bitter as cheerfully as the sweet, when we
see it to be His Majesty's good pleasure. This seems exceedingly difficult—not the mere doing God's will, but the taking
pleasure in what is wholly and entirely contrary to our own
natural wishes. And so indeed it is. But love, if it is perfect,
has virtue to make us forget our own pleasure in the pleasure of
pleasing one whom we love. And as a matter of fact so we find
it ; for when we see we are pleasing God, even the greatest sufferings become sweet to us: and those who have attained to this
state love God thus amidst persecutions and dishonours and
wrongs.

This is so certain, and is so well known and plain, that I

need not dwell on it. What I wish to shew is the reason why, as I think, obedience acts most quickly or is the chief means there is of attaining to this so blessed condition. It is this. As we are by no means masters of our own will, so as to be able to employ it purely and simply and wholly for God, until we have subjected it to reason, so obedience is the true way thus to subject it. For this cannot be done by good reasons, because our natural temperament and our self-love produce so many that we should never arrive there : and they very often make what is most reasonable seem unreasonable, if we are not inclined to it, only because we are not inclined to act on it. (I had so much to say here that we should never get done with this internal contest and with describing all that the devil, the world, and the flesh do to warp our reason.) What, then, can be done ? This : that just as in a very doubtful matter of law, the litigants, weary of strife, choose an arbitrator and put the matter into his hands ; so should our soul choose one, whether Superior or confessor, resolving to strive no longer nor take thought for itself, but to trust the Lord's words when He said " He that heareth you heareth Me," and to put aside its own will. Our Lord counts this submission a great thing ; and justly so, because it makes Him master of the free will which He has given us. So we exercise ourselves in this ; and, sometimes completely conquering ourselves, sometimes with a thousand conflicts, thinking what is decided for us foolish, we come to submit ourselves to what is enjoined on us, through this painful exercise ; but, painfully or not, at last we do it. And the Lord on His part aids us greatly, so that just as we come to submit our will and reason for His sake, so He makes us masters of them. Then, being masters of ourselves, we are able to give ourselves over perfectly to God, offering Him a pure will that He may unite it to His own ; beseeching Him to send down the fire of His love from heaven to consume the sacrifice, giving up everything which might displease Him ; because now there is nothing left to us which, although with sore struggles, we have not laid on the altar, so that, so far as in us lies, it no longer touches the earth.

It is plain that no one can give what he does not possess ; but he must needs first possess it. Then believe me, there is no better way of winning this treasure than by digging and toiling to get it out of the mine of obedience ; for the more we dig the more we shall find ; and the more we submit ourselves to human beings, having no will but that of our betters, the more we shall be masters of our will so as to be able to conform it to the will of God.

See now, Sisters, whether the giving up the pleasure of solitude is not amply rewarded. I can tell you that the lack of solitude will be no hindrance to you in training yourselves for the attainment of that true union which, as I have said, consists in making my will one with the will of God. This is the union which I myself desire, and would wish you all to possess, and not occasional very enjoyable raptures which take place, to which people give the name of union : and they will really be union, if afterwards the condition which I have described ensues. But if when the suspension is over, very little obedience is found, and self-will remains, then I think the self-will will be united to self-love and not to the will of God. May His Majesty grant that I may practise what I know in this matter !

The second source of this dislike is, I think, that, as in solitude there are fewer occasions of offending God,—some there always must be, as the evil spirits and ourselves are never absent—the soul seems to keep itself purer : and if it is apprehensive of offending Him, it is a great comfort not to have occasions of stumbling. And certainly this seems to me a more adequate reason for wishing not to converse with anyone than the former—the great delights and spiritual sweetnesses which solitude affords.

Here, my daughters, is where true love is to be seen : not in corners, but in the midst of temptations. And believe me that although there may be more faults committed, or even some slight falls, yet our gain is incomparably greater. Remember, in what I say it is always taken for granted that it is in obedience and for charity's sake that you go into temptation. If not, I grant that solitude is best. And indeed we ought to be desiring it even while we are doing as I say. In truth this desire is ever present in souls which really love God.

I say that it is a gain for this reason—that it makes us see what we are, and how much our strength is capable of. For when a person is continually in solitude, however saintly he may seem to himself to be, he does not know whether he has any patience or humility, nor has he any means of knowing. It is as if a man were very valiant, how could he know it if he had not proved it in battle ? St Peter was sure he was so, but see what he was when the temptation came ! But he came out from that fall with no trust in himself, and from that he went on to put his trust in God, and afterwards suffered martyrdom, as we know.

Alas, my God, if we only knew how great is our wretchedness ! If we do not know it, there is danger in everything : therefore it is good for us to be made to do things which shew us how abject we are. And I consider one day of humbling knowledge of ourselves which has cost much sorrow and pain to be a greater boon from our Lord than many days of prayer : how much more when the true lover loves wherever he is, and always keeps his beloved in mind ! It would be a poor thing

if prayer could be carried on only in corners. I myself find
that I cannot now spend many hours in it. But, O my Lord,
how powerful before Thee is one sigh, sent forth from a spirit
which is troubled because not only are we in exile, but have
not even opportunities of being alone, that we might enjoy
communion with Thee !

This is what shews clearly that we are His bondservants,
for love of Him willingly sold to the virtue of obedience, since
for its sake we give up, in a measure, the joy of communion
with God Himself. But that is nothing, when we consider
that He in obedience came from the bosom of the Father to
become our bondservant. How then can this gift be repaid or
requited ! We must walk warily in our active works, even of
obedience and charity, lest we should be careless, not continually
turning to God in our inmost heart. But believe me, what
helps a soul to advance is not the spending long hours in
prayer, but it is a great help to be employed also in active
works, so that the soul is better disposed to enkindle its love
in a very short space of time than by spending many hours in
meditation. All must come from His hand. May He be blessed
for ever and ever !

CHAPTER VI

Of the harm it may do spiritual people not to know when to
resist the spirit. Of the soul's desire for Communion, and the
delusions there may be in this. Contains matters important
to those who are in charge of these Convents.

I HAVE long and carefully tried to find out whence proceeds
a sort of great absorption in thought which I have observed in
certain people to whom the Lord gives great sweetness in
prayer, and who do not neglect to prepare themselves for

receiving His graces. I am not speaking now of a soul's being suspended and enraptured by His Majesty, for I have elsewhere spoken of this at some length : and of such things as this there is really nothing to be said, because we ourselves can do nothing, even if we do our utmost to resist, if it is a real rapture. It is to be observed that in this case the force which deprives us of all power over ourselves lasts but a short time. But it often happens that a prayer of quiet begins, as it were a spiritual slumber, which absorbs the soul in such wise that, if we do not know what ought to be done in this case, we may waste much time and, by our own fault, spend our strength and gain little.

I wish I knew how to explain myself on this point, but it is so difficult that I do not know whether I shall succeed : but I know very well that if the souls who have been in this delusion are willing to believe me, they will understand me. I know of some, and very virtuous souls too, who have been seven or eight hours in this state, and think it all to have been a rapture : and any other religious exercise has laid such hold upon them that they have yielded themselves to it immediately, thinking they must not resist the Lord ; and so little by little they might die or turn silly, if they got no help.

What I know about the matter is that, when the Lord begins to bestow joys on the soul, we being by nature so fond of delights, it gives itself up to that pleasure so entirely as not to be willing to move or lose it on any account; for it really is a greater pleasure than any worldly pleasures. This takes place sometimes in a soul by nature weak, or whose mind—or rather, imagination—is not lively but of a sort which, when it has once laid hold on something, dwells on it without distraction (as is the case with many people who, when they begin to think of something, not necessarily of God, remain absorbed and, as it were, gazing at something without knowing what they are gazing at—a sort of people slow by nature, who, from inattention, forget what they were going to say). And so it is when they are thinking of God, agreeably to their own disposition or nature or weakness. Or suppose they are given to melancholia, they will entertain a thousand pleasing delusions.

Of a melancholic humour I will say a little by and bye. But even without that, what I have described takes place, and even in the case of people who are worn with penance : when, as I have said, love begins to afford them a sensible pleasure, they let themselves be carried away by it overmuch, as I have said. To my mind, it would be a much better loving if they did not let themselves go on mooning: for they could very well resist it at this point in their prayer. For just as in bodily weakness we experience a faintness which does not allow of our speaking or moving, so it is here, if we do not resist ; for if our natural temperament is weak, the vehemence of the spirit lays hold on it and overcomes it.

I may be asked, What is the difference between this and rapture ; for to all appearance it is the same ? So it is, in appearance ; but not in reality : for rapture or the union of all the powers of the soul lasts but a short time, as I say ; and leaves behind it great effects, interior light, and many other benefits ; and the understanding does not work at all, but it is the Lord Who is working in the will. In the present case it is very different : for although the body is made captive, the will and memory and understanding are not, but their operation is irregular, and if by chance they alight on some subject, there they will stop and stay.

I see no advantage in this physical weakness—for it is nothing else—except that it comes from a good beginning : it would be better to employ the time profitably than to be so long half asleep. More can be gained by one act, or by often arousing the will to love God, than by letting it remain passive. Therefore I would advise Prioresses to do their utmost diligence to stop these long drowsinesses : for all they do, in my opinion, is to blunt the faculties and the understanding so that they cannot perform the soul's bidding, and therefore deprive her of the benefits which they ordinarily reap when they are taking care to please the Lord. If the Prioresses see that it comes from weakness, they should put a stop to their fasts and disciplines— I mean, such as are not of obligation—and the time may come when they will be able to give them all up with a good conscience—and they should set them tasks which will take off their minds from themselves.

And even if Sisters are not subject to these swoonings, yet if their mind is too much engrossed, even with deep matters of prayer, it must necessarily happen that they often are not mistresses of themselves. In particular, if they have received some unusual grace from the Lord or seen some vision, they will be always thinking they are seeing it, when that is not the case, but it was only once they saw it. Anyone who finds herself going on in this dreamy torpor for long must try to change the current of her thoughts ; for so long as she is occupied with things Divine there is no harm in this : but let her thoughts be first of one thing, then of another, just as they employ themselves in her own affairs. And God is as well pleased with our thinking sometimes of His creatures and of His creative power, as with our thinking on the Creator Himself.

Oh wretched misery of man, which is such through sin that even in what is good we require rule and measure lest we bring ruin on our health so as to lose the fruition of our good!

And indeed many of us, and especially those of weak head or imagination, need self-knowledge; and it is more to our Lord's service, and very necessary. So if anyone sees that, when her thoughts are fixed on some mystery of the Passion, or the glory of heaven, or any such thing, she goes on for a long time without being able, even if she wishes it, to turn them on anything else, or leave off being immersed in this, let her realise that she must divert them as best she may, or the time will come when she will realise the harm of it, and that its origin was what I have said—great weakness either of the physical frame, or else of the mind, which is much worse. For just as a lunatic, if he gets anything fixed in his mind, is not master of himself, and cannot distract himself, nor think of anything else, nor can any reasoning influence him, because he is not master of his reason ; so it may happen in this case, although it is a pleasurable madness.

Oh what harm may such an one do himself if he has a melancholic temperament ! I can see no good whatever in it. For the soul has a capacity for delighting in God Himself. If, then, it is not for one of the reasons I have given above, why should the soul, since God is infinite, be chained to only one of His mysteries or attributes, when there are so many for us to dwell upon ? And the more things of God we meditate on, the more of His greatnesses we come to see. I do not say that in one hour or even in one day we should meditate on many subjects, for this would probably mean that we should not get the good of any of them. As these questions are very nice, I would not have you misunderstand, or think I am saying what it has never entered into my head to say. I am sure that it is so important to understand this chapter rightly, that although it gives me trouble to write, I do not grudge it. And I hope that anyone who does not understand it at the first reading will not grudge reading it over and over, especially Prioresses and Novice mistresses who have to guide Sisters in their methods of prayer. For if they are not careful at the beginning, they will find how long it takes to set right such weaknesses as these.

If I were to narrate the many instances of this evil which have come to my knowledge, it would be seen what cause there is for my making so much of it. I will only relate one ; and from this the rest can be gathered. There were in one of our monasteries a choir nun and a lay Sister. Both were highly advanced in prayer, together with mortification and humility and other virtues. The Lord shewed Himself very gracious to them, and revealed to them His perfections. Above all, they were so detached and so engrossed in His love that, though we watched them closely, we saw no trace of failure to correspond—as our weakness can—to the graces which our Lord bestowed upon them. I have said so much of their goodness in order that those who do not possess it may be the more in fear.

They began to have great impetuous longings for our Lord, which they could not control. They thought these longings were satisfied when they made their Communion: and so they prevailed with their confessors to let them communicate frequently. Thereby their pain came to increase so greatly that they thought they would die if they were not given their Communion daily. Their confessors seeing such souls with such great longings thought—although one of them was very spiritually minded—that that was the right remedy for their suffering. It did not stop here : for the tension came to such a pitch in one of them that they had to give her her Communion early in the morning to keep her alive, according to her own view. And they were not people who would feign, nor would they have told a lie for anything in the world.

I was not there at the time, and the Prioress wrote to tell me what was going on. She said she could do nothing with them ; and that such and such people said that, as there was nothing else to be done, they should be relieved in this way. By the Lord's will, I understood the matter at once : but for all that, I said nothing until I could go to them, for fear I might be mistaken ; and it would not have been right to oppose the confessor's approval of it, until I could give him my reasons. He was so humble that when I went there and spoke to him, he believed me at once. The other was not so spiritual, nothing indeed to compare with him ; and there was no means of persuading him : but I cared little for that, because I was not under the same obligation in regard to him. I began to talk to the two Sisters, giving them many and, to my mind, sufficient reasons to make them see that it was a mere fancy to think they would die without this relief. But they had it so firmly fixed in their minds that nothing in the way of reasoning sufficed or could suffice to move them. I soon saw it was useless : so I told them that I had the same longings as they, and that I would abstain from Communion so that they might believe that they also need not communicate except when all the Sisters did : that we would all three die together ; for I thought that would be much better than that a custom of that kind should take root in our houses, where there were Sisters who loved God quite as much as they did, and would desire to do just as they did.

The harm which their custom had already done them had come to such a pitch—and the devil must have had a hand in it—that when they did go without making their Communion, they really seemed as if they would die. I shewed great severity : for the more I saw that they did not--because they thought they could not—accept submissively what obedience required of them, the more clearly I saw it was a temptation. They got through that day with great difficulty, the next with rather less ; and thus it went on lessening : so that, even when I made my Communion (because I was ordered to do so ; for, seeing them so weak, I would not have done it) they endured it very well. By and bye they and all the nuns saw that it was a temptation. And a good thing it was that it was set right in time : for shortly after, there arose in that house, not by the Sisters' fault, difficulties with the ecclesiastical superiors —of which I may perhaps speak hereafter—and they would have been displeased with such a custom and would not have allowed it.

Oh how many instances of this kind I could give ! I will give only one more. It was not in one of our monasteries, but in a Cistercian. There was a nun, quite as good as those of whom I have spoken. Through many disciplines and fasts, she came to be so weak that, every time she made her Communion or whenever there was an occasion to inflame her devotion, she used to fall on the ground, and there to remain for eight or nine hours, in what she and everyone else thought to be a trance. This happened so often that I believe great harm would have come of it, if it had not been stopped. The fame of these trances spread about all the neighbourhood. I myself was sorry to hear of it, because it pleased the Lord that I understood what it really was, and I was afraid of what might come of it. The nun's confessor was like a father to me, and he came to tell me the story. I told him what I thought: that it was waste of time; that it could not possibly be a trance, but was only weakness ; and that he should make her give up the fasts and disciplines, and should cause her thoughts to be distracted. She obediently did as he bid her : and after a little while, as she gained strength, there was no shadow of a trance.   While if it had really been a trance, there would have been no stopping it until it was God's will that it should cease; because the force of the spirit is so great that our own strength cannot cope with it.   Also, as I have said, a trance leaves behind it great fruit in the soul; while this other experience leaves no more than if it had never taken place, but only fatigue in the body.

Then let us learn from this to hold in suspicion anything which so overcomes us that we see it does not leave our reason free; and remember that we shall never gain liberty of spirit by such means.   For one of the properties of this liberty is the being able to think about all kinds of things and find God in them.   Anything but this is bondage of spirit : and, let alone the harm it does to the body, it binds the soul so that it cannot grow.   It is as when people on a journey come to a bog or quagmire which they cannot pass.   So, in a way, is it with the soul; which, to advance through this, would have not only to walk, but to fly.   Oh when they say or think they are engrossed with God, and cannot help it because they are so rapt, and can by no means divert their thoughts—and this is a common experience—let them consider what I repeat again.   There is no need for fear if this state lasts for only one day, or four, or a week; for it is no wonder that a weak nature should remain in a maze for so long : but if it persists beyond this, it must be stopped.   What is good in all this is that there is no sinful guilt in it, nor loss of merit; but it has the disadvantages which I have mentioned, and many besides.

In the matter of Communions, it is very serious if a soul, because of its love, is not submissive to the confessor and the Prioress in this matter : if, although it feels its loneliness, it is not enough to make it go to them.   In this matter, as in others, the Sisters must be continually mortified, and must be made to understand that it is better to give up their own will than to take their own pleasure.   Our self-love also may be mingled in this.   It has been so with me : for at one time it often happened that when I had made my Communion, even while the Host must still have been whole, if I saw others communicating, I wished I had not done so in order that I might communicate again.   At the beginning I did not think I need attend to this.   But when it happened so often, I afterwards came to reflect, and saw that it was more for my own satisfaction than for the love of God : because when we go to Communion, we usually feel a certain emotion and sweetness ; and this was what drew me.   Because if it had been in order to have God within my soul, I had Him already ; if to obey what is commanded us in regard to Communion, I had done so already ; if to receive the graces which are given to us in the Blessed Sacrament, I had already received them.   In short, I came to see clearly that there was nothing in it but the desire of experiencing that sensible sweetness over again.

This reminds me that in a place where I lived, where there was one of our monasteries, I knew a woman who was a great servant of God, according to popular estimation, and so she must have been.   She had no confessor in particular, and she made her Communion daily, going for it sometimes to one church, sometimes to another.   I noticed that ; and I would rather have seen her obeying one confessor than making so many Communions.   She lived alone, and, as it seemed to me, did what she pleased : only that, as she was a good woman, all she pleased was good.   I spoke to her about it more than once, but she paid no attention, and justly so, because she was much better than I am.   However, I thought I was not

mistaken in this. The saintly Brother Peter of Alcantara
came to the place, and I got him to talk to her, and I was
not satisfied with the direction he gave her. But that might
have been because, wretched that we are, we are never
thoroughly satisfied with any but those who go on in the same
way as we do: for I believe that that woman did more
penance and served our Lord more in one year than I in many.
After a time she fell into a mortal sickness—this is what I am
coming to—and she took pains to get mass said daily in her
house and to receive the Blessed Sacrament. As her sickness
proved to be protracted, a certain ecclesiastic, a great servant
of God, who had often said the mass, at last thought it was
not right that she should communicate daily in her house.
It must have been the devil who suggested this; for that day
happened to be her last, on which she died. When she saw
mass over and herself left without the Lord, she was so angry
and went into such a passion with the priest that he came,
greatly scandalized, to tell me about it. I was very unhappy
about it ; for even now I do not know whether she was ever
reconciled. I believe she died immediately.

From this I came to understand the harm of doing our
own will in anything, especially in so great a thing as this.
For anyone who so often approaches to the Lord ought to be
so alive to her own unworthiness that she would not do it
on her own judgement, but would let the obedience of
following direction supply what is lacking in our fitness to
approach so great a Lord—a lack which must always be great.
This good woman had an opportunity of greatly humbling
herself, and it might have done more for her than that
Communion, if she had thought that the priest was not in
fault, but that the Lord, seeing how wretched and unworthy
she was to receive Him in so poor a lodging, had thus ordered

it. Thus did a certain person[1] whose wise confessors often kept her from her Communion, because her rule was to make it often[2]. Although she felt this very keenly, she, on the other hand, desired God's glory more than her own; and so did nothing but praise Him for awakening her confessor's watchfulness over her, so that His Majesty should not enter so wretched a lodging. And by the help of such considerations she obeyed with great peace in her soul, although with a loving and tender pain. But not for all the whole world would she have gone against what was bidden her.

Believe me, the love of God—I mean, what seems to us love, but it is not—which stirs our passions in such wise that we commit any sin, or that the peace of our soul is troubled, and it is so full of feeling as to be inaccessible to reason—this sort of affection is plainly self-seeking. And the devil will not be asleep, but will attack us when he thinks it will do us the most harm, as he did to this woman. Indeed it frightened me terribly, not that I believe it sufficed to hinder her salvation, for God's goodness is great, but the temptation came at a very bad time.

I have spoken of it here that the Prioresses may take warning, and that the Sisters may fear and consider and examine themselves on their motives in approaching to receive so great a gift. If it is to please God, they know already that He is better pleased with obedience than sacrifice. Then if this is so and I gain more, why should I be troubled? I do not mean that a humble sorrow would be wrong: for not all have attained to the perfection of feeling none, only because

---

[1] From St Theresa's rather depreciatory way of speaking of this person, and from her praise of her confessors, it may safely be conjectured that she was speaking of herself.

[2] [Daily. Tr.]

they are doing what they understand to be more to God's pleasure. For it is plain that none will be felt if the will is entirely detached from all selfish likings : but on the contrary, the soul will greatly rejoice because it has an opportunity of pleasing the Lord by so costly a sacrifice ; and it will humble itself and will abide as well satisfied with communicating spiritually. But as in the beginnings—and even more at the last—these strong desires of drawing near to the Lord are a gift from Him, some emotion and pain may well be permitted to souls when they are deprived of Communion, although they should abide in peace and should draw from it matter for acts of humility. I say, in the beginnings, because this is the most important, for the Sisters are not so strong in the other points of perfection of which I have spoken.

But if there should be with this desire any strong feeling or anger or temptation to think wrongly of the Superior or the confessor, believe me that it is a manifest temptation. And if anyone should make up her mind to communicate in spite of her confessor's telling her not, I should be sorry to have the gain she would get by it: for in such matters we are not to be our own judges. He who holds the keys for binding and loosing is to be judge. May it please the Lord to give us light to be wise in matters so important : and may we never lack His help, that we may not turn His gifts into occasions of displeasing Him.

CHAPTER VII

How to deal with melancholic nuns. Needful for Prioresses.

THESE my Sisters of St Joseph's at Salamanca, where I am living while writing this, have earnestly begged me to say something about how melancholic[1] nuns should be treated. Because although we are always extremely careful not to admit those who suffer from it, it is so cunning that it feigns death when this serves its purpose, so that we do not find it out until it is too late. I think I have said something about it in a little booklet of mine[2], but I cannot remember. There is no harm, anyhow, in speaking of it here, if the Lord is pleased that I should speak aright. It may be that I have said it at some other time: I would say it a hundred times over if I thought I could succeed in saying anything profitable. The devices which this temperament invents to get its own way are so many that they have to be studied so as to be able to endure it and control it, so that it may not do harm to others.

It must be observed that not all people of this temperament are so troublesome: for when it lights on humble and gentle subjects, though they are troublesome to them-

---

[1] [It would perhaps be too great a liberty to render St Theresa's "*melancolia*" by *hysteria*. Nevertheless, if this rendering is kept in mind, much light is thrown on what she says. Tr.]

[2] It has been conjectured from these words that St Theresa had written some other treatise now lost. But in my opinion she is referring to the first copy of *The Way of Perfection*, a *quarto* volume (which is in the Escorial) instead of being a *folio* like the other writings.

selves, they do no harm to others, especially if they are of
good understanding. And besides, there are different degrees
of this temperament. I fully believe that in some people the
devil takes it as his handle for getting them into his power;
and that if they are not exceedingly careful, he will do so.
For, as the chief effect of this temper is to overcome the
reason, and so this becomes obscured; what then, under such
conditions, will not our passions do?

Not having the use of one's reason seems the same as
being mad, and so it is: only that in those of whom we are
speaking the evil has not come to such a pitch, and it would
be a much less evil if it had. For having to behave as a
reasonable being, and having to treat some one as such when
she is not so, is an intolerably difficult situation. For to those
who are altogether sick of this malady, compassion is to be
shewn, but they do no harm; and if there is any way of
keeping them under control, it is to put them in fear. Those
in whom this malignant evil is only begun but has not taken
such firm hold, yet must be treated in the same way, when
other means fail; as the evil is of the same quality and root,
and springs from the same stock. The Prioresses must avail
themselves of the penances in use in the Order; and must
aim at so bringing them under control that they may recognize that they will not succeed in getting everything nor
anything they want. For if they find that their clamour and
the desperate things which the devil says in them to ruin
them have sometimes succeeded, then they are lost. And
one of such is enough to disquiet a whole monastery. For
as the poor creature has in herself nothing with which to
defend herself from the devil's suggestions, the Prioress must
take the greatest pains to direct her, not only outwardly but
inwardly. As reason is obscured in the sick nun, it must be

the clearer in the Prioress, so that the devil shall not begin
to obtain power over that soul, by means of this malady.

It is a dangerous thing. For this temper is sometimes
of such violence as to overcome the reason altogether; and
when this is so, they are not to blame, as madmen are not,
whatever follies they commit. But people are to be blamed
when their reason is not quite overcome, but only weakened,
and they are at times quite well. They must not be allowed
to take liberties when they are at their worst, lest when they
are well they should not be able to master themselves: for
this artifice of the devil's is much to be dreaded; and thus, if
we consider it, what they are mostly at is the getting their
own way, and saying whatever comes into their head, and
finding out faults in others to hide their own with, and
pleasing themselves with whatever they have a fancy for:
acting, in short, as one who has in himself no power to
control himself. Then, with passions unmortified and every
one of which wants to get its own way, what will happen if
there is no one to control them?

I repeat, as one who has seen and dealt with many
people suffering from this malady, that there is no other
remedy for it but to bring them into subjection by all possible
ways and means. If words will not suffice, then punishments;
if slight ones will not suffice, then severe; if one month's imprisonment will not suffice, then four: for no greater good
can be done for their souls. Because, (as I have said, and say
again, for it is important that the nuns themselves should
understand it): although once or more than once they may be
really not responsible for their actions; as it is not a con-
firmed madness of a kind which makes wrong-doing blameless
(although it may be so at times, yet not habitually), the soul
is in great danger. Except it is, as I say, a case of such

entire loss of reason that the nun is constrained to do what
she says or does when she cannot help herself.   It is a great
mercy of God to those who suffer under this malady, when
they submit themselves to some one who can control them;
for this is their only safety in the danger of which I have
spoken.   And for the love of God, if any of them should
read this, let her consider that her salvation may depend
on it.

I know some whose understanding is all but completely
unsound, but who are so humble-minded and fearful of offending God that, although they dissolve in tears when they are
alone, they do nothing but what they are told, and bear their
infirmity as others do: but this being a greater suffering, their
glory will be the greater; and having their purgatory here,
they will not have it hereafter.   But I repeat that those who
will not do this of their own accord must be compelled to it
by the Prioress, and must not be led on by imprudent kindnesses till they come to upset everyone by their disorderliness.

For besides the danger to the nun herself of which I have
spoken, there is another most serious evil: that when the
other Sisters see her, as they think, in good health, but do
not realise what inward struggles she goes through, our nature
is so wretched that every one will be tempted to affect melancholia, so that she may be borne with; and in fact the devil
will make her actually think herself melancholic.   And so the
devil will succeed in making a havoc which, by the time it is
found out, will be difficult to undo.   And this is so important
that no negligence must be tolerated in a melancholic Sister:
but if she disobeys the Superior, she must be punished for it
like the sane, and must never be let off; if she speaks wrongly
to any of her Sisters, the same; and so in everything else of
the kind.

It may seem unjust that the sick should suffer as the sane, when they cannot help what they do: so must it be, then, to confine and beat madmen, but they ought to be allowed to kill everybody. Believe me; for I have proved it, and, having tried all sorts of remedies, find none but this to answer. And a Prioress who out of pity allows such as these to begin to do as they please—at last, at last, it will be unendurable, and when it comes to setting it right, that will only be after much harm has been done to the others. And if madmen are confined and punished in order that they may not kill people, and it is right to do so, although we are very sorry for them because they cannot help it, how much greater precautions must be taken that these Sisters may not injure souls with their wilfulnesses?

And I really believe that very often, as I have said, it is not so much their malady which makes some of them act thus as their natural disposition, wilful, proud, and ill-disciplined: for I have seen them control themselves and behave properly for some one whom they feared; then why cannot they do so for God?

I am afraid that the devil is seeking to make prey of many souls under colour of this temper, as I have said. For it is more common than it used to be; and the reason is that all self-will and licence are now called *melancholia*. So I have thought that, in our houses and in all religious houses, we ought not to take this word on our lips, because it seems to carry with it licence; but that it should be called *a dangerous illness*—and how dangerous it is!—and be treated as such. For it is sometimes quite necessary to use some sort of medical treatment to dissipate the violence of the malady and make it endurable, and the patient should be kept in the infirmary. But she must recognize that when she comes out to join the

Community she will have to be submissive like the rest; and if she is not, her malady will not avail as an excuse; because, for the reasons given above, this is necessary: and I could give more.

Without the Sisters themselves perceiving it, the Prioresses should help them along with tender compassion, just like a true mother, and should keep thinking of ways of doing them good. I seem to be contradicting myself, because so far I have said that they are to be treated with severity. So I say again, that they must not suppose that they can get their own way, nor must they get it. It must be clearly laid down that they are to obey; for it is in their feeling they need not that the evil lies. Still, as they have not the strength to do violence to themselves, the Prioress may refrain from commanding them to do anything which she knows they will refuse, but try to lead them on discreetly and by affection to all that is really necessary; so that, if possible, they may obey her from affection, which will be much better: and this is usually the case if she shews them much affection, and makes them see it by her words and deeds.

And it must be borne in mind that the best remedy at the Prioresses' disposal is to give them plenty to do, so that they may have no opportunity for idle imaginations; for the whole evil comes from these. And although they may not do the work so well, yet let some faults be put up with, that other worse faults may not have to be endured in them when they are past help. For I know this to be the most efficacious remedy that can be used. And it must also be arranged that they shall not spend much time in prayer, not even so much as others spend; because they mostly have a weak imagination, and it is very bad for them: and if this is not done, they will be fancying things which neither they nor anyone who listens to them will be able to make sense of. Care must be taken that they eat fish but seldom; also they must not be allowed to keep such prolonged fasts as the others.

It may seem disproportionate to give so much advice about this evil and about no other, when in our wretched life there are so many serious evils, especially in the weakness of women. I have done it for two reasons: the first, that they seem to be in good health, because they will not own to this malady. And as, having no fever, they are not obliged to stay in bed nor send for the doctor, the Prioress must be their physician; because this malady is more inimical to all excellences than those which keep people in bed in peril of death. The second reason is that in other sicknesses people get well or die: in this, it is a wonder if they recover, nor do they die of it; but they come to lose their reason completely—a sort of dying which is the death of everybody else.

They suffer death enough within themselves with their miseries, fancies, and scruples: and thus they may reap exceeding spiritual gain, although they always call them *temptations*: but if they could once understand that these come from nothing but their malady, it would be a great relief to them because they might be able to disregard it. Indeed I am very sorry for them; and so ought all to be who live with them, considering that they themselves might be thus dealt with by the Lord, and helping them along without their perceiving it, as I have said. May it please the Lord that I have hit the mark in what has to be done for so grievous a sickness!

CHAPTER VIII

Counsels in regard to revelations and visions.

IT seems to frighten some people only to hear the word *vision* or *revelation*. I do not know why they reckon it so dangerous a road when God leads a soul by this way, nor whence has arisen this terror. I do not now intend to treat of the difference between good and evil visions, nor of the marks which very learned men have given me to know them by; but of what anyone who finds herself in such circumstances had better do : because there are few confessors she can go to who will not frighten her. For it is a fact that they are not so shocked to hear that the devil has been setting before us all sorts of temptations, of the spirit of blasphemy, of foolish and ugly things, as they are scandalized to hear that some angel has appeared or spoken to us or that we have seen in a vision Jesus Christ our Lord on the cross.

No more do I mean now to treat of the great blessings brought to the soul by revelations which come from God, for this is well known : but of images produced by the devil to deceive us, making use of the likeness of Christ our Lord or His saints. For my part, I hold that His Majesty will not permit this, nor give him power to deceive anyone by such images, unless it is by the person's own fault ; but that it is the devil himself who will be mistaken. I mean that no one will be deceived if he is humble : so there is nothing to be terrified about, but we should trust in the Lord, and pay little attention to such things, except by turning them to His greater praise.

I know of some one[1] whose confessors caused her sore distress over such things, when afterwards, they were seen to have come from God, because of the great fruit and good works which resulted from them. It was hard for her when in some vision she beheld His likeness, to cross herself and treat it with contempt; for so she had been told to do. Afterwards, when she spoke of it to a very learned Dominican, Master Fray Domingo Bañez, he told her that it was wrong for anyone to do so; because it is right to reverence the likeness of our Lord wherever we may see it, even if the devil had depicted it—for he is a great artist; and that, intending to do us harm, he would, on the contrary, have done us good service if he depicted a crucifix or some other likeness of our Lord so life-like that it remained engraved in our heart.

This reasoning greatly commended itself to me: because when we see a very good picture, we should not fail to think highly of it, even if we knew that it was painted by a bad man; nor should we so make account of the painter as to lose our edification. For the good or evil is not in the vision, but in whoever beholds it and does not humbly profit by it: for if he is humble, it can do him no harm even if it is from the devil; and if he is not, it can do him no good even if it is from God. Because if he is puffed up by that which is meant to make him abase himself, seeing that he is unworthy of that favour, it is like the spider, who turns all that he eats into poison, and not like the bee, who turns it all into honey.

I must explain myself more fully. If our Lord of His goodness is pleased, in order that some soul may know and love Him better, to appear to it, or to reveal to it some secret

---

[1] Herself. *Life*, ch. xxix. Not only Bañez condemned this, but also the venerable Juan de Avila, as he has recorded.

of His, or to bestow on it any special consolations or graces ; and if, as I have said, that soul, because of what ought to humble it and make it feel how unworthy of this favour is its abjectness, should consider itself straightway as a saint, and should suppose that this favour has been done it on account of some service it has rendered, then it is plain that, like the spider, it turns to evil the great good which it might thence have derived.

Then say that the devil, in order to stir up pride, produces these apparitions. If then the soul, thinking they come from God, humbles itself and acknowledges itself to be unworthy of so great a favour, and strives earnestly to serve God better : because it sees itself enriched while it is unworthy to eat the crumbs which fall from the table of those people to whom, as it has heard, God has granted such favours—unworthy, I mean, to be the servant of any of them—if it humbles itself and begins in earnest to do penance and to be more in prayer, and to be more careful not to offend our Lord, because it thinks this favour comes from Him, and to obey Him more perfectly : then I can answer for it that the devil will not do it again, but will go away ashamed, leaving no harm done to the soul.

When a Sister is told to do something or told the future, in that case she must tell it to a sensible and learned confessor, and not do or believe anything but what he tells her. She should tell the Prioress of it, that she may appoint her such a confessor. And she may rest assured that if she does not do what the confessor tells her and allow herself to be guided by him, her experiences come from an evil spirit or a terrible melancholia. For, supposing that the confessor were mistaken, she would not be mistaken in keeping to what he said, even if it had been an angel of God that had spoken to her: for His Majesty will give light to the confessor or will otherwise provide for the accomplishment of His word. And there is no danger in acting thus; but in acting otherwise there may be great danger and great harm.

Let it be considered that the weakness of nature is very weak, especially in women, and shews more in this way of prayer; so we must be careful not at once to suppose every little fancy to be a vision: for, believe me, when it really is so, there can be no question about it. Where there is any touch of melancholia, much greater caution is necessary: for I have known of things about such fancies which have made me wonder and wonder how people can possibly believe in such good faith that they have seen what they have not seen.

Once there came to me a highly esteemed confessor, who heard the confessions of a certain person; and she had told him that our Lady often came and sat on her bed, and stayed more than an hour talking to her, and telling her things to come and much besides. Out of such a number of follies one came true; and so all the rest were firmly believed. I saw at once what it was, but I dared not say so; for we live in a world where we have to consider what people may think of us, for our words to have any effect. So I said to the confessor that he should wait to see whether those prophecies came true, and ask about other effects of the visits, and find out what sort of life that person lived. In the end, when he came to find out, it was all folly.

I could tell so many things of this kind as would be ample proof of my point: that a soul should not readily give credence, but should keep its judgement in suspense, and know its own mind very well before it speaks, lest, without intending it, it should deceive the confessor: for, however learned he may be, that does not suffice for understanding these things, if he has no experience in them. Not many years ago, but quite lately, a man made fools of some very learned and spiritually minded people with things of this kind, until he came to speak with someone who had experience in such favours of the Lord, and who saw clearly that it was madness, together with delusions, although at that time it was not acknowledged, but carefully concealed. Shortly afterwards, the Lord made it plainly manifest; but the person who had perceived it had much to suffer first, from not being believed.

For these and similar reasons, it is important that each Sister should clearly describe to the Prioress her manner of prayer. And the Prioress should carefully consider her disposition and spiritual attainments, in order to inform the confessor, so that he may understand better : and she should choose her a suitable confessor, if the ordinary one is not capable of dealing with such things. She must take great care that matters of this kind do not get abroad (not though they may really come from God and be confessedly miraculous) nor be made known to confessors who have not the sense to keep silence about them : for this is most important, more so than they know. Nor must Sisters talk among themselves about these things. But the Prioress must always be ready to listen to them discreetly, inclining rather to commend those who are distinguished for humility and mortification and obedience than those whom God is leading by this very supernatural way of prayer, even though they also may have all these virtues. For if it is the spirit of the Lord, it will bring with it the humility to relish being thought little of; so it will do them no harm, and it will be good for the others. Because as these cannot attain to that way of prayer—for God grants it to whom He will—they may feel discouraged about having only those virtues : and although these too are the gift of God, yet more can be done towards the attainment of them, and they are of great value in the Religious life. May His Majesty bestow them upon us! He will not deny them to anyone who, with perseverance and carefulness and prayer, seeks for them with trust in His mercy.

CHAPTER IX

Of the Foundation of St Joseph's at Malagon.

How I have wandered from my purpose ! And yet the counsels I have given may be more to the purpose than the accounts of the foundations. Well, I was at St Joseph's of Medina del Campo, very happy at seeing the Sisters tread in the same steps as those at St Joseph's of Avila, of sincere religion, fraternity, and zeal ; and happy at seeing how our Lord provided what was necessary for His house, both for the church and for the Sisters. Some women entered the convent whom our Lord seemed to have chosen as being the right sort for the foundation of such a house ; for I have learned that on the good beginning of a house depends its subsequent well-doing ; for later comers go on in the ways they find there.

There was at Toledo a lady[1], sister of the Duke of Medinaceli, in whose house, by order of my Superiors, I had stayed, as I have narrated more at length in the account of the foundation of St Joseph's[2]. This had made her conceive a special affection for me, which must have had something to do with the interest which she took in my doings : for His

[1] Doña Luisa de la Cerda, widow of Arias Pardo and owner of Malagon.

[2] *Life*, ch. xxxiv.

Majesty often brings about such effects from things which to us, who know not the future, seem of little use. This lady, understanding that I had a licence to found convents, began begging earnestly that I would establish one in her own town, Malagon. I was not at all inclined to consent; because the place is so small that we could not be maintained there without an endowment, to which I was strongly opposed.

When I discussed the matter with learned men and with my confessor, they told me that I was doing wrong: that since the Holy Council[1] permitted endowment, I ought not to refuse to found a convent where the Lord might be so well served, because of my own opinion. To this was added the lady's urgent requests; so that I could not help accepting the foundation. She granted us a sufficient endowment: for I always like convents to be either altogether without means, or else with enough to supply the nuns with necessaries without their having to beg of anyone. I took all possible precautions that no Sister should be able to possess anything of her own, but that the Constitutions might be kept in every respect as in the houses founded in poverty.

When all the legal documents were completed, I sent for some Sisters to begin the foundation, and we went with that lady to Malagon. There the house was not ready for us, so we were more than a week in an apartment in the Castle. On Palm Sunday, 1568, the procession of the place came for us, and we went, with our veils over our faces and our white cloaks, to the parish church, where a sermon was preached; and thence they carried the Blessed Sacrament to our convent. It moved everyone to devotion. I stayed there some time. One day when I was in prayer, after my Communion, I under-

---

[1] [Of Trent. Tr.]

stood from our Lord that He would be greatly served in that house. I think I was there not quite two months; for my spirit was urging me to make haste to found the house of Valladolid, for the reason which I will now relate.

CHAPTER X

Of the Foundation at Valladolid of the Convent of the Conception of our Lady of Carmel.

FOUR or five months before the foundation of the Convent of St Joseph at Malagon, a young man of noble family who was talking to me said that, if I liked to found a convent at Valladolid, he would be very glad to give me a house of his, with a very large and good garden, which contained a large vineyard, and he would like to give me possession of it at once. It was of considerable value. I accepted it, although I had not quite made up my mind to found a convent there, because it was about a quarter of a league from the town. However, I thought that when once we had taken possession there, we might be able to move into the town. And as he made the offer so spontaneously, I did not like to refuse to carry out his good work or hinder his devotion.

About two months after this, he was taken ill so suddenly that he could not speak nor make his confession clearly, although he made many gestures shewing that he was praying to the Lord for forgiveness. He died very shortly, a long long way off from where I was staying. The Lord told me that his salvation had been in grave peril; but that He had had mercy on him on account of the service he had done to His Mother in giving that house for a convent of her Order: he would be kept in purgatory until the first mass

was said there; when he would be released. The grievous
pains of that soul were so continually borne home to me, that
although I was wishing to found a house at Toledo, I gave it
up for the time, and made all the haste I could to found at
Valladolid as best I might.

I could not be so quick as I wished, because I was
unavoidably detained for a good time at St Joseph's at Avila,
of which I was in charge, and afterwards at St Joseph's at
Medina del Campo, for I travelled that way. There one day
while I was in prayer, the Lord told me to make haste, for
that soul was in great suffering. So although I was not very
well equipped for it, I put it in hand, and entered Valladolid
on the Feast of St Lawrence.

But when I saw the house, I was filled with dismay, for
I saw it would be foolish to let nuns live there, unless a great
deal was spent upon the place. And although it was a very
pleasant place, the garden being so delightful, it could not
fail to be unhealthy; for it was close to the river. Tired
though I was, I had to go to hear mass at a monastery of our
Order, at the entrance of the town : and it was such a long
way that it redoubled my distress. For all that, I said nothing
to my companions, so as not to discourage them : for, though
weak, I had some confidence that the Lord Who had told me
what I have said, would make it come right. I sent for
workmen in great secrecy, and began to have mud walls built
for purposes of enclosure and whatever was necessary.

The ecclesiastic of whom I have spoken, Julian of Avila,
was with us, and one[1] of the two friars who, as I have said,
wished to become Barefoot brothers. He was learning our
way of living in these houses. Julian of Avila employed
himself in getting the Ordinary's licence, which he had given

[1] St John of the Cross.

me good hopes of, before I set out. It could not be accomplished so quickly but that a Sunday came before it was obtained : but we were given leave to have mass said in the room which we had for a chapel ; and so it was said for us.

I was very far from imagining that what had been told me of the young man's soul would be accomplished then : for, although I had been told it would be at the first mass, I supposed this meant the mass when the Blessed Sacrament would be reserved. But when the priest came with the Blessed Sacrament in his hands to where we were to communicate, and when I came up to the priest to receive It, I saw in a vision this young man, his face shining and full of joy, with clasped hands, and he thanked me for what I had done to enable him to come out of purgatory, and depart into heaven. And certainly, when I first heard that he was in the way of salvation, I was very far from thinking so, and was in great distress, considering that such a life as his demanded a different kind of death. For, though there was much good in him, he was much mixed up in worldly matters. It is true, he had said to my companions that he continually had death before his mind. It is wonderful what pleasure our Lord takes in any service done to His Mother ; and great is His mercy. May He be praised and blessed for all, Who thus rewards with eternal life and glory the poverty of our works, and makes them great though they are worth little.

Well, on the Day of the Assumption of our Lady, the 15th of August, 1568, possession was taken of the convent. We did not stay there long, because we almost all fell ill. There was a lady there, Doña Maria de Mendoza, wife of the Knight Commander Cobos, and mother of the Marquis of Camarasa, a good Christian, and very liberal, as her abundant alms testified. She had done me kindnesses in past times when I had had to do with her, because she was sister to the Bishop of Avila, who helped us much with our first convent, and has done so in all the affairs of the Order. She saw our plight, and that we could not stay there without serious difficulties, because of being too far off for alms, and because of sickness. And, being so charitable, she proposed to us to give that house to her, and she would buy us another : and so she did, one which was worth much more; and she has provided us with all necessaries up to the present time, and so she will do as long as she lives.

On St Blaise's Day we moved into it, with a great procession, amidst the devotion of the people, which is still maintained, because the Lord grants many mercies in that house and has drawn to it souls whose sanctity will be known in His good time to the praise of the Lord Who makes use of such means to advance His works and give blessings to His creatures.

For a very young Sister entered that house who shewed what the world is worth by despising it. And I think good to narrate it here in order to shame those who love the world, and that girls into whose hearts the Lord may put good desires and inspirations may learn from her example to carry them out.

There was at Valladolid a lady named Doña Maria de Acuña, sister of the Count de Buendia, and wife of the Governor[1] of Castille. He died, leaving her with one son and two daughters, and very young. She began to lead a life of such sanctity, and bringing up her children so virtuously as to deserve that the Lord should choose them for Himself. I am wrong : she had three daughters. One soon became a nun ; another would not marry, but lived a very edifying life with her mother. The son began very early to see what the

---

[1] [Adelantado.   Tr.]

world was, and to be called by God to the Religious life so strongly that no one was able to put him off. His mother, however, was delighted, and must have helped him much with her prayers to the Lord; although not openly, because of his relations. Indeed, when the Lord chooses a soul for Himself, no creatures can prevail to hinder it. So it happened here: for when by much persuasion they had kept him back for three years, he entered the Company of Jesus. Doña Maria told one of her confessors, who told me, that never in her life had such joy come to her heart as on the day when her son was professed. O Lord, what a mercy Thou grantest to those to whom Thou givest such parents, who so truly love their children that they would have them possess their estates and inheritances and riches in that blessed life which has no end! It is a matter deeply to be regretted that the world is so wretched and blind that parents reckon their honour to consist in the continuance of the memorials of their possession of the dunghill of this world's goods, which sooner or later must come to an end—and all temporal things, however lasting, come to an end, and are to be held of no account— and desire to keep up their vanities at the expense of their poor children, and audaciously rob God of souls whom He desires for Himself. And these souls they rob of so great a good that, although there were no eternity in which God invites them to dwell with Him, it would be a great happiness to find themselves free from the weary customs of the world, which are the more wearisome the greater their possessions. Open their eyes, O my God. Shew them what their love should be for their children, that they may not deal so ill with them; and that their children may not bring it up against them before God in the last judgement, where, however unwillingly, they will understand what everything is really worth.

As then, God in His mercy drew out of the world Don Antonio de Padilla, the son of Doña Maria de Acuña, at the age of about seventeen, the property came to the eldest daughter, Doña Luisa de Padilla. The Count of Buendia had no children, and Don Antonio inherited his title as well as the governorship of Castille. Since that is not to my point, I will not enter on all that he suffered at the hands of his relations before accomplishing his purpose : those who know what worldly people feel about having an heir to their family will realise this well enough.

O Jesus Christ our Lord, Son of the Eternal Father, true King of creation, what didst Thou leave in the world for us Thy children to inherit? What hadst Thou, O my Lord, but toil and suffering and insult? And even to go through the anguish of death Thou hadst nothing but the hard wood. Surely, O my God, we who aspire to be Thy true children and not renounce our inheritance—it does not beseem us to fly from suffering. The arms Thou bearest are five wounds. Ah then, my daughters, this must be our device also if we are to inherit His kingdom. Not with ease, not with pleasures, not with honours, not with riches can we gain that which He purchased with so much blood.

O ye of high birth, for the love of God open your eyes ! Mark the true knights of Jesus Christ and the princes of His Church. A St Peter, a St Paul did not take the way which you are taking. Do you think, peradventure, that a new way is to be made for you ? Believe it not. See how our Lord began shewing you the way through people so youthful as those of whom we are now speaking. Don Antonio I have sometimes seen and spoken with : he would gladly have had greater possessions in order to renounce them. Blessed youth and blessed damsel, who, at an age at which the world

is used to ruling over those who dwell in it, were counted
worthy by God of grace to reject it! Blessed is He Who so
abundantly wrought in them!

When, then, the family honours devolved on the elder
daughter, she cared as little for them as her brother: for from
a child she had been so much given to prayer, through which
our Lord gives light to know the truth, that she esteemed it
all as lightly as her brother. Alas, my God, what difficulties
and vexations and law suits and even risk of life and honour
many would have gone through for the succession to this
inheritance! But these two went through not a little to gain
permission to renounce it. Such is this world; it would shew
us its own absurdities plainly enough, if we were not blind.
With a very good will, that she might be left free from this
inheritance, did she renounce it in favour of her sister, who
was about ten or eleven : for there was no other heir. Her
relations, in order that their wretched family name might not
perish, immediately arranged to marry the little girl to an
uncle, brother of her father; and they got a dispensation
from the sovereign Pontiff, and betrothed them.

It was not our Lord's pleasure that the daughter of such
a mother and the sister of such a brother and sisters should
remain more mistaken than they were; and thus what I am
about to relate came to pass. The child had begun to take
pleasure in her worldly dress and adornments, which would
naturally please one of her tender years : but in less than two
months after her betrothal, our Lord began to give her light,
although at the time she did not understand it. Having
spent a day very happily with her betrothed, whom she cared
for with an affection beyond her years, a great sadness came
over her on considering that as this day had come to an end,
so would every day. Oh, how great is God! From the very

pleasure which the pleasures of perishing things gave her, she was led to turn against them. She began to experience a sadness so deep that she could not conceal it from her betrothed ; nor did she know whence it arose, nor what to tell him about it, although he questioned her.

At that time her betrothed had to take a journey which obliged him to go very far away ; and she felt it keenly, because she cared for him so much. But suddenly our Lord revealed to her the cause of her sadness, which was that her soul was attracted to that which has no ending ; and she began to reflect that her brother and sister had taken the safer course, and had left her amid the perils of the world. This on the one hand ; and on the other hand the thought that there was no help for it—for she did not know until later, when she made enquiries, that it was possible for her, although betrothed, to become a nun—this kept her in sadness ; and above all, the affection which she had for her betrothed kept her undecided ; and so she went on sorrowfully. But as our Lord had chosen her for Himself, He kept lessening this affection and increasing her desire of giving up all.

At that time she was only moved by the desire to save her soul and to find out the best means for this ; for she thought that if she were more immersed in worldly things, she might forget to seek that which is eternal. At this tender age God imbued her with wisdom to seek how she might gain that which has no end. Happy soul, so early to emerge from the darkness in which so many who are old die !

When she saw her heart was at liberty, she resolved to give it entirely to God, and began to speak of it to her sister : for hitherto she had kept silence. Her sister, thinking it a childish fancy, dissuaded her from it, and told her, among other things, that she could very well be saved in the estate of matrimony. The child answered, "Then why did you yourself renounce it?" And for some time her desire went on increasing, although her mother dared not say anything : but perhaps it was she who, by her holy prayers, was carrying on the conflict.

CHAPTER XI

Continues the story of Doña Casilda de Padilla and how she succeeded in carrying out her holy desires for the Religious life.

At that time it happened that the habit was given to a lay Sister, Sister Estefania of the Apostles, in the Convent of the Conception. I may perhaps later on tell the story of her vocation ; because, although these two were in different positions—for Sister Estefania was a labourer's daughter—yet the great graces which God bestowed on her deserve to be recorded of her, to the glory of His Majesty. When she took the habit, Doña Casilda—for that was the name of this beloved of our Lord—went to the service with her grandmother, the mother of her betrothed. She took a great liking to the convent, thinking that the nuns there could serve the Lord better from being few and poor. However, at that time she had not made up her mind to quit her betrothed ; for, as I have said, it was the giving him up which most held her back.

She reflected that before her betrothal she used to observe times of prayer, because her mother in her goodness and saintliness observed them and brought up her children to it : from the age of seven she used to make them go into the oratory at certain times, and she taught them how to meditate on the Passion of our Lord, and made them go often to confession. Her desire was to dedicate them to God : and thus she saw the good fruit of her longing. She has told me that she used continually to offer them to God, beseeching Him to take them out of the world; for she was already disenchanted as to the world's value. I sometimes think when they find themselves in the fruition of everlasting joy, knowing that they owe it to their mother, what thanks they will give her, and what her special joy will be in seeing them there. And I think of those whose parents, on the contrary, have not brought them up as the children of God—Whose they are more than their parents'—and what cursing and despair there will be when they see each other in hell.

Then, to return to what I was saying, when she found that it was irksome to her even to recite the Rosary, she was sorely afraid that she would grow worse and worse. And she seemed to see clearly that her salvation would be assured if she came into this house; and so she quite made up her mind. And one morning when she and her mother and her sister together came thither, it happened that they went inside the house, without the least idea of what she was going to do. When she found herself within, nobody could get her out again. Her weeping and entreaties to be allowed to stay were such that they did not know what to do. Her mother, although secretly rejoicing, was afraid of the relations, and did not wish her to remain, as things were, lest they should say it was by her persuasion : the Prioress also was of the same mind, thinking her a child, and that she needed more probation. This was in the morning. They had to stay until the evening; and they sent for her confessor, and for the master Father Fray Domingo, who was mine, the Dominican whom I mentioned at the beginning. I was not there myself. This Father saw at once that it was the work of the Spirit of God. (And he helped her greatly, going through much at the hands of her

relations. So indeed ought all those who profess to serve
God to do, when they see a soul to be called by God, and
they ought not to be so much influenced by worldly prudence.)
He promised to help her to return some other day. And he
got her to go away for this time, with great persuasion, lest
the blame should be laid on her mother.

Her desires kept increasing in strength. Her mother began
to speak of it to her relations; privately, so that the secret
should not come to the knowledge of the betrothed. They
said it was childishness, and she must wait until she was old
enough; for she had not completed her twelfth year. The child
said, They had thought her old enough to be married and left
in the world; how was it they did not think her old enough
to give herself to God? She so spoke that it was plain to see
it was not herself who was speaking. The thing could not be
kept so secret but that the betrothed got to know of it. When
she heard that, she felt she could bear to wait no longer. So
one day, on the Feast of the Conception, when she was staying
with her grandmother, who was also her mother-in-law, who
knew nothing about this, she begged and besought her to let
her go into the country with her nurse for a little amusement.
Her grandmother, to content her, did so, sending her in a
carriage with her servants. The child gave some money to
one of them, asking him to get some vine-branches or faggots
and wait with them at the door of this convent, and she had
the carriage driven round by a way which brought her back
past the house. When it arrived at the door, she told the
servants to ask at the grating for a jar of water, without
saying who it was for, and she herself hastily alighted. They
said they would give it to her outside; but that she would not
have. The faggots were already there; and she told the
servants to ask the Sisters to come to the door for them.

She stood close by : and when they opened the door, in
she went, and went and threw her arms round the statue of
our Lady, weeping and imploring the Prioress not to send her
away.　Loud were the cries of the servants and their knocking
at the door.　She went and spoke to them through the grating,
and said she would not come out for anything in the world,
and they must go and tell her mother.　The women who had
gone out with her made piteous lamentations ; but she cared
for none of it.　When they told the news to her grandmother, she went there immediately.　But neither she, nor an
uncle, nor her betrothed, who, when he came, succeeded in
talking to her at the grating, could do more than distress her
while they were with her ; but they left her more determined
than before.　Her betrothed, after many piteous lamentations,
told her that she could serve God more by giving alms.　She
answered that he might give them himself : and in answer to
the rest she told him that her strongest obligation was her
own salvation, that she knew herself to be weak, and that
among the temptations of the world she would not be saved ;
and that he could not complain of her, since it was only for
God she had left him, and this was doing no wrong to him.
When she found that nothing convinced him, she got up and
left him.　He made no impression upon her ; rather on the
whole he put her against him.　For when God gives the light
of truth to a soul, the devil's temptations and obstacles only
help it the more, because it is God Himself Who fights for it.
Thus in this case it was clearly seen, for it appeared not to be
herself who was speaking.

　　When her betrothed and her relations saw of how little
use it was to try to get her out by her own consent, they took
measures for doing so by force.　So they obtained an order
from the King to take her out of the convent and restore her to

liberty. During all this time, from the Feast of the Conception until Holy Innocents' Day, when they took her out, she was never given the habit; but she kept all the observances of the Rule, just as if she had received it, with the greatest satisfaction. On Holy Innocents' Day, the officers of the law came for her, and took her to the house of a nobleman, she weeping abundantly and asking why they tormented her, seeing it would avail them nothing. There much persuasion was brought to bear on her, both by members of Religious Orders and others; some thinking it was childishness, and others wishing her to enjoy her worldly position. It would take me too long to recount the arguments used and the way in which she extricated herself from them all. She amazed everyone with the things she said. When at last they saw it was of no use, they placed her in her mother's house, to be kept there for some time. Her mother was fairly tired of all this disquiet, and gave her no help, but rather seemed to be against her. It may be that this was in order to test her better: at least, this is what she has since told me, and she is so saintly that whatever she says is to be believed. But the child did not understand this. Her confessor, too, was strongly opposed to her desires ; so that she had no help but from God, and from a maidservant of her mother's, who comforted her.

Thus she went on in great trouble and affliction until she had completed her twelfth year, when she heard that as they could not now hinder her from taking the veil, they were talking of taking her to the convent where her sister was, because it was not so severe. When she heard that, she determined to carry out her purpose by any possible means. So one day, when she had gone to mass with her mother, and her mother had gone into a confessional in the church to make

her confession, the girl asked her nurse to go and request one
of the Fathers to say a mass for her. As soon as she saw her
back turned, she put her clogs up her sleeve, picked up
her skirts, and went off as fast as ever she could go to this
convent, which was a long way off. Her nurse, finding she was
gone, went after her, and when she got near her, she begged a
man to stop her for her. The man afterwards said that he
had found himself unable to stir: and so he let her go. She
ran through the outer gate of the convent and shut it and
began to call out; and by the time the nurse arrived she was
inside the house; and they gave her the habit immediately.
Thus the good beginning which our Lord had wrought in her
was brought to its completion.

His Majesty speedily began to reward her with spiritual
graces, and she to serve Him with the greatest joy and the
deepest humility and detachment from all things. May He
be blessed for ever Who made her, once so fond of the most
elaborate and richest garments, to take pleasure in the poor
habit of serge! Not that this could conceal her beauty: for
our Lord had endowed her with natural graces as well as
spiritual; her personal qualities and intelligence being so
attractive as to move everyone to praise God for them. May
it please His Majesty that many may thus respond to His
call![1]

---

[1] St Theresa wrote some very interesting letters, published in her
Correspondence, about this nun. The one most worthy of attention is
one to Father Bañes, written at Salamanca, on her way to make the
foundation at Segovia in 1574. And, after all, this nun, yielding perhaps
to the insidious suggestions of her relations, quitted the Carmelite habit,
and betook herself to a Franciscan convent at Burgos, where she died, not
without being very sorry for what she had done in her fickleness.

CHAPTER XII

Of the life and death of Beatriz of the Incarnation, a nun whom the Lord led to this same house. She lived so perfect a life and her death was such that she ought to be had in remembrance.

A GIRL called Beatriz Onez, some relation to Doña Casilda, entered this convent as a nun. She came some years earlier. Her spirit filled everyone with amazement, seeing what great virtues the Lord was working in her. The nuns and the Prioress declare that in all her life there they never saw in her anything which could be considered an imperfection: nor, whatever might happen, did they ever see her behave but with a cheerful modesty which indicated clearly the inward happiness of her soul. A silence without gloom: for, although she spoke very little, it was so done that it could not be noticed as a singularity. She never was found to have spoken a word which could be found fault with: nor was any obstinacy found in her; nor did she ever make an excuse, although the Prioress, to try her, used to blame her for things she had not done, as is the custom in our houses by way of mortification. She never complained of anything, nor of any Sister; nor did she ever by word or look give offence to anyone, whatever office she held, nor give anyone occasion to think ill of her: nor was there ever any fault to accuse her of in chapter, although the correctors of faults in that house say they used to take notice of the most trifling things. In all circumstances, her outward and inward composure were extraordinary. This arose from her continually having eternity present to her thoughts, and the end for which God has created us. The praises of God were ever in her mouth, and an overflowing thankfulness; in a word, she was continually in prayer.

In the matter of obedience she never failed, but did all she was told promptly, exactly, and cheerfully. The greatest charity towards her neighbour: so that she used to say she would let herself be cut into a thousand pieces for anyone, if thereby he might not lose his soul and the fruition of her Brother Jesus Christ—for thus she used to call our Lord. Her very severe sufferings, from terrible sicknesses and sharp pains, of which I shall presently speak, she bore with as much goodwill and satisfaction as if they had been great pleasures and delights. Our Lord must have given her courage; for no otherwise would it have been possible to bear them with such joy.

It happened at Valladolid that certain people, for great crimes, were taken to be burnt. She must have heard that they were going to their death not so well prepared as was fitting; and she was so terribly distressed that she went to our Lord in great sorrow and earnestly besought Him for the salvation of their souls; and prayed that instead of the punishment they had deserved, or, that she might be worthy to obtain her request—for I do not accurately remember her words—she might suffer all her life all the pains and sufferings she could bear. That same night she had her first attack of fever; and until her death she was never without suffering. The criminals made a good end: whereby it appears that God heard her prayer.

Directly after this, an internal abscess formed, so acutely painful that it took all the courage our Lord had given her to bear it patiently. Being internal, no remedies they could give could do any good, until, in the Lord's good pleasure, it broke and discharged, which gave her some relief. Her appetite for suffering was not easily satisfied. Thus, on one Holy Cross Day, while listening to a sermon, the desire waxed so strong that, when the sermon was over, she went and threw herself

on her bed in a passion of weeping; and when they asked
what it was, she begged them to pray that God would send
her severe sufferings, and then she would be satisfied.

To the Prioress she spoke of all the affairs of her soul;
and that was a comfort to her.

In all her sickness she never gave the least trouble in the
world, nor did anything but what the infirmarian wished, even
to the drinking a little water.

It is a very common thing for souls who are given to
prayer to desire sufferings when they are without them: but
it is not many who, when those same sufferings are upon them,
can rejoice in bearing them. Some of the Sisters were there
at a time when she was so worn out that she had not long to
live, and had most acute pains, and an abscess in the throat,
so that she could not swallow; and she told the Prioress, who
was encouraging her to bear her great pain, that she was
not suffering at all, and that she would not on any account
exchange with any of the Sisters who were in good health.
She was so conscious of the presence of the Lord for Whom
she was suffering, that she dissimulated her sufferings as well
as she could, that no one might perceive how great they were:
so she made very little sign of suffering, except when the
pain forced it out of her.

She thought there was nobody in the world worse than
herself; and thus, in everything that we could judge of, her
humility was deep. She took great delight in speaking of
other people's virtues.

In matters of mortification she was very severe with herself. From anything in the nature of recreation she withdrew
herself so quietly that no one who was not on the look out for
it would notice it. She seemed not to live or converse with
creatures, so little did she concern herself about them; for,

however things might turn out, she went through them so peace-
fully that she was always the same: so much so that a Sister
once told her that she was like the people who make such
a point of their honour that, if they were hungry, they would
rather die of it than have anyone know. For the Sisters
could not believe that she really minded certain things so
little as she seemed to mind them.

All her work and her duties were done with but one end—
not to miss the good of them. Thus she used to say to the
Sisters, "The least thing we do is priceless, if done for the love
of God. We should not so much as move our eyes, Sisters,
but for love of Him and to please Him." She never meddled
with anything which was not her business; and so she never
noticed anybody's faults but her own. She so disliked being
well spoken of herself that she was careful not to speak of
others in their presence, so as not to give them pain.

She never sought relief by going into the garden or by means
of any created thing; because, as she used to say, it would be a
sort of discourtesy to distract herself from the pains which our
Lord gave her. So she never asked for anything besides what
was given her, but was content with that. She said too, that
it would really have been a cross to her to receive comfort from
anything but God. It is a fact that, when I questioned the
Sisters of that house, there was not one who had perceived in
her anything but what befitted a soul of high perfection.

When, then, the time came when our Lord was pleased to
take her from this life, her pains increased: and the Sisters
used from time to time to visit her, in order to praise God for
the contentedness with which they saw her endure so many
afflictions together. In particular, the chaplain who was the
confessor of the convent, a great servant of God, was very
anxious to be present at her death; for, having heard her
confessions, he reckoned her a saint. It pleased God to fulfil

his desire: for, while she was still in possession of her faculties, though having received unction, they sent for him to be at hand that night, if necessary, to absolve her and help her to die. A little before nine, about a quarter of an hour before her death, the chaplain and all the Sisters being present, all the pains left her, and she lifted up her eyes in a profound peace. An expression of joy, as it were a shining, overspread her countenance, and she seemed to be beholding some glad sight, for she smiled twice. So great was the spiritual joy and bliss experienced by all who were present, including the priest, that they could only say they felt as if they were in heaven. And in that same joy, with eyes raised to heaven, she expired. Her countenance was like an angel's: and so, according to our faith and according to her life, may we believe that God took her to rest in reward for her earnest desires to suffer for His sake.

The chaplain declares, and has repeated it to many people, that at the moment when her body was laid in the tomb he perceived a strong and very sweet odour arising from it. The sacristan Sister also declares that of all the candles which were burnt for her funeral rites and burial not one suffered any diminution of the wax. All can be believed of the mercy of God. When I spoke of these things to one of her confessors, a Jesuit, who had been her confessor and spiritual adviser for many years, he said it was no wonder, and he was not surprised, because he knew that our Lord held frequent converse with her. May it please His Majesty, my daughters, that we may learn to profit by the example of so good a companion, and by many others which our Lord gives us in these houses! Perhaps I may say something about the others, in order that Sisters who are somewhat slack may bestir themselves to imitate them, and that we may all give thanks to our Lord, Who thus makes His greatness shine forth in a few poor weak women.

CHAPTER XIII

How and by whom was founded the first House of Barefoot Carmelite friars, in 1568.

BEFORE I went to that foundation at Valladolid, I had already agreed, as I have before said, with the Father Fray Antonio of Jesus, then Prior of the Carmelite Monastery of St Anne's at Medina, and with Fray Juan of the Cross, that if a friars' monastery of the primitive Rule were founded, they should be the first to enter it. As I had no means of getting a house, I did nothing but commend it to our Lord. For, as I have said, I was well satisfied with those Fathers; because in the year after I had spoken about it to Brother Antonio of Jesus, the Lord had tried him with difficulties and he had borne them with great perfection: while of Brother John of the Cross, no trial was needed, because, even while he was living among the unreformed Fathers of the Cloth[1], he always lived a life of great perfection and strictness.

It pleased our Lord, having given me the chief thing, brothers to begin with, to provide for the rest. A gentleman of Avila, Don Rafael, to whom I had never spoken, came to know—I do not know or remember how—that we desired to found a monastery of Barefoot friars, and he came to me to offer to give me a house he had in a little place of perhaps not twenty inhabitants. He used it for a farmer who collected the rent in kind from that part of his property. I gave praise to our Lord and thanked him much, although I saw what sort of a house it must be. He told me that it was on the way to Medina del Campo; and as I was going there for

[1] The Calced Carmelites were spoken of as Fathers *of the Cloth* (del Paño) because their habit and cloak were usually of cloth, instead of serge, which was worn by the Discalced.

the foundation at Valladolid, since it is on the direct route, I could see it. I said I would: and so I did: for I set out from Avila in June with one companion and the chaplain of St Joseph's, Father Julian of Avila, the priest who, as I have said, helped me in these journeys.

We started early in the morning. As we did not know the way, we went wrong: and as the place is little known, we could not get much information about it. So we travelled that day with great weariness, for the sun was very strong: when we thought we were close to the place, we found we had as far again to go. I shall never forget the fatigue and perplexity we went through in that journey. So we arrived but little before nightfall. When we went into the house, it was in such a condition of extreme dirtiness that we dared not spend the night there: also there were a great many harvesters there. It had a fair entrance[1], and a room with an alcove with a garret above, and a little kitchen: this was the whole of the edifice which was to serve as our monastery. On thinking it over, I thought that the entrance might be made into a chapel and the attic into a choir for saying Office, for it would do well for that, and the room to sleep in. My companion, although she was much better than I, and much given to penance, could not bear to think of my making a monastery there; and so she said to me, "Assuredly, Mother, there is no one, however good, whose spirit could stand this: do not think of it." The Father who was travelling with me thought the same as my companion: but when I told him what I planned, he did not oppose me.

We went to spend the night in the church, because we were so very tired that we did not want to spend it watching.

---

[1] [The entrance had no floor above it, but went up to the roof, and the attic had openings or squints into it. The house had only two stories. Tr.]

When we got to Medina, I spoke at once to Father Fray Antonio and told him what had taken place, and said that if he had the courage to live there for a time, I was certain that God would soon make things better: it was everything to make a beginning. That which the Lord has now done seemed to me, so to say, as present and as certain as I now see it: and indeed much more than what I have seen up to the present: although at the time that I write this there are, by God's goodness, ten monasteries of Barefoot[1] friars. I told him that I did not believe the late Provincial or the present one would give us a licence (for the foundations had to be with their consent, as I said at the beginning) if they saw us in a very well-appointed house—let alone that we had no means of getting one; but that in that little place and house they would think it did not matter. He answered—for to him God had given more courage than to me—that he was ready to live not only there but in a pigsty. Fray Juan of the Cross was of the same mind.

Now we sought to obtain the leave of those two Fathers whom I have mentioned; for it was on that condition that our Father General had given us the licence. I trusted in our Lord to obtain it: and so I bade Father Fray Antonio take pains to do all he could to get together something for the house, while I went with Fray Juan of the Cross to the foundation of Valladolid, which I have narrated: and as we were there some days with workmen to repair the house, without enclosure, I had an opportunity of shewing Father Fray Juan of the Cross all our ways of going on, so that he should carry away a thorough knowledge of everything, of our mortification as well as of our sisterliness, and of our Recreation which we have all together, which is all so quietly done that it serves

---

[1] The first were Duruelo and Mancera, then Pastrana (1569), Alcalá (1570), Baeza (1572), Seville (1573). Afterwards some unreformed monasteries accepted the reform.

but to shew the Sisters' faults and to afford a little refreshment to enable us to endure the rigour of the Rule. Fray Juan was so good that I, at least, could have learned much more from him than he from me: but this was not what I did; I only shewed him the Sisters' way of going on.

God was pleased that Fray Alonso Gonzalez, the Provincial of our Order, whose leave I had to get, should be at Valladolid: he was an old man, of very good stuff and straightforward. When I asked him, I said so much to him of the account he would have to give to God if he hindered so good a work, and His Majesty so disposed him to agree, that he softened greatly towards our projects. When Doña Maria de Mendoza came with her brother the Bishop of Avila, who has always favoured and protected us, they succeeded in arranging it with him and with Father Fray Angel de Salazar, the late Provincial, from whom I feared all the difficulty. But afterwards there arose circumstances which necessitated the good offices of Doña Maria de Mendoza. And these friends, I believe, helped us much: notwithstanding, even without this timely help, the Lord, I believe, would have disposed his heart towards us, as He did that of the Father General, far though it had been from his mind.

Oh, válame Dios! how many things I have seen in these foundations which seemed impossible, and how easy it has been to His Majesty to make the ways plain! And how am I covered with confusion that, having seen all that I have seen, I am not better! Now that I see it written down, I am amazed, and I desire that our Lord should make everyone understand how in these foundations what we creatures have done is nothing. The Lord has ordered it all, working from such poor beginnings that His Majesty alone could have raised it to what it is now. May He be blessed for ever!

CHAPTER XIV

Continues the account of the first Foundation of friars: and tells
something of the life which they lead there, and of the good
work which our Lord began in those parts; to the honour and
glory of God.

SINCE I had won over the wills of these two, I felt as if
nothing was now lacking. We arranged that Fray Juan of
the Cross should go to the house and get it ready so that
they might get into it somehow; for I was in a great hurry
for them to begin, because I was much afraid that something
might happen to hinder us: and so he did. Father Fray
Antonio had already collected some of what was necessary.
We helped him as we could, but that was not much. He
came to speak to me at Valladolid, very happy, and told me
what he had got. It was very little. Only with hour-glasses
was he well provided: for he was taking five, to my great
amusement. He said he did not like to go without the means
of keeping the appointed Hours. I do not believe he had got
anything to sleep on.

There was little time spent in furnishing the house because, however much they might have wished to do, he had
no money. When he had done, Father Fray Antonio resigned
his Priorship and promised to observe the primitive Rule:
for, although they advised him to make trial of it first,
he would not. He went off to his little house with the
greatest content in the world: Fray Juan was already there.

Father Fray Antonio has told me that when he came in
sight of the little place it gave him a great inner joy: it
seemed to him that he had already done with the world, in
leaving all and stationing himself in that solitude. Neither

one nor the other of them felt the house uncomfortable; but
rather they seemed to themselves to be living very pleasantly.

Oh, válame Dios, how little difference these edifices and
luxuries make to one's mind! For the love of Him I beseech
you, my Sisters and Fathers, never leave off being very circum-
spect in this matter of large and sumptuous houses: let us keep
before us the example of our true founders, those holy fathers
from whom we are descended: for we know that by that road
of poverty and humility they attained to the fruition of God.
Truly I have seen more ardour and also more inward joy
where bodily conveniences have seemed to be wanting than
later when these had been acquired and a large house. What
good does its size do us when one cell is all that we habitually
use? What can it matter to us that it should be spacious
and well built? Nothing: for we are not to spend our time
gazing at the walls. If we consider that it is not an everlasting habitation, but is only for the short span of this life
at its longest, it will be good enough for us; seeing that the
less we possess here, the more joy we shall have there in that
eternity, where according to the love with which we have
imitated the life of our good Jesus will our mansions be.
Since we say that these beginnings are meant to reform the
Rule of His mother the Virgin, our Lady and Protectress, let
us not do to her, nor to our holy fathers who have gone before,
so great a wrong as to fail to live after their pattern. And
although, through our weakness, we cannot do so in everything, yet in things which neither make nor mar health, we
must be very careful; for at the most it is only a little bit of
pleasant toil, as those two Fathers found it: and when we
have once made up our mind to go through it, the difficulty
is over; for all the hardship is only a little at the beginning.

On the first or second Sunday of Advent in the year 1568

—I do not remember which of these Sundays it was—the first mass was said in that little porch of Bethlehem—for I think it was no better. In the following Lent, when I was going to the foundation of Toledo, I went that way. I arrived one morning. Father Fray Antonio of Jesus was cleaning out the doorway of the chapel with the happy face which he always has. I said to him, "How is this, Father? What has become of your dignity?" He answered, telling me his great happiness, in these words, "I execrate the time when I possessed it."

As I entered the chapel, I stood amazed to see the spirit which the Lord had inspired there: and not only I, but two merchants, friends of mine, who had come with me from Medina, did nothing but shed tears. There were so many crosses, so many skulls! I shall never forget a small wooden cross there was for holy water, which had fastened to it a paper image of Christ which seemed to excite more devotion than if it had been of the finest workmanship. The Office choir was the garret, half of which was lofty enough for standing to say the Hours: but they had to stoop a great deal to enter it and to hear mass. They had made at the two extreme corners next the chapel two hermitages, where they could only be prostrate or sitting: these were filled with hay, because the place was very cold and the roof was close over their heads; they had two openings facing the altar; and two stones to rest their heads on: and there were their crosses and skulls. I found that when Matins was finished they did not go away again before Prime, but remained there in prayer, so absorbed in it that sometimes when they returned to their places for Prime their habits were covered with snow, and they had not noticed it.

They said the Hours with another Father of the unreformed Rule, who went with them to live there but did not change his habit because he was very delicate; and with another young Brother, not in orders, who lived there also. They used to go to preach at many neighbouring places which were destitute of any teaching: and that was another reason why I was pleased that the house should have been founded in that place; for they told me that there was no monastery near, nor any means of maintaining one, which was a great pity. In so short a time they had gained such great esteem that it gave me the greatest joy when I heard of it. They used to go, as I said, to preach a league and a half or two leagues off, barefoot—for at that time they wore no sandals, although they were afterwards made to wear them—and in much snow and frost; and when they had preached and heard confessions, they returned home to their meal very late. They were so happy that they minded all this very little. Of food they had plenty, for the people of the neighbourhood provided them with more than they needed; and some gentlemen who lived in those parts and came to them for confession, offered them better houses and situations.

Among these was one Don Luis of Ciñco Villas. This gentleman had built a chapel for a picture of our Lady, which was indeed worthy of veneration. His father had sent it from Flanders by the hand of a merchant to his grandmother or mother, I forget which. He liked it so much that he kept it for himself many years; and then, at the hour of death, he directed that it should be placed in a great altar piece, one of the finest things that I have ever seen in my life— and many other people say the same. Father Fray Antonio of Jesus, when, at Don Luis' request, he went to the place and saw the picture, liked it so much—and quite rightly— that he consented to move the monastery to Mancera (that was the name of the place), although there was no well-water

there, nor did there appear any possibility of obtaining it.
Don Luis built them a monastery, a small one, agreeably to
their Rule; and fitted it up. He did it very nicely.

I cannot refrain from telling how the Lord gave them
water; for it was considered a miracle. One day after
supper, when Father Fray Antonio was in the cloister with
his Brothers, and they were talking about their need of water,
the Prior rose and took up a staff, and carried it in his hands,
and he made the sign of the cross over it, I think; but I do not
remember for certain whether he made the cross. Anyhow, he
made a sign with the staff and said, "Now dig here": and
when they had dug a very little depth there issued forth a
spring so abundant that it is difficult to get rid of it when the
well has to be cleaned, and it is inexhaustible; and it is very
good drinking water. They use it for every purpose, and, as I
said, it never fails. Afterwards when they had enclosed a
garden, they tried to obtain water in it, and made a well, and
spent a great deal; but up to the present time they have
found none worth speaking of.

Well, when I saw that little house, in which, only a short
time before, one could not have remained, now full of such a
spirit that, whichever way I looked, I found something to
edify me; and when I learned what manner of life theirs was,
and their mortification and prayer and the good example they
set (for a gentleman and his wife whom I knew, who lived
near, came to see me there, and could not say enough of their
saintliness and the good which they did in those villages)—
when I learned this, I could not sufficiently thank our Lord,
and I felt within me the greatest rejoicing; because I thought
I saw initiated a beginning which would be to the great good
of our Order and to the service of our Lord. May it please
His Majesty to carry it on as it is now going on, and my

anticipation will indeed come true. The merchants who had gone with me told me that they would not have missed going for all the world. What a thing virtue is, that such poverty gave them more pleasure than all the wealth they possessed, and satisfied them and rejoiced their soul!

The Fathers and I discussed several matters. In particular, I, being weak and worthless, besought them not to be so severe in their penance; for they carried it to extremes. And I told them that I had spent much earnest desire and prayer on the work, that the Lord would send me some one to begin it; and that now I saw so good a beginning, I feared that the devil was seeking to kill them before that which I hoped for was effected. Being faulty and of little faith, I did not sufficiently consider that it was God's work, and therefore His Majesty would see to carrying it on. The Fathers, as they had those qualities which were lacking in me, paid little attention to my advice to give up their exercises. So I departed in the very greatest joy; although I did not give God worthy thanks for mercies so signal. May it please His Majesty that, in His goodness, I may be worthy to do Him some service for all that I owe Him! Amen. For I well understood that this was a much greater favour than that which He had granted me in enabling me to found convents of nuns.

CHAPTER XV

Of the Foundation of the Monastery of the glorious St Joseph
in the city of Toledo, in 1569.

THERE was in the city of Toledo a merchant, a man much respected and a servant of God, who chose never to marry, but lived the life of a very good Catholic. He was a very truthful and honest man; and by legitimate trade he increased his wealth with the intention of using it for some work which should be pleasing to the Lord. His name was Martin Ramirez. A mortal sickness seized him. There was at Toledo a Father of the Company of Jesus, Paul Hernandez, who, while I was staying there, had heard my confession at the time when I was arranging for the foundation at Malagon. He had a great desire that a convent of our nuns should be founded at Toledo. Hearing of Martin Ramirez' illness, he went to speak to him, and told him how greatly to the Lord's service it would be to make this foundation, and that he could leave to its charge the chapelries and chaplainships which he desired to found; and that in it could be celebrated certain festivals; and all the rest which he had made up his mind to leave to one of the town parishes. He was already so ill that he saw he had not time to arrange for this, so he left it all in the hands of a brother of his, Alonso Alvarez Ramirez; and, this done, God took him. He acted wisely; for this Alonso Alvarez is a very discreet and God-fearing man, very truthful and liberal and accessible to reason. And as I have had a great many dealings with him, I can say this most truthfully as an eyewitness.

When Martin Ramirez died, I was making the foundation of Valladolid, where Father Paul Hernandez of the Company

TOLEDO

from photograph by Messrs W. M. Spooner & Co.

wrote to me, and Alonso Alvarez himself, giving me an account of what had taken place, and telling me to come quickly,
if I wished to accept that foundation: and so I started soon
after the repairs of the house were completed. I arrived at
Toledo on the eve of Lady Day, and I went to the house of
Doña Luisa[1], the foundress of Malagon, which is where I had
stayed at other times. I was most joyfully welcomed, because
her affection for me is very great. I took with me two companions, great servants of God, from St Joseph's of Avila.
An apartment was at once given us, as usual, where we lived
enclosed just as in a monastery.

I began at once to talk over the business with Alonso
Alvarez and a son-in-law of his, Diego Ortiz, who, although
a very good man and a theologian, was more wedded to his own
opinion than Alonso Alvarez, and did not yield so quickly to
reason. They began to demand of me a great many conditions
which I did not think suitable to consent to. We kept
going on with the negotiations, and seeking a hired house
to take possession of; and, although they hunted a great
deal, they could never find one that would do. No more
could I prevail with the Governor to give me the licence
—for there was no Archbishop[2] at this time—although
the lady with whom I was staying earnestly solicited it, and
also a gentleman who was a Canon of the church, Don Manrique, son of the Governor of Castille[3]. A great servant of
God was he, and is, for he is still alive; and, some years after

[1] De la Cerda. *See* ch. ix.

[2] The Archbishop was the celebrated Dominican, Bartolomé Carranza:
but his office was in abeyance, because he had been since 1557 in the prison
of the Holy Office at Valladolid. Thence he was sent to Rome, where he
died in 1576. So St Theresa says there was no Archbishop in 1569,
meaning that practically there was none.

[3] [Adelantado. Tr.]

the foundation of that house, he, although of very weak health, entered the Company of Jesus, where he is now.   He was a great person in Toledo, because of his great capacity and worth.   For all this I could not succeed in obtaining the licence; for when they had got the Governor to be a little propitious, the members of the Town Council[1] were not so. On the other hand, Alonso Alvarez and I could not come to terms because of his son-in-law, to whom he left too much. At last we came to disagree altogether.

I did not know what to do: for I had come for no other purpose but to found; and I saw that if I went away without, it would be much noticed.   In all these difficulties I minded not getting the licence more than anything else: because I believed that, when possession was taken, the Lord would provide, as He had done in other places.   So I determined to speak to the Governor.   I went into a church which was close to his house, and sent to beg that he would be so good as to speak to me.   It was already more than two months that we had been trying to persuade him, and things only got worse every day. When I found myself in his presence, I said that it was an evil thing that there should be women who desired to live in such strictness and perfection and enclosure, and that those who were enduring nothing of the kind, but were living in luxury, should desire to hinder works so well pleasing to our Lord.   These and many other things I said to him, with great decision, which was given me by the Lord.   It so moved him that before I parted from him he gave me the licence.

I went away well content: for I felt as if I had got every-

---

[1] The Council was originally formed to deal with political and feudal cases ; but through the Archbishop's Primacy and his landed property— he being a member of the Council—it became an ecclesiastical court for administration and litigation.

thing, when really I had nothing, for it might have been as much as three or four ducats that I had in hand. With this I bought two pictures, for we had no sort of image to put on the altar, and two straw mattresses and a blanket. Of a house there was no sign : with Alonso Alvarez I had already broken off. There was a friend of mine, a merchant, of the same place, who never had wished to marry, nor cared for anything but to do good to the prisoners in the gaol and many other good works. His name was Alonso de Avila. He told me not to be anxious about a house, for he would seek one for me. He fell me ill.

Some days before this, a very saintly Franciscan friar, Brother Martin of the Cross, had come to Toledo. He stayed some days, and when he went away, he sent me a young man[1], called Andrada, whose confessions he heard, begging him to do whatever I asked him. The young man was not rich, but very poor. One day when I was in church at mass, he came and spoke to me, and told me what that excellent man had told him, and assured me that anything whatever that he could do for me, he would, though he had nothing but himself to help us with. I thanked him; and it amused me much, and my companions more, to see what sort of assistance the holy man had sent us; for his appearance was not that of a person for Barefoot nuns to associate with.

Well, when I found myself with the licence and without anyone to help me, I did not know what to do, nor whom I could ask to seek a hired house for me. I remembered the young man whom Brother Martin of the Cross had sent me, and I spoke of him to my companions. They laughed at me a great deal, saying that I must do no such thing, that it would only serve to make our affairs public. I would not

---

[1] [A student. Tr.]

listen to them; for I trusted that his being sent by that
servant of God was not without significance, and that he
was meant to do something. So I sent to fetch him, and
told him, with all the secrecy that I could enjoin on him,
what had taken place, and that therefore I begged him to
seek a house for me, and I would give the name of a surety
for the rent. The surety was that good Alonso de Avila, who,
as I said, had fallen ill. He thought it an easy thing, and he
said he would seek one.

Early next morning, when I was at mass in the Jesuits'
church, he came to speak to me and said that he had already
got a house and had brought me the keys, that the house
was near at hand and that we should go to see it. So we
did: and it was such a good one that we lived in it about
a year. Often when I think over this foundation, the ways of
God amaze me. For about three months—at least more than
two, for I do not remember exactly—such wealthy people had
gone up and down Toledo hunting for a house, and had no
more found one than if there had been no houses in the town:
and all at once came this young man, who was not rich but
very poor, and it pleased the Lord that he should find it at
once. And it pleased Him that when it might have been
founded without difficulty if Alonso Alvarez and I had agreed,
this was not the case, but very far from it, in order that
the foundation might be made in poverty and difficulty.

Well, as we were satisfied with the house, I at once gave
orders to take possession before anything was done in it, so
that there might be no hindrance; and in a very short time
the said Andrada came to tell me that that day the house
would be cleared out so that we could take our furniture
there. I told him that there was but little to be done, since
we possessed nothing but two mattresses and a blanket. He

must have been astonished. My companions were vexed at my telling him, and said, How could I have done such a thing! for he would not care to help us, when he saw how poor we were. I paid no attention to this: nor did he think anything of it; for He who gave him that good will must needs lead him on until he had finished his work. And indeed in all that he did in getting the house in order and bringing in workmen, I do not think we were a bit more earnest than he was.

We borrowed what was necessary for saying mass; and we went with a workman[1] at nightfall with a little bell for taking possession, of the sort which they ring for the elevation, for we had no other; and we spent the whole night—I in great apprehension—getting ready: and we found nowhere to make the chapel but in a room to which the entrance was through another adjoining cottage occupied by some women, which the lady who owned it had let to us also.

We had not dared to say anything to the women, lest they should tell of us: and when we had everything ready just before dawn, we began to open the door, which was blocked up and opened into a tiny court. When the women, who were in bed, heard the knocks they arose in terror. We did our best to soothe them, but it was almost time for mass. Although they were rude, they did us no harm; and when they saw what it was for, the Lord pacified them. Afterwards I saw how badly we had done: for at the time, with the preoccupation which God sends in order that the work may be done, one does not think of what may go wrong.

Well, the trouble came when the lady to whom the house belonged heard that a chapel had been made in it; for she was the wife of a country gentleman. She made a great to-do.

[1] A mason.

It pleased the Lord that she was pacified on bethinking herself that, if she did not annoy us, she might sell us the house advantageously. Then, when the members of the Council heard that the monastery was established for which they had never been willing to grant a licence, they were furious, and they went to the house of a church dignitary, to whom I had imparted my plans in confidence, telling him what they meant to do to us. It was because the Governor, after he had given me the licence, had slipped off on a journey and was not in the town, that they betook themselves to this gentleman, indignant at such audacity as that an insignificant woman should have founded a convent there against their will. He made as though he knew nothing about it, and appeased them as well as he could, saying that I had done the same in other places, and surely in this case not without sufficient papers.

They sent us—I forget how many days after—an injunction forbidding mass to be said until we had shewn them the authorization by which we had founded. I answered them very mildly that I would do what they bid me, although I was not obliged to obey in this matter: and I begged Don Pedro Manrique, the gentleman of whom I have spoken, to go and speak to them and shew them the papers. He smoothed them down[1], the foundation being already made: for if not, we should have had trouble.

We went on some days with the mattresses and the blanket, without more to cover us, and one day we had not even a bit of wood enough to broil a sardine, when the Lord moved some one, I know not whom, to put in chapel for us a little faggot, with which we did better. At night we

---

[1] He shewed them, that is, that it would not look well to forbid it when it was already done.

suffered a little from cold, for it was cold: however, we covered ourselves with the blanket and with the serge cloaks which we wear over our habit, which have often been useful to us. It will be thought impossible that, being in the house of a lady who cared so much for me, we should have begun in such poverty. I do not know how it was, except that it pleased God that we should find out the good of that virtue. I did not ask her for anything, because I do not like giving trouble; and she perhaps did not think of it—for I owe her more than what she might have given us then.

It was a very good thing for us: because the interior consolation and happiness which we experienced was so great that it often makes me call to mind what the Lord keeps locked up in virtues. As it were a kind of sweet contemplation was caused by that want we were in: although it lasted but a short time; for very soon Alonso Alvarez himself and others provided us with what we wanted: more, indeed; for I felt so sad that it seemed just as if I had found many jewels of gold, and they had taken them from me and left me poor, so distressed was I that our poverty was come to an end. So were my companions: for, seeing them look sad, I asked what was the matter, and they said, "What is the matter, Mother? That we seem to be no longer poor."

From that time forward there grew within me the desire to be very poor, and there remained with me a sovereign contempt for worldly wealth: since the lack of it increases our interior wealth, which certainly brings with it a very different sufficiency and peace.

At the time when I was negotiating with Alonso Alvarez about the foundation, there were many people who disapproved of it and told me so, because the Alvarez family were not noble or gentle; although, as I have said, they were thoroughly good people of their estate, and in so considerable a town as Toledo I should not lack what was wanted. I did not pay much regard to what they said, because, glory be to God, I have always esteemed virtue above lineage. But there had been so much said about it to the Governor that he only gave me the licence on condition that I should found here as I had done in other places[1].

I did not know what to do, because when the convent was founded, the Alvarez family began again to treat of their business; but as it was already founded, I took advantage of this to give them the principal chapel, but said they should have no voice in what concerned the convent; which is the arrangement to this day.

It was a difficult matter to settle: for there was already a great personage who desired to have the principal chapel, and there were many different opinions about it. Our Lord was pleased to give me light on this question, and thus one day He said to me, Before the judgement seat of God of how little account will be those lineages and dignities! and He blamed me severely for having given ear to those who had spoken of this: for it was not a matter for such as already held the world in contempt. With these and many other considerations I made myself heartily ashamed, and I determined to arrange to give them the chapel as I had begun to do. And I have never repented it; for we have seen clearly what difficulty we should otherwise have experienced in buying a house; for with their help we bought the one where the nuns now live, which is one of the best houses in Toledo, and cost 12,000 ducats. And as so many masses and festivals are celebrated there, it is a joy to the nuns and brings joy also

---

[1] [In other places the founders were of gentle birth. Tr.]

to the people of the town. If I had given weight to the vain opinions of the world, it would have been impossible, so far as we can see, to have been housed so advantageously, and we should have done a wrong to him who with such good will did us this charity[1].

CHAPTER XVI

In which, to the honour and glory of God, are narrated some things which took place in the Convent of St Joseph at Toledo.

It seems a good thing to narrate some instances of the practice of certain nuns in our Lord's service, so that those who come after may endeavour always to imitate these good beginnings.

Before the house was bought, there came in a nun, Anne of the Mother of God, who was about forty, and had spent all her life in the service of His Majesty. And although in her house and way of living there was no lack of comfort, for she

---

[1] The house to which they removed was in the quarter of St Nicholas, opposite the Mint. They went there in 1570. Alonzo Ramirez and his son-in-law gave 12,000 escudos for it from what Martin Ramirez had left. Certain chapelries and obligations to keep such and such festivals were made a condition of the foundation, until the visit of the Father General Rossi. These obligations brought on the nuns so many annoyances that they had to leave that chapel, and in 1594 they removed to the house of Alonso Franco, close to the Misericordia, in the *plaza* of Sancho Minaya. Neither did they succeed in settling there, the neighbourhood being very low and noisy. Finally, in 1607, St Theresa's niece, Beatrix of Jesus, being Prioress, bought a house in the parish of St Leocadia, close to the Cambron Gate, and there the convent has been ever since. The first chapel was kept under the name of St Joseph's Oratory or Martin Ramirez' Chapelries.

was wealthy and lived alone, yet she chose rather the
poverty and obedience of our Order, and so came to speak to
me. She was far from strong: but when I saw a soul so good
and so resolute I thought it a good beginning for a new foundation; and so I admitted her. It pleased God to give her
much better health amidst her austerities and obedience than
she had when she was in liberty and comfort.

What edified me, so that I mention her here, was that
before the time for her profession, she made a deed of gift of
all that she possessed—and she was very rich—to this monastery, as an act of almsgiving. I did not like her doing this,
and was not willing to consent, telling her that perhaps either
she might repent of it, or we might not be willing to let her
be professed, so that it was a bad thing to do; although, if she
should go away, we should not let her go without taking back
what she had given us. I purposely made the worst of it:
first, that it might not prove an occasion for some temptation; and next, to prove her spirit the better. She answered
that, if this did happen, she would beg her bread for the love
of God: and I could never get anything more out of her than
that. She lived in great happiness and with much better
health.

The nuns in this convent practised obedience and mortification to such a degree that, at one time when I was staying
there, the Superior had to be very careful of her words,
for even if she spoke without reflection the nuns would
carry it out at once. Once they were looking at a pond
there was in the garden, and the Superior said, "Now, suppose I told her (a Sister who was standing by) to throw herself
in!" No sooner said than the nun was in, and got so wet
that she had to change her clothes. I was there on another
occasion, when the nuns were going to confession, and the one

whose turn came next went, while she was waiting, to speak
to the Superior[1]. The Superior said, Why, how was this?
was this a good method of recollection? She should put her
head into the well, and there think over her sins. The Sister
understood that she was to throw herself into the well, and
went off in such a hurry to do it that if they had not gone
after her quickly she would have done it, thinking to do to
God the greatest service in the world.

Other such things could be told, and instances of great
mortification: so much so that it became necessary for
certain learned men to explain to them the limits of obedience, and put restraints on them: for they were doing some
out of the way things which, but for their good intention,
would have been demerits rather than merits. This has
occurred to me to say in this place; but it is not only in this
convent, but in all, that such things are done that I could
wish I myself had nothing to do with the nuns, that I might
tell of them to the honour of our Lord in His handmaids.

While I was there, one of the Sisters was taken with
mortal sickness. When she had received the Sacraments
and Extreme Unction had been administered, her joy and
peace were so great that we could speak to her almost as if
she were in the next world, begging her to commend us in
heaven to God and to the Saints to whom we had a devotion.
A little before her death I went in to stay with her. I had
been praying to our Lord before the Blessed Sacrament to
grant her a good death. When I went in, I saw His Majesty
at her pillow, in the middle of the bed's head. He was holding His arms a little open, as though protecting her; and He
said to me that I might be quite certain He would thus

---

[1] St Theresa wrote at first *to speak to me*, then scratched it out and
wrote as in the text.

protect all the nuns who died in these convents, and that they need have no fear of temptations in the hour of death. This made me very recollected and comforted. After a little time I went and spoke to her, and she said, "Oh, Mother, what great things I have to see!" Thus she died, like an angel. And in some nuns who since then have died, I have observed a quietude and repose as if they were in a trance or in the prayer of quiet, shewing no sign of any temptation. So I trust that in the goodness of God He will give us this grace through the merits of His Son and of His glorious mother, whose habit we wear. Therefore, my daughters, let us strive to be true Carmelites, for our day's journey will soon be at an end: and if we realised the misery which many suffer at that hour, and the wiles and deceits with which the devil tempts them, we should highly esteem this gracious promise.

One thing which comes into my mind I should like to tell you, because I knew the person concerned, who was in some way akin to kinsmen of mine. He was a great gambler, and he had a certain amount of learning, which the devil made use of to deceive him, beginning to make him believe that a death-bed repentance availed nothing. He held this so stoutly that in no wise could they prevail on him to make his confession: nothing sufficed. Yet the poor fellow was extremely repentant and sorry for his sinful life; but he said, what was the use of confessing when he knew that he was damned? His confessor, a learned Dominican, did nothing but argue with him, but to no purpose, the devil taught him such subtle answers. This went on some days, and the confessor did not know what to do: but he and others must have earnestly prayed to the Lord for him: for he found mercy from Him. When the disease, which was a pain in the side, became very severe, the confessor came once more, and he must have thought out more arguments to ply him with: but it would have availed little if the Lord had not had pity on him and softened his heart. When the confessor began to talk and reason with him, he sat up in bed as if he had not been ill, and said, "To make short, do you say that my confession may avail me? Well, then, I will make it." And he sent for a clerk or notary —I do not remember which—and made a solemn oath to gamble no more and to amend his life: of this they were to be witnesses. And he made a very good confession, and received the Sacraments with such devotion that, so far as we can judge, according to our faith, he was saved. May it please our Lord, my Sisters, that we may live our life as true daughters of the Virgin, and keep our Rule, that our Lord may give us this grace which He has promised us. Amen.

CHAPTER XVII

Of the Foundation of the two Monasteries at Pastrana, the monks and the nuns'. This was in 1569.

WELL, as soon as the house at Toledo was founded, I had spent a fortnight up to Whitsun Eve, furnishing the chapel, and putting up gratings and other things, and there had been a great deal to do—for, as I said, we lived for about a year in that house—and I was fatigued with going about with the workmen; and at last, all was finished. That morning, when we sat down to breakfast in the refectory, it was such a great comfort to see that I had nothing more to do and that at that Whitsuntide I could for a space rejoice with our Lord, that I could hardly eat, my soul felt so happy.

I did not deserve this happiness; for while I was enjoying it, they came to say that a servant of the Princess of Eboli[1], Ruy Gomez de Silva's wife, was there. I went to him: and it was to say that she was sending for me; for she and I for some time past had been talking about founding a convent at Pastrana. I did not think it would have been so soon. I was sorry: for it was very risky to leave a convent founded so recently and against opposition; and so I determined at once not to go, and told him so. He said that that could not be suffered; because the Princess was there[2] already, and had come for no other purpose: it would be putting a slight on her. For all this, it did not enter my head to go; and so I told him to go to breakfast, and I would write to the Princess, and he might go. He was a very just man, and although it did not please him, yet he accepted it, when I had given him my reasons.

The nuns who had just come to live in the convent could not see that it was in any way possible to leave the house so soon. I went before the Blessed Sacrament to ask of the Lord that I might so write as not to give offence; for that would have been a very bad thing for us, because the friars were just beginning. And on all accounts it was a great thing to keep Ruy Gomez' favour, because he had so much influence with the king and with everyone. I do not remember whether I thought of this; but I know that I was very anxious not to displease the Princess. While I was praying, it was said to me from our Lord, That I must not fail to go, that my going would effect more than that foundation, and that I must take with me the Rule and Constitutions.

When I heard this, although I saw strong reasons for not going, I dared not do otherwise than as I was used in similar

---

[1] Doña Ana de Mendoza.   [2] [At Pastrana. Tr.]

matters; that is, to be guided by the advice of the confessor. So I sent for him, without telling him what I had heard in prayer: for I am always better satisfied not to do this, but to beseech the Lord to give them light according to what they can know of their own knowledge; and His Majesty, when He desires a thing to be done, puts it into their heart. This has often happened to me: and so it was now; for taking all into consideration, he thought I had better go, and so I determined to go. I left Toledo on the second day of Whitsuntide. The way was through Madrid: and my companions and I lodged at a Franciscan convent with the lady who built it and lived in it, Doña Leonor Mascareñas, a great servant of our Lord, who had been the King's governess. I had lodged there before, at other times when there had been occasion to pass that way, and she had always shewn me much kindness.

This lady told me that she was glad I had come at that time, because there was a hermit there who greatly desired to know me, and she thought that the life which he and his companions lived was very much the same as what our Rule prescribed. As I had only two friars, it came into my mind that it would be a great thing if he possibly might be one; so I begged her to arrange an interview. He was living in an apartment which she had given him, with another young Brother, Juan de la Miseria, a great servant of God, but very simple in worldly matters. Well, having opened communications, he came to tell me that he was intending to go to Rome.

And before I proceed further, I desire to narrate what I know of this Father, Mariano de San Benito. He was an Italian physician and was of great skill and ability. Being in the service of the Queen of Poland, steward of all her household, he never was inclined to marry, but held a

Commandery of St John[1]. Our Lord called him to leave all
for the better saving of his soul. Then he had to go through
troubles; for he was accused of being concerned in a murder,
and was kept two years in prison. He sought the assistance
of no lawyer, nor of anyone to undertake his defence, but only
God and His justice. They got witnesses who said that he
had sent for them to murder the man. It happened just as
with Holy Susanna's old men, that when they were asked
separately where he was at the time, one said he was sitting
on a couch, and the other said he was at a window. At last
they came to confess how they had got it up: and he assured
me that it had cost him a great deal of money to save them
from punishment; and that the very man who had planned
the attack on him had fallen into his hands, for he had certain
information laid against him, and that in the proceedings he
had done all he could not to harm him.

These and other virtues—for he is a pure and chaste
man, shy of having dealings with women—must have won for
him the light which our Lord gave him on the character of
the world, that he might be led to leave it. So he began to
consider which Order he would enter, and, as he told me, when
he thought over first one and then another with a view to his
own needs, in every one he found some drawback. He heard
that near Seville there were some hermits living together in
a stretch of waste ground called the Tardon, with a very
saintly man, Father Mateo[2], for their Superior. Each lived

---

[1] [Of Jerusalem. Tr.]

[2] The Venerable Father Mateo de la Fuente, the restorer of the Order
of St Basil in Spain. He was born about 1524 at Alminuete, near Toledo,
and studied at Salamanca. He began living as a hermit near Cordova,
but, finding himself to be gaining admiration, withdrew into the wilds of
the Sierra Morena. At the command of his director, Juan de Avila, he
took others with him, and they inhabited a waste place full of thistles

apart in his own cell without saying the Divine Office, but they had an oratory where they met for mass. They neither had any endowment nor asked or received alms, but lived by the work of their hands, and each ate alone, very poorly. When I heard of it, it seemed to me the very picture of our holy founders. He went on eight years in this manner of life.

When the Holy Council of Trent took place, and it was decreed that all hermits were to join some Order, he was minded to go to Rome to request that these might be left as they were, and this was his intention when I spoke to him. Then when he told me his manner of life, I shewed him our primitive Rule, and told him that without putting himself to so much trouble he might keep all his, since it was the same as ours; especially in the matter of living by the work of his hands, which was what he cared much for, telling me that the world was lost through idleness, and that it was their idleness which made it think so little of monks. As I was of the same mind, we agreed at once, and indeed altogether; for when I had given him my reasons for believing that he could please God greatly in our habit, he said he would think over it that night. I saw that he had already almost made up his mind, and I concluded that this was what I had heard in prayer, That I was going for more than to found a convent of nuns. It gave me the greatest satisfaction: for I felt sure it would be greatly to our Lord's service if he entered the Order.

His Majesty, desiring this, so moved him during that night, that next day he sent for me, quite determined, although surprised to find his intention so quickly changed, and that by a

[cardos], thence called *Cardon*, afterwards *Tardon*. They cultivated the ground, on the principle "He that will not work, neither let him eat." When St Pius V ordered all hermits to adopt the Rule of some Order, they took that of St Basil.

woman (as even now he sometimes tells me); as if this were the cause, and not the Lord, Who has power to change the heart. Great are His judgements. For he had been so many years without knowing what estate to take upon himself (for the life which he was then living was no estate, for they took no vows and were under no obligation but to live there in retirement). And so suddenly did God move him and gave him to understand how much he would serve Him in our estate, and that His Majesty had need of him to carry forward what was begun. For he has helped us much, and up to the present it has cost him many labours, and will cost him more before he has done with it, so far as one can judge from the present hostility to the primitive Rule. For through his ability, skill, and good life, he has great influence with many people who help and protect us.

Then he told me how Ruy Gomez had given him at Pastrana—the very place to which I was going—a good hermitage and site to make a settlement of hermits, and that he would like to make it one of our Order, and take the habit. I thanked him and gave great thanks to our Lord, because with the two licences which our most reverend Father General had given me for two monasteries, there was only one made. And from thence I sent a messenger to the aforesaid two Fathers, the Provincial and the late Provincial, entreating them to give me a licence, since the foundation could not be made without their consent: and I wrote to Don Alvaro de Mendoza, the Bishop of Avila, who was our great friend, begging him to obtain it of them. It pleased God that they thought it well. They must have deemed that in so remote a place it could not do them much harm. Father Mariano gave me his word to go there as soon as the licence came: with this I departed well content.

I found there the Princess and Prince Ruy Gomez, who gave me a warm welcome. They allotted to us a separate apartment, in which we stayed longer than I had expected; for the house was so small that the Princess had ordered a good deal of it to be pulled down and built up again: not the walls, however, but a good many things.

There I remained three months, going through considerable difficulties because the Princess asked of me several things which our Rule does not admit of; so I determined to come away without founding rather than do it. But Prince Ruy Gomez with his good sense—for he possesses much, and is open to reason—prevailed on his wife to give way, and I yielded on some points: for I was more eager to have the monastery of the monks than that of the nuns, for I knew how important it was, as has since been seen. During this time, the aforesaid hermits, Mariano and his companion, arrived; and, the licence having come, the Prince and Princess consented that the hermitage which they had given should be established for hermits of the Barefoot friars. I sent for Father Fray Antonio of Jesus, who was the first there was at Mancera, to begin the foundation of this monastery. I prepared them habits and cloaks and did all that I could that they might be able to take the habit without delay. During that time[1] I had sent to the convent of Medina del Campo for more nuns, for I had not taken with me more than two. At Medina there was a Father already in years, for although he was not very old, he was not young, but he was a very good preacher. His name was Brother Baltasar of Jesus. When he heard that this monastery was to be founded, he came with the nuns with the intention of becoming a Barefoot friar himself; and so he did when he came.

---

[1] [Before Brother Antonio arrived. Tr.]

When he told me his intention, I praised God. He gave
the habit to Father Mariano and his companion, both of
them as lay Brothers: for neither would Father Mariano
hear of being a priest, but wanted to enter the Order to
be least of all, nor could I persuade him. Afterwards, at
the command of our most reverend Father General, he was
ordained priest.

Well, when both monasteries were founded, and Father
Fray Antonio of Jesus had arrived, novices began to come in to
the monks' house (of what sort, some of them, will be told
hereafter), and to serve the Lord in such reality as, if it please
God, will be written by one who knows how to tell it better
than I; for about these matters I know very little. As for the
nuns, their convent was in great favour with the Prince and
Princess, and the Princess was assiduous in taking care of
them and shewing them kindness, until Prince Ruy Gomez
died. Then the devil—or it may have been that the Lord
permitted it, His Majesty knows why—in a sudden passion of
grief at his death, the Princess entered the convent as a nun[1].
In the grief which she was in, the rules of enclosure, to which
she was not used, cannot have been much to her taste: and
in consequence of the Holy Council's decrees, the Prioress[2]
could not give her the freedom she desired. The Princess
came to be so displeased with her and with them all, that

[1] This violent fit of grief and devotion blazed up and cooled down in
three days. It pleased Providence that all communications between
Theresa and the Princess should be broken off. When Mother Isabel de
Santo Domingo heard that the Princess was turning nun, she exclaimed,
" The Princess a nun! It is all over with the convent." And so it was.

[2] St Theresa, writing to Bañez, says "The nuns of Pastrana, although
the Princess has now returned to her own house, are like prisoners. The
Prior of Atocha, who has been there, did not venture to see them. The
friars too are in evil case. I do not see why such vassalage should be
endured."

even after she had taken off the habit and was in her own house, they were an offence to her; and the poor Sisters lived in such uneasiness that I tried in every way I could, with entreaties to the Superiors, that they would move the convent from Pastrana and establish one in Segovia, as will presently be narrated. Thither they went, leaving behind them whatever the Princess had given them[1], and taking with them some nuns whom she had ordered them to receive without dowry. The beds and trifling articles which those same nuns had brought in, they took with them. They left the people of the place very sorry for their departure.

It gave me the greatest satisfaction in the world to see them in peace: for I knew perfectly well that it was not at all their fault that the Princess was offended, but that when she was wearing the habit they treated her just as before she took it. The occasion was only what I said above; and the Princess's distress and that of a servant whom she took with her was, so far as is known, to blame for it all. To make short of it, the Lord Who permitted it must have seen that this convent was out of place there, for His judgements are deep and contrary to our understanding. I should not have ventured there on my own judgement alone without that of learned and saintly people.

[1] Before starting for Segovia the nuns gave into the hands of the mayor of Pastrana an inventory of everything the Princess had given them.

CHAPTER XVIII

Of the Foundation of St Joseph's at Salamanca, in 1570. Weighty counsels for Prioresses.

WHEN those two foundations were accomplished, I returned to the city of Toledo, where I remained some months, until the aforementioned house was bought and all could be left in order. While I was attending to this, a Rector of the Company of Jesus wrote to me from Salamanca telling me, and giving his reasons, that it would be a good thing to have a convent of our nuns there. Although the great poverty of the place[1] had kept me from founding a monastery in poverty there, yet I considered that so is Avila poor, and yet we had never wanted there, nor do I believe that God will allow His sevants to want. And our needs being so modest, with the fewness of the nuns, and their helping to support themselves by the labours of their hands, I determined to make the foundation: and I betook myself from Toledo to Avila, and thence I sought to obtain the licence from the Bishop of Salamanca[2]. When the Father Rector told him

[1] This remark of Theresa's is very striking. The bull of Pope Alexander IV, authorizing the university, gives a very different account. But the multitude of convents, colleges, hospitals, parochial foundations, chapelries, and entailed charges had left hardly a yard of land in private hands. Agriculture and trades had disappeared, people got their living by teaching, and morals were corrupted. St Theresa, being a daughter of Avila, hardly 20 leagues from Salamanca, could not have been ignorant of the difficulties and straits which such and such convents were beginning to experience; since, though much was given in alms, it came to little for each. For the rest, the city and country are by no means poor, but among the richest in Spain.

[2] The Bishop was Don Pedro Gonzalez de Mendoza, son of the Duke

about our Order, and that the foundation would be to God's service, he behaved so well as to give it at once.

It seemed to me that, having the Ordinary's licence, I had the convent founded, so easy did it appear. So I sought at once to rent a house, and a lady whom I knew let me have one. There were difficulties, because it was not the time for hiring houses, and some students were occupying it: but she got them to agree to give it up as soon as whoever was to come into it arrived there. They did not know what it was to be taken for: for I took the greatest care that nothing should be known until we had taken possession, because I know by experience what the devil does to hinder one of these convents. And although in this instance God did not permit him to hinder it at the beginning, because it pleased Him that the house should be founded, yet the troubles and opposition which we have since gone through have been so great that even now they are not altogether overcome, although at the time I am writing the house has been founded some years. So I believe God is greatly pleased with it, since the devil cannot bear it.

Well, having the licence, and being sure of the house, and trusting in God's mercy—for there was no one there to help me in any way, and much to be done in preparing the house —I started for Salamanca, taking with me only one companion, in order to go with greater secrecy: because I found it was better not to bring the Sisters until possession was taken; for I had learned a lesson from what had befallen me at Medina del Campo, having found myself in great difficulties there.

del Infantado. He was appointed by Philip II, and consecrated in 1560. He took part in the Council of Trent. He was Bishop of Salamanca 14 years. Three other convents besides St Theresa's were founded there in his time.

Because, if there should be any obstacles, nobody but myself would have to go through the difficulty, with no more than one nun, without whom I could not go. We arrived on the Eve of All Saints, having travelled a good piece of the way on the preceding night in bitter cold, and having slept at a village, I being very unwell.

I do not set down in these foundations the great hardships of the journeys, with cold, with heat of the sun, with snow— for it happened once to us to have it snow the whole day long —sometimes with losing our way, sometimes with great sicknesses and fevers. For, glory be to God, it is only my usual lot to be in poor health; but I saw clearly that our Lord used to give me strength. Because it has sometimes happened to me, when a foundation was on hand, to find myself in such sicknesses and pains that I was greatly distressed, for even in my cell I seemed not to be fit for anything but bed. And I would turn me to our Lord, complaining to His Majesty and saying, How could He desire me to do what I was not able to do? And then His Majesty gave strength to do it, although with difficulty; and with the zeal with which He filled me, and the anxiety, I seemed to forget myself.

So far as I remember, I never refrained from founding for fear of the trouble, although I had a great dislike to the journeys, especially the long ones; but when I had once set out, I thought little of them, seeing in Whose service they were undertaken, and considering that in that house the Lord would be praised, and the Blessed Sacrament would be there. To see one church more is a peculiar joy to me, when I call to mind the many which the Lutherans are doing away with. I do not know how any trouble, however great, can be feared, in consideration of so great a benefit to Christendom: for although many of us do not recognize Jesus Christ, very God and very Man, to be, as He is, in the Blessed Sacrament in many places; to us who do so, it must be a great joy. Certainly it often is so to me in chapel, when I see souls so pure as these engaged in praising God: for their purity cannot fail to be perceived in many ways, such as their obedience, and the happiness which it gives them to be in such strict enclosure and solitude, and their rejoicing when some opportunity of mortification presents itself. When the Lord gives the most grace to the Prioresses to practise them in this, I see the greatest happiness; and it is the case that the Prioresses sooner weary of giving them mortifications than they of obeying, for they never can have enough of it.

Although it is not connected with the story of the foundation of which I have begun to speak, some considerations on this subject of mortification present themselves to me, and it may be, my daughters, that they will be useful to the Prioresses; so, in order not to forget it, I will put them down here. For as there are different talents and virtues in the Superiors, so they seek to guide their nuns by these different ways. The one who is very ascetic will think anything which she commands in order to bend the will an easy thing, as it would be to herself, and yet perhaps it may do the Sisters a great deal of harm. This we must bear well in mind, that what we ourselves should feel harsh, we must not lay upon others. Discretion is a great matter in ruling, and in our Houses it is very needful; I may say, more so than in others, because the Sisters have to give a stricter account to the Prioress, both as regards internal and external matters.

Other Prioresses who are very spiritually minded would like to have nothing but praying. Indeed, the Lord leads souls by different ways. But the Prioresses must remember that they are not set there to choose the way according to their own taste, but to guide the nuns by the way of their Rule and Constitution, although they themselves may have to do violence to themselves, and would rather pursue another course.

I was once in one of these Houses with a Prioress who was very ascetic and guided all the nuns in that way. On one occasion the whole convent had to take the discipline during the seven penitential Psalms with prayers, and other things of the same sort. So does it befall them, if the Prioress is engrossed in prayer, although it is not the time of prayer, but after Matins, that then she keeps the whole convent, when it would be much better for them to go to bed again. If, as I say, she thinks much of mortifications, everything has to be kept up to the mark; and these little sheep of the Virgin are silent like so many little lambs, and certainly it rouses in me great emotion and shame, and is sometimes a great trial: for the Sisters do not notice it, because they are occupied entirely with God; but I fear for their health, and I would have them only to fulfil the Rule, which is plenty for them to accomplish; and that anything beyond this should be mildly done.

This matter of mortifications is specially important, and, for the love of our Lord, let the Prioresses look to it: for in these Houses discretion is a very important thing, and the consideration of each one's ability; and if the Prioresses do not walk very carefully in these matters, instead of doing the Sisters good, they will do them great harm and bring them into disquiet. They have to remember that this matter of mortifications is not of obligation: this is the first thing they have to consider; and although it is very necessary if the soul is to gain liberty and high perfection, yet this is not accomplished in a short time; but they ought to keep helping each one little by little, according to the measure of understanding and spirituality which God gives to each.

Probably they may think that understanding is not necessary for this. They are mistaken; for there are some who have much ado first to come to the understanding of perfection and also of the spirit of our Rule; and afterwards perhaps these will become the most saintly: because at first they did not know when it was right to exculpate themselves, and when not, and other small points which, when they understand them, they will perhaps carry out with ease. But if they are not able to understand them, they will not even see that these things belong to their perfection; which is worse. There is in one of these Houses a nun who is one of the greatest servants of God there is in them, so far as I can judge, great in spirituality, and in the graces which His Majesty bestows on her, humble and given to penance: yet she cannot succeed in understanding some points in the Constitutions. Our accusing each other of Faults in Chapter seems to her uncharitable, and she says that she cannot say anything against the Sisters. And there are other things of this kind which I could relate of some other Sisters who are great servants of God; who in other matters, as I see, could give odds to Sisters who understand these things very well.

And the Prioress must not think that she understands souls straight off: let her leave this to God, Who alone is able to comprehend them: but let her seek to lead each one in the way in which His Majesty leads her, always provided that she does not fail in obedience or in the more essential points of the Rule and Constitutions. That one of the eleven thousand virgins who hid herself did not fail to be a saint and a martyr, but rather suffered more, perhaps, than the other virgins, in coming afterwards all alone to offer herself for martyrdom.

Well, now, to return to mortifications. Sometimes the Prioress commands a Sister, to mortify her, something which, though small in itself, is serious to her: and suppose she does it, it leaves her so troubled and upset that it would have been better not to have commanded it. Let the Prioress at once take warning by this not to attempt to make her perfect by main force; but let her conceal her own views and go on little by little until the Lord works in her soul, lest that which she does to perfect her should only cause her disquiet and bring misery to her spirit, which is a very terrible thing; while she might be a very good nun without that particular perfection. And when she sees what the others do, little by little she will come to do the same, as we often have seen: and even if not, she will be saved without that virtue. For I know one of them who all her life has had great virtues and has served our Lord many years already, and in many ways; and yet she often has such imperfections and wrong feelings that she can do nothing with herself, and she knows it and mourns over it with me. I think God lets her fall into those faults without sin—for there is no sin in them—that she may humble herself and may have something to shew her that she is not altogether perfect. So, as some will bear great mortifications, and the greater the happier they will be, because the Lord has given to their souls strength to conquer their will; so others cannot bear even little ones, and to impose them would be like loading a child with two bushels of corn: not only could he not carry them, but would break down and fall to the ground. So, my daughters (to the Prioresses I am speaking), forgive me: for it is the things which I have seen some do which have made me enlarge so much on this point.

Another thing I could impress upon you, and it is very

important, that, although it should be only as a test of obedience, you should not command anything which, if it were done, might be a venial sin—and I have known of some things which would have been mortal sins if they had done them : at least the Sisters themselves might perhaps have been saved as having done them in their simplicity; but not the Prioress. For there is nothing she tells them which they do not immediately carry out. And as they hear and read of the things which the Saints in the desert did, so all things whatsoever seem right to them when commanded them, at least right that they should do them. Moreover let the Sisters be instructed that anything which would be a mortal sin if done not in obedience, they cannot do in obedience, except it were such a thing as omitting to hear mass or to keep Church fasts; for the Prioress may have good reasons for such as these. But throwing themselves into a well and things of that sort are wrong to do, because nobody has a right to think that God will perform a miracle for her as He has done for the Saints. There are plenty of things by which perfect obedience can be trained : and I would commend anything which keeps off from these dangers.

Once when a Sister at Malagon asked leave to take the discipline, the Prioress (no doubt others had been asking the same) said, "Let me alone." When she went on begging, she said, "Go along[1], let me alone." The Sister with great simplicity went and walked for some hours, until a Sister asked her, Why was she walking so much ?—or some such words—and she said that she had been told to do it. At that moment the bell rang for Matins, and when the Prioress asked why she had not come, the other Sister told her what had taken place.

---

[1] [Lit. "*Go and walk*." Tr.]

So it is necessary, as I said before, for Prioresses to be very careful with souls, having charge of those whom they see to be so obedient, and to take care what they do.

To another Prioress a nun went to shew her one of those very large worms, telling her to look how pretty it was, and the Prioress said joking, Then let her eat it. She went off and fried it very well. The cook asked her, Why she was frying it? and she said, To eat it: and so she meant to do; while this was very far from the Prioress' intention: and it might have done her much harm. It pleases me the more that the nuns should possess this virtue of obedience to an extreme degree, because I have a special love of it: and so I have done all I could that they might have it: but it would have been of little use if the Lord had not of His great mercy given grace to all the Sisters in common to desire it. May it please His Majesty still to increase it.

CHAPTER XIX

Continues the account of the Foundation at Salamanca.

I HAVE made a long digression, because when something occurs to me which it has pleased the Lord I should know by experience, I do not like not setting it down. It may be that what I think right is right. Always ask counsel, my daughters, of learned men; for in learning you will find the way of perfection with discretion and truth. It is very necessary for Prioresses, if they would fulfil their office aright, to make their confession to learned men. If not, they will make blunders enough, thinking them sanctity. Also they ought to arrange for their nuns to go to confession to learned men.

Well, on the Eve of All Saints, in the year which I have said above, about midday, we arrived in the city of Salamanca. From our lodging I sent for a good man there, called Nicholas Gutierrez, of whom I had requested that he would get the house cleared for us. He was a great servant of God, who by his good life had gained from His Majesty peace and contentment amid great troubles, for he had been through many : he had seen great prosperity, and had come to poverty, and bore himself in it as cheerfully as in his riches. He laboured much in this foundation with abundant devotion and good will.

When he came, he told me that the house was not yet empty, for he had not been able to get the students to turn out of it. I told him how important it was that they should give it up to us at once, before it became known that I was in the town ; for I always went in fear of some hindrance, as I have said. He went to the lady who owned the house, and made such efforts that it was left empty that very evening ; and about nightfall we entered it. It was the first convent which I founded without reserving the Blessed Sacrament ; because I used to think that it was not taking possession if It was not reserved, but now I had learned that that did not matter. This was a great comfort to me, seeing how unfit for it the students had left the place. They cannot have been at all nice in their ways : for the house was in such a state that we had no little work that night[1]. Next morning early the first mass was said, and I sent to fetch more nuns, who were to come from Medina del Campo.

[1] One of these students was afterwards a Bishop, Don Juan Moriz, of Barbastro. In the fifth volume of the *Año Teresiano*, p. 74, there is an interesting letter by him, in which (he was asking for St Theresa's canonization) he says, " Forty years ago, when I was a student at Salamanca, I turned out of the house where I was lodging that she might come in to found a convent."

The night of All Saints' Day I and my companion remained in the house alone. I can tell you, Sisters, that it makes me inclined to laugh when I think of the terror of my companion, Maria of the Sacrament, who was a nun older than I, a great servant of God. The house was very large and rambling, and had many garrets[1], and my companion could not get the students out of her head, thinking that, as they were so angry at having to go out of the house, one of them might have hidden in it. They could very well have done so as regards hiding places. We locked ourselves into a room where there was straw, which was the first thing I had provided for founding the house, because with it we could do without a bed. We slept in it that night with a blanket apiece which had been lent us.

Next day some nuns who lived next door, who, we had thought, would not like our coming, lent us bedclothes for our companions who were coming, and gave us alms: and all the time that we were in that house they bestowed on us many kindnesses and alms. The name of their house was Saint Isabel[2].

When my companion found herself locked into that room, she seemed to be a little reassured as to the students; yet notwithstanding, she did nothing but look from one side to

[1] The house, which to this day bears St Theresa's name, is between the churches of San Juan de Barbalos and that of St Thomas, now demolished. The house is even worse and more inconvenient than in St Theresa's time, the entrance to it being across an open sewer.

[2] They were Franciscan Tertiaries. Although the house was suppressed in 1857, it has since been re-established. There were houses of this Rule at Béjar and other places: and they still exist at Alba de Tormes, where the cell is still shewn in which St Theresa slept when she went to make her foundation there. The habit is violet or mulberry, in memory of the queen St Elizabeth.

the other : and the evil spirit must have helped to put thoughts of dangers into her mind in order to upset me ; for with my weak heart, a little suffices. I asked her why she was looking about, when nobody could get in. She said, "Mother, I am thinking, if I died here now, what would you do all alone ?" This, if it should come to pass, seemed to me a dreadful thing. It made me reflect a little, and be frightened too ; for even when I am not nervous, dead bodies always give me a curious feeling, even when I am not alone. And with the tolling of the bells into the bargain—for, as I said, it was the night of All Souls—the devil got a good start for making us lose our wits with childish trifles : when he sees that people are not afraid of him himself, he seeks other devices. I answered her, "Sister, when this comes to pass, I will think what to do : now let me go to sleep." As we had had two bad nights, sleep soon drove away our fears. Next day they were ended by the arrival of more nuns.

The convent was in that house three years, or it may have been four ; for I remember very little about it, because I was sent to the Incarnation at Avila[1]. I never, of my own will, would leave any convent, nor have I ever left one, until I could leave it in a house of its own, enclosed and fitted up to my liking. For in this God has given me the grace to like to be always foremost in the labour of it, and I have got together everything, even to the most trifling things, for the nuns' comfort and convenience, just as if I myself had to live all my life in that house : and so it has always given me great pleasure when they were settled in very well.

I felt deeply for what those Sisters suffered at Salamanca : not for lack of maintenance, for I saw to that from where I

---

[1] This was in 1571. She was sent for to be Prioress.

was, because the house was quite out of the way for alms; but for want of health, because the house was damp and very cold, and as it was so large this could not be remedied ; and the worst was, that the Blessed Sacrament was not reserved, which, under such strict enclosure, is a great deprivation. This was not the Sisters' feeling, but they bore all with a contentment to praise God for : and some of them said to me that it seemed to them wrong to wish for another house, for they lived there as happily as if they had had the Blessed Sacrament.

Well, the Superior, seeing their goodness and the troubles which they endured, and moved with pity, sent to the Incarnation for me. The nuns had already arranged with a gentleman there to let them have a house, only it was one which needed more than a thousand ducats to be spent on it before they could go into it. It was entailed property, but the owner agreed that we should be allowed to enter it, even if the king's licence should not have arrived, and that we might very well put up walls. Father Julian of Avila, the one who, as I have said, used to go with me to these founda- tions, had come with me, and I arranged that he should accompany me that we might see the house, to say what had to be done ; for I understand these matters well by reason of my experience.

We went in August, and with all the haste we could make, we had come to Michaelmas, which is the time when houses in those parts are let, and yet the house was not finished by a long way; but as we had not hired the one we were in for another year, another tenant had already taken it, and was hurrying us. The whitewashing of the chapel was all but finished. The gentleman who had sold us the house was away. Certain people who wished us well told us that we were acting unwisely in departing so soon: but where needs must, counsels can ill be taken if no remedy is provided. We removed on Michaelmas Eve, a little before daybreak. It was already made known abroad that Michaelmas would be the day when the Blessed Sacrament was to be reserved, and who the preacher was to be. It pleased the Lord that in the evening of the day when we removed there was such violent rain that carrying across the necessary things was done with difficulty. The chapel was newly built, and it was so badly roofed that most of it let the rain through. I can tell you, daughters, that I found myself very imperfect that day: for as the date had been given out, I did not know what to do; but I kept on lamenting, and I said to our Lord, as it were complaining, That I would He would either not command me to engage in these works, or would set this trouble right. That good man Nicholas Gutierrez, in his equanimity, as if it were nothing, told me very gently not to distress myself, for God would set it right. And so it was: for on Michaelmas Day, at the time when the people were to come, the sun began to shine. This moved me to devotion, and I saw how much better that dear good man had done with his trust in our Lord than I with my worry. There were a great many people and there was music, and the Blessed Sacrament was reserved with great solemnity. And as this house was well situated[1], the convent began to be known and cared for: in particular, the Countess of Monterey, Doña Maria Pimentel, favoured us greatly, and a lady named Doña Mariana, whose husband was mayor.

---

[1] It was opposite the Convent of the Madre de Dios, therefore near the beautiful but now dismantled Palace of Monterey. St Theresa stayed in this palace for some time, and in it she worked a great miracle. The convent was afterwards demolished when the Count de Fuentes built the magnificent convent of Recollet Augustinians.

The very next day, to temper our joy at having the Blessed Sacrament, came the gentleman who owned the house, so furious that I did not know what to do with him, and the devil would not allow him to listen to reason—for we had fulfilled all our agreement with him. Of little use was it to try to tell him so. When certain people had talked to him, he was a little pacified, but afterwards went back to his former mind. I made up my mind to leave the house to him, but this pleased him no better, because he wanted the money given him immediately[1]. It was his wife's house, and she had

---

[1] [The fundamental laws of Castile (the Siete Partidas) and the Leyes de Toro which were in operation almost unchanged in the Nueva Recopilacion of the time of Philip II, gave to married women absolute right to the enjoyment of all property belonging to them, whether entailed (de Mayorazgo) or not, during their life. There existed, however, a certain right of the husband *after the death of his wife* to a life interest in a portion (one-fourth) of the usufruct of the estate, and this of course gave the husband a pretext in some cases for interfering in the disposal of the property by the wife to whom it belonged.

This I gather is what happened in the case of Pedro de la Vanda. He was absent from Salamanca when his wife made the bargain to sell the house to Ana de la Encarnacion, but when he returned as the Nuns were moving in—St Teresa having then arrived—he apparently, considering that the purchase price ought to be paid down instead of by instalments, raised the objections he did to the terms and plunged the poor Nuns into the long and ruinous litigation that ensued. St Teresa herself in one of her letters says that the origin of the trouble was a *dispute between D. Pedro and his wife*, the latter being content to abide by the bargain that she herself had made, whilst her husband was not. When a mayorazgo was what is called a "Mayorazgo Regular," *in* CASTILE only, the succession of the entail followed the old Spanish tradition by which females inherited after males (as in the case of the crown of England) and this form of entail could only be broken by obtaining a royal license on the petition of the owner and the heirs in tail then in existence.

This was, however, purely a matter of payment and form when the parties interested were agreed. I do not know, but it is possible that

wished to sell it for the benefit of two daughters, and it was on this ground that they had asked for the licence. The money had been deposited with the person whom he had named.

It has turned out that, although this was more than three years ago, the purchase is not yet completed, nor do I know whether the convent will stay there[1] (that is why I mention this), I mean to say in that house, or where it will settle. What I do know is that in no convent of the primitive Rule which the Lord has yet founded have the nuns been through so much by a long way. Those who are there are, by God's mercy, so good that they bear it all cheerfully. May it please His Majesty that this may be to their advancement! For it matters little whether we have a good house or not: rather

Pedro de la Vanda by marital right and by his claim for a share of the income of the house in case of his wife's death, may have tried to stop the granting of the King's license to break the mayorazgo. So far as I know, the ground of his objection to the bargain that his wife had made with the Nuns and Ana de la Encarnacion was that the purchase money ought to be paid down and not by instalments.

I think I should add that the " *Licencia Marital* " of the husband was necessary before a wife could legally alienate the property belonging to her, not only because in case of her death he had a fourth life interest in the usufruct but also by *derecho marital*. If the husband unreasonably withheld this license the wife had the right of recourse to the tribunals, which could if necessary authorise the sale if desired by the wife-owner independently of the husband's permission.

What happened in the present case, as I gather, was that Pedro de la Vanda did not desire to quash the sale but to exert his right to modify the terms which his wife had made with the nuns. MARTIN HUME.]

[1] As a matter of fact, it did not ; and in letters written by the Saint in latter years can be seen what difficulty there was in finding a house, until they built the convent which they still possess outside the walls. This was partly laid in ruins by the Portuguese last century during the wars of succession, with the rest of the suburb of Villamayor.

it is a great pleasure when we find ourselves in a house which
we can be turned out of, remembering how the Lord of the
world had no house. The being in a house which was not
our own has sometimes happened to us, as may be seen in the
story of these Foundations; and it is the truth that I have
never seen a nun distressed about it. May it please His
Divine Majesty that we may not fail to attain the eternal
mansions, of His infinite goodness and mercy. Amen, amen.

CHAPTER XX

*Of the Foundation of the Convent of our Lady of the Annunciation
at Alba de Tormes, in 1571.*

NOT two months after the All Saints' Day when we had
taken possession of the house at Salamanca, I was entreated
on behalf of the Duke of Alba's bursar and his wife to make
a foundation and convent at Alba; and I was not much
inclined to do it, because the place was so small that the
convent would have to be endowed, and I would rather that
no convent was endowed. The Father Master Fray Domingo
Bañez, my confessor, of whom I have spoken at the beginning of this book, who happened to be at Salamanca, chid
me, and said that, since the Council [of Trent] had sanctioned
endowments, it would be wrong to refrain from founding a
convent on that account: and that I did not understand; for it
would make no difference to the nuns' being poor and very
perfect.

Before I go farther, I will say who the foundress was, and
how the Lord led her to found it.

¹JHS.

Teresa de Layz, the foundress of the convent of the Assumption² of our Lady at Alba de Tormes, was the daughter of noble parents, very aristocratic³ and of good descent. As they were not so wealthy as the position of their family required, they had taken up their abode in a village called Tordillos, two leagues from the said town of Alba. It is such a pity that, because worldly affairs are held in such vain estimation, people will rather endure the lack which there is in such small villages of good teaching and many other things which are means of giving light to the soul, than sacrifice one jot of the punctilios which what they call honour⁴ carries with it!

Well, as they already had four daughters, when Teresa de Layz came to be born, it was a great distress to her parents to find that she also was a girl. It is certainly much to be lamented that mortals, without understanding what is best for them, as though they were altogether ignorant of God's counsels, not knowing the great advantages which may come from daughters nor the great evils from sons, yet do not seem to be willing to leave these things to Him Who made all and knows all, but are dreadfully disappointed at what they should rejoice over. Like people whose faith is slumbering, they do not go on to consider nor remember that it is God who thus ordains it, so as to leave it all in His hands. And even if they are too blind to do this, it is great ignorance not to see how useless it is to make lamentations. Oh, my God, how differently we shall judge of these things in the day when the truth

---

¹ In the original MS. there is this break, the story recommencing with the monogram.

² [A slip for *Annunciation*.   Tr.]

³ [" *Muy hijos de algo*."   Tr.]

⁴ [*Honra*. See note to p. 187.   Tr.]

of all things shall be known! And how many fathers will find themselves going to hell because they have had sons, and how many mothers in like manner will find themselves in heaven through their daughters!

Well, to return to what I was saying, things came to such a pass that, as if the little girl's life were a thing which mattered little to them, on the third day from her birth she was left alone and without anyone's giving a thought to her from morning to night. In one thing they had done well, that they had had her baptized by an ecclesiastic directly she was born. At night, when a woman who had the care of her came, and heard what had happened, she went running to see whether she was dead, and with her some other people who had been to see the mother, who were witnesses of what I am about to relate. The woman took her up in her arms weeping, and said, "How is this, my child, are you not a Christian?" meaning, How cruel it had been! The baby lifted up her head and said, "Yes, I am[1]": and she spoke no more until the age when children usually speak. Those who heard her were left in astonishment; and from that time forth her mother began to care for her and make much of her, and she often said thus, That she would like to live to see what God would do with this child. She brought up the girls excellently, teaching them all that belongs to a good life.

When the time came for them to seek a marriage for her, she did not desire it, nor was she willing. But she came to hear that Francisco Velasquez, her present husband, who also is the founder of this convent, had proposed for her; and when she heard his name, she determined to marry, if they would marry her to him, although she had never seen him in her life. But the Lord saw this to be fitting, in order that

[1] [In Spanish, *Si soy*. Tr.]

the good work might be done which they both together have done to His Majesty's service. For besides being a good man, and wealthy, he loves his wife so much that he does her pleasure in everything : and with good reason; for everything which can be desired in a married woman the Lord bestowed on her in abundance.

She takes great care of her household; and her goodness is great. When her husband took her to Alba, his native place, and the billeting officers of the duke happened to billet a young gentleman in her house, she disliked it so much that she began to hate the place. For she being young and very good looking, the devil began to put evil thoughts into his mind: and if she had not been so good, some harm might have come of it. But when she perceived it, she begged her husband, without telling him anything, to take her away from Alba. He did so, and took her to Salamanca, where they lived very happily, and with many of the good things of this world, because he held an office which made everyone wish to please and entertain them. They had only one sorrow—that the Lord had given them no children : and great were the devotions and prayers which she offered that she might have them : and she never besought the Lord for anything else but to give her offspring in order that when she herself was dead they might continue praising His Majesty; for it seemed to her a grievous thing that His praises should end with her life, and there should be no one after her to praise His Majesty. And she herself told me that she never set before her any other reason for desiring it : and she is a woman of great truthfulness, and such a good Christian and so good that it often makes me praise our Lord to see what she does and to see a soul so desirous of pleasing Him continually. She never ceases to employ her time well.

Well, she went on desiring this for many years, and commending it to St Andrew, who, she was told, was an intercessor in such matters. After she had offered many prayers, one night when she was in bed, it was said to her, Do not seek to have children, for thou wouldst destroy thy soul. This left her astonished and afraid; yet for all this the desire did not leave her, because she thought, when her end was so good, why should she be destroying her soul? And so she went on imploring it of our Lord, and in particular making special prayers to St Andrew.

Once when she was desiring this same thing—she knows not whether awake or asleep: however it may have been, the vision is shewn to have been a true one by what followed— she thought she found herself in a house where in the patio, under the gallery, there was a well, and she saw in that place a meadow and green grass, with white flowers here and there in it, all so beautiful that she could not say enough of what it was to look at. Beside the well St Andrew appeared to her in the form of a very venerable and beautiful person, so that it gave her great delight to behold him: and he said to her, Other children are these than those whom thou desirest.

She wished that the great joy which she felt in that place might never come to an end; but it did not last long. And she understood clearly that that Saint was St Andrew, without anyone's telling her; and likewise that it was the will of our Lord that she should found a convent. By which we may know that it was an intellectual as well as an imaginary vision, and could not be a fancy nor an illusion of the devil. In the first place, it was not a fancy, because of its great effect; for from that moment she never again desired children; but she remained so convinced in her heart that this was the will of God that she neither asked for them nor wished for them any

more. Likewise it is seen not to have been the devil, both by
the effect which it caused, for nothing in which he is concerned
can do good; and here is the convent established, in which
our Lord is greatly served: and also because this was more
than six years before the convent was founded; and he is not
able to know the future.

Being deeply impressed by the vision, she said to her
husband that, since God was not pleased to give them
children, they had better found a convent of nuns. He,
being so good and loving her so much, was well pleased
with this, and began to consider where it should be. She
wished it to be in the place where she was born: but he
set before her certain real difficulties, that she might see it
would not be wise to make it there.

While they were considering this, the Duchess of Alba
sent for him; and when he came, she asked him to return to
Alba to hold a certain office and position which she would
give him in her household. He, when he had been to see
why she had sent for him, and had been told about it, accepted it, although it was much less profitable than the office
which he held at Salamanca. His wife, when she heard of
it, was miserable, because, as I have said, she hated the place;
but when he assured her that she would be given no more
guests, she was a little comforted, though for all that she was
very unhappy, because she liked living at Salamanca better.
He bought a house and sent for her. She came very unhappy, and was more so when she saw the house, because
although it was well situated and spacious, it had no out-
buildings. So she spent that night very unhappy.

Next day early when she went into the patio, she saw the
well in the very same place where she had seen St Andrew
beside it, and everything else just exactly as she had seen it :

I mean the place, not the Saint, nor meadow or flowers, although in her imagination she retained them and retains them still. Having seen this, she was astonished, and she determined to found the convent there; and she was in great comfort and peace, no longer wishing to go elsewhere: and they began buying other houses adjoining until they had got ample space. She was very anxious as to what Order it should be of, because she wanted the nuns to be few in number and strictly enclosed. When she spoke of it to two monks of different Orders, very good and learned men, they both told her that it would be better to do some other good work, because nuns for the most part were discontented: and plenty of other things they said; for as the devil disliked the foundation, he wished to prevent it, and he made them think the reasons they gave very reasonable. And, since they insisted so strongly on its not being a good thing, and the devil took still more pains to hinder it, it made her doubt and fear and decide not to do it: and so she told her husband. And they made up their minds, since men such as these had told them it was not a good thing, and their own intention was only to please our Lord, that they would let it alone. And so they agreed to marry a nephew of hers, the son of one of her sisters, whom she loved much, to a niece of her husband's, and to give them a great part of their property, and to leave the rest for the good of their own souls. They chose this nephew because he was very good and was young in years.

They were both quite resolved on this, and had altogether settled it. But since our Lord had ordained otherwise, their agreement availed little; for in less than a fortnight the nephew fell into an illness so severe that in a very few days our Lord took him to Himself. In this great extremity she was convinced that it was her determination to leave undone what God desired of her, in order to give money to her nephew, which had been the cause of his death; and so she was in great fear. She called to mind the prophet Jonah and what had befallen him for not being willing to obey God; and she thought God had punished her in like manner by taking from her that nephew whom she so dearly loved. From that day she determined that nothing should prevent her from founding the convent; and her husband the same: although they did not know how to carry it out. For it seems that God put into her heart that which now is actually done: but when she told it to other people and pictured to them what she wanted the convent to be like, they laughed at her, supposing that she could not find the kind of things she required. So in particular did a confessor of hers, a Franciscan, a man of learning and high character: and she was very disconsolate.

At that time this friar happened to go to a certain place where he was told of the convents of our Lady of Carmel which were in course of foundation. He inquired very carefully about them, and came back and told her that he had now discovered that she could found the convent, and just as she wished. He told her what was being done and that she had better arrange to discuss it with me; and so she did.

We had difficulty enough in coming to an agreement: because I have always maintained that convents which are founded with an endowment should have sufficient for the nuns not to be dependent on their relations or anyone else; but that they should be given in the house all that is needful for food and clothes and a very good provision for the sick: because many inconveniences arise from the lack of necessaries. For founding many convents in poverty without endowment, I have never lacked heart and confidence, being convinced that God will not fail them: but for founding them with an insufficient endowment, I do altogether lack it. I consider it better that they were not founded at all.

In the end they came to reason, and gave endowment enough for the numbers ; and—what cost them much—they left their own house to give it to us, and went to another very bad one. The Blessed Sacrament was reserved and the foundation made on the day of the Conversion of St Paul, in the year 1571, to the honour and glory of God ; and there, to my thinking, is His Majesty well served. May it please Him ever to carry it forward !

I had begun to narrate some particulars about some Sisters of these convents, thinking that, when these came to be read, those who are now living would no longer be alive, and that those who came after might be animated to carry forward such good beginnings. Afterwards I thought that there would be some one who would tell it better and more in detail, and without the fear which I have had, for I feel that I may be considered prejudiced in their favour; and so I have left out many things which anyone who has seen and heard them cannot but hold for miraculous, because they are supernatural. Of these I have not wished to tell any, nor of things which our Lord has clearly been seen to accomplish through their prayers.

I rather suspect that in my reckoning of the dates of these foundations there may be some error, although I have done my best to remember. As it is not very important, and can be corrected later, I give them from memory as well as I can ; it makes little odds if there should be some mistake.

CHAPTER XXI

Of the Foundation of the Carmelite Convent of the glorious
St Joseph, at Segovia. It was founded on St Joseph's Day,
1574.

I HAVE already told how, after the convents of Salamanca
and Alba were founded, and before the one at Salamanca was
settled in a house of its own, the Master Father Fray Pedro
Fernandez, who was at that time Apostolic Commissary,
ordered me to go to the Incarnation at Avila for three years, and
how, seeing the extreme need of the house at Salamanca, he
ordered me to go back there, that they might move to a house
of their own. While I was there one day in prayer, it was
said to me by our Lord that I was to go and found at Segovia.
To me this seemed an impossibility, because I could not go
unless I was sent, and I had understood from the Apostolic
Commissary, Master Fray Pedro Fernandez, that he did not wish
me to make any more foundations ; and I saw too, that as the
three years which I had to spend at the Incarnation were not
completed, there was great reason not to wish it.

While I was thinking over this, the Lord told me to tell
him, and he would do it. He was at Salamanca at the time,
and I wrote to him saying that he already knew that I held
instructions from our Most Reverend General not to omit
making a foundation whenever I saw a suitable opening
anywhere ; that at Segovia the Bishop and the town council
had consented to the foundation of a convent ; that if his
Paternity ordered me to do so, I would found it : that I
informed him of this in order to satisfy my own conscience ;
and that I should be at rest or content with whatever he
commanded. I believe these were my words, or thereabouts,

and that I thought it would be to the service of God. Well did it appear that His Majesty desired it: for he at once told me to found it, and gave me the licence: which greatly surprised me, from what I had heard him say in regard to this matter. From Salamanca I arranged to have a house hired for me: because, since the foundations of Toledo and Valladolid, I had seen that it was better to seek one of our own after we had taken possession, for many reasons, the first one being that I had not a penny to buy houses; but when a convent is already founded, the Lord soon provides it. Besides, one can thus choose a situation more to our purpose.

There was a lady there named Doña Ana de Jimena, who had been the wife of a country gentleman. She had once been to see me at Avila, and she was a great servant of God, and her vocation had always been to be a nun. So, when the convent was established, she entered it, with a daughter of hers who was leading a very good life; and for the unhappiness which she had been through as a wife and a widow, the Lord rendered her double happiness when she found herself in Religion. The mother and daughter had always lived in retirement and in the service of God. This saintly woman took the house and provided all that she saw was needful for us, both for the chapel and for ourselves; so that I had little trouble about this. But in order that there might be no foundation without some, He permitted me to go there with severe fever and loathing of food, and excessive interior troubles of dryness and darkness in my soul, and bodily ills of many kinds, which continued at their worst for three months: and the half year that I was there, I was ill all the time.

On St Joseph's Day we reserved the Blessed Sacrament. I would only enter the town secretly at night on the Eve,

SEGOVIA

from photograph by Messrs W. M. Spooner & Co.

although I had the permission of the Bishop and of the town council. The permission had been given long ago; but as I was at the Incarnation and had a Superior other than our Father the Generalissimo, I had not been able to make the foundation. And I had the permission of the Bishop—the one who was Bishop when the town council gave its consent —by word of mouth, as he gave it to a gentleman who asked it for us, by name Andres de Jimena. He did not concern himself to get it in writing: nor did I think it mattered. But I was mistaken: for when it came to the knowledge of the Vicar-general[1] that the convent had been founded, he came at once, very angry, and would not consent to let mass be said any more, and wanted to send to prison the priest who had said it, a Barefoot friar[2] who had gone with Father Julian of Avila, and another servant of God who went with me, by name Antonio Gaytan.

This Antonio Gaytan was a gentleman of Alba, and our Lord had called him when he was living much mixed up in the world: and a few years later he had it so under his feet that he only thought how he could do it greater service. Since in the account of subsequent foundations he will have to be mentioned, because he has helped me much and toiled much, I have said who he is: but if I had to say his virtues, I should not have done so soon. What profited us most on this journey was his being so ready to endure hardness that amongst the servants who travelled with us there was not one who did so much as he did of what had to be done. He is always much in prayer, and God has given him such grace that everything which would have put out anyone else gave him pleasure and came easy to him. So it was with all his

---

[1] [The Bishop being absent. Tr.]
[2] [St John of the Cross. Tr.]

trouble in these foundations: so that it is plain that God called him and Father Julian of Avila to this work— Father Julian, however, has been in it from the foundation of the first convent. It must have been on account of such companions that it pleased our Lord all should go well with me. Their discourse on the journeys consisted in speaking of God and teaching those who went with us and those whom we met: and so in every way they kept doing service to His Majesty. It is well, my daughters, those of you who shall read the story of these foundations, that you should learn what you owe them; so that, since for no advantage to themselves they so toiled for the good which you enjoy of living in these convents, you may commend them to our Lord and they may reap some profit through your prayers. For indeed, if you knew the weary nights and days they have passed, and their hardships on the road, you would do this with a very good will.

The Vicar-general would not leave our chapel without setting a constable at the door. Why, I know not. It a little served to frighten those who were there: but as for me, nothing which happened after taking possession ever troubled me much; my fears were all beforehand. I sent for some people, relations of one of the Sisters whom I had taken with me, who were some of the chief people of the town, that they might speak to the Vicar-general, and tell him that I had the Bishop's permission. He knew that very well, as he afterwards said; but he would have wished us to inform him beforehand. I believe it would have been much worse if we had. At last they settled with him to leave us in possession of the house, but he took away the Blessed Sacrament. This we did not mind.

We lived thus for some months until we bought a house,

and with it lawsuits in plenty. We had had one with the Franciscans about a house which was bought near theirs: about this other we had one with the Ransomers, and with the town council, because they held a mortgage on the house. Oh Jesus, how troublesome it is to contend with many opinions! When at last all seemed to be settled, it began over again; because it did not suffice to give them what they asked for, but straightway some other difficulty was made. It seems nothing as I relate it, but to go through, it was a great deal.

A nephew of the Bishop's who was Prior and a Canon of the church did all he could for us, so also did a Licentiate, Herrera, a very great servant of God. At last, by paying a great sum of money, that difficulty was settled. We still had the Ransomers' suit against us: so that we had to move into the new house with the greatest secrecy. When they found we were there—we went a day or two before Michaelmas—they thought good to come to terms with us for a payment.

The chief distress which these hindrances gave me was that it wanted only seven or eight days to the end of my three years at the Incarnation, and at all costs I was bound to be there at the end of them. It pleased the Lord that all was so well settled that there remained no contentions, and in two or three days more I was off to the Incarnation. For ever blessed be His name Who has done me so many favours, and may all His creatures praise Him! Amen.

CHAPTER XXII

Of the Foundation of the Convent of the Glorious St Joseph del
Salvador at Veas, on St Matthias' Day, 1575.

At the time when, as I have said, I had been sent from
the Incarnation to Salamanca, while I was there, a messenger
came from the town of Veas with letters for me from a lady
of that place and from the parish priest and from other people,
begging me to go and found a convent there, because they
already had a house for it, and there was nothing wanting
but to go and found it. I questioned the man. He told me
great things of the country, and rightly, for it is most delightful, and the climate good: but seeing how many leagues it
was off from Salamanca, I thought it out of the question,
especially as it would have to be done by order of the
Apostolic Commissary: for, as I have said, he was against
foundations, or at least not in favour of them. So I intended
to answer that I could not, without saying anything to him.
Afterwards I reflected that as he was at Salamanca at the
time, it would not be right to do so without asking his
opinion, because of the injunction which our Most Reverend
Father General had laid upon me not to omit to found.

When he had seen the letters he sent to tell me that he
did not think their feelings should be hurt; that he was
edified by their devotion; and that I should write to them
saying that when they had obtained leave from their Order[1],
we would be ready to make the foundation. I might be
certain, he said, that they would not get leave; for he had

---

[1] [The Knights of St James.   Tr.]

heard of the Knights Commanders from other parties who had tried for many years and not succeeded in getting it: and they should not be answered harshly.

I sometimes think of this, and how it comes to pass that of what our Lord wills, even when we will it not, we become the instrument without intending it, as in this case was the Father Master Fray Pedro Fernandez, the Commissary. And so when they had obtained the licence, he could not refuse, but the foundation was made in that way.

This convent of the Blessed St Joseph of the town of Veas was founded on St Matthias' Day in the year 1575. It had its origin in the following manner, to the honour and glory of God. There was at Veas a gentleman of noble lineage and abundance of worldly wealth, called Sancho Rodriguez de Sandoval. He was married to a lady named Doña Catalina Godinez. Among other children whom the Lord gave them were two daughters; the elder, Doña Catalina Godinez, the younger, Doña Maria de Sandoval, who were the foundresses of the said convent.

The elder girl was fourteen when our Lord called her for Himself. Up to that age she was very far from giving up the world, but rather held so high an opinion of herself that any marriages which her father attempted to arrange for her seemed to her not good enough.

One day when she was in a chamber within the one where her father was (although he was not yet up), by chance she happened to read on a crucifix which was there the title which is written over the cross; and suddenly, as she read it, the Lord entirely changed her. For she had been thinking over a match which was proposed for her, which was an exceedingly good one, and saying within herself, "With how little my father is satisfied, with just an eldest son! While

10—2

I myself intend my family to begin with me." She was not inclined to marry, because she thought it beneath her to be subject to anyone. Nor did she know whence this pride arose. Our Lord very well knew whence to cure it, blessed be His mercy!

Thus when she read the title, a light seemed to have come into her soul to know the truth, just as though the sunlight had come into a dark room: and in this light she fixed her eyes on the Lord Who was on the cross dripping with blood, and she thought how evil entreated He was, and thought of His great humility, and what a different way she was taking, walking in pride. She must have spent some time thus; for the Lord threw her into a trance. In this trance His Majesty gave her a genuine and deep knowledge of her own wretchedness, and she would have had everyone know of it. He gave her a desire to suffer for God so great that she could have wished to suffer all that the martyrs had gone through, and with this, so profound a self-abasement of humility and self-abhorrence that, if it had not been for offending God, she could have wished to be an outcast woman, that everyone might abhor her. And thus she began to abhor herself, with a great desire for penance, which she afterwards put in practice. Then and there she vowed poverty and chastity, and desired to see herself in such subjection that she would have been pleased if she could have been carried off to the Moors' country for it. All these virtues have so endured in her that it can well be seen to have been a supernatural favour of our Lord, as will presently be told in order that all may praise Him.

For ever blessed be Thou, my God, Who in one moment unmakest a soul and makest it anew! What is this, O Lord? I would fain ask here what the Apostles asked Thee when

Thou healedst the blind man, saying, Did his parents sin? I ask, Who had merited so sovereign a favour? Not she, for I have already said what were the thoughts from which Thou didst deliver her when Thou didst thus deal with her. Oh the depth of Thy judgements, Lord! Thou knowest what Thou doest, and I know not what I am saying, forasmuch as Thy works and judgements are unfathomable. Be Thou for ever glorified Who canst do even more; where should I be, if this were not! But it might be in part her mother; for she was so good a Christian that it may be Thy goodness was pleased, in lovingkindness, that in her life-time she should see such great virtue in her daughters. Sometimes I think Thou bestowest such favours on those who love Thee: doing them the grace of giving them something wherewith to serve Thee.

While she was in this state, there came such a loud noise overhead in the room that it seemed as if it was all tumbling down. All the noise seemed to come down through a corner to where she was, and she heard loud roars which went on some time; so that her father, who, as I have said, was not yet up, began to shake with fear, and, as though beside himself, put on a gown and took his sword and went in and looking very white he asked her what it was? She answered that she had seen nothing. He looked into another room within hers, and seeing nothing, he told her to go to her mother; and to her mother he said that she must not let her be alone, telling her what he had heard.

Well can it be understood from this what the devil must feel when he sees a soul lost out of his power whom he reckons already as his prey. As he so hates our good, I am not surprised that, when he saw the pitiful Lord doing so many mercies together, he was taken by surprise and made so great a demonstration of his feeling: especially as he must have

known that, through the wealth of graces contained in that
soul, he would have to go without other souls which he considered his own.   For it is my own belief that our Lord never
does so great a favour without its extending to others besides
the person himself.

She never told anything of this: but it left her with the
greatest desire for the Religious life, and she greatly besought
it of her parents.   They would never give consent.   At the
end of three years during which she had greatly besought it,
when she saw that they would not allow this, she dressed
herself, one St Joseph's Day, in plain sober clothes.   She told
only her mother, whom it would have been easy to persuade
to let her be a nun: her father she dared not.   In this dress
she went to church, in order that, since she had been seen in
it publicly, it might not be taken from her: and so it turned
out, for they said nothing about it.

During those three years she kept hours of prayer, and
mortified herself in every way she could, as the Lord taught
her.   She used to go into the yard and wet her face and
set herself in the sun, so that for her ill looks she might cease
to be harassed with offers of marriage.   She had a great dislike to giving orders to anyone, yet, as she kept house for
her parents, she had to give orders to the women servants, because she could not do otherwise.   Then, when she thought of
this, she would watch until they were asleep, and go and kiss
their feet, being distressed that, being better than her, they
should serve her.   As in the daytime she was kept occupied
with her parents, when the time for sleep came she would
spend the whole night in prayer; so that for a long time she
went with so little sleep that it would seem impossible if it
were not supernatural.   Her penances and disciplines were
many; for she had no one to keep her in check, nor did she

speak of it to anyone. Among other things, during the whole
of one Lent she wore next her skin one of her father's coats
of mail. She used to go apart to pray in a lonely place where
the devil played strange tricks upon her. Often she began
her prayers at ten in the evening, and was not aware of the
hour until day broke.

In these exercises she spent about four years, when the
Lord began to let her serve Him in other greater ones, giving
her most serious sicknesses and very painful, such as continual
fever, dropsy, and heart disease, and a cancer which was
excised. These sicknesses lasted about seventeen years; for
she was hardly ever well. Five years after God had done her
that favour, her father died: and her sister, who was then
fourteen (that is, a year after she herself had made that
change) also put on a plain dress, though she was very fond
of amusements, and also began to practise devotion. Her
mother aided her in all her good practices and desires.
Thus she approved of their employing themselves in one
work which was most virtuous, but very foreign to their
quality; namely, teaching girls to sew and read, without
payment, but only for the sake of teaching them to pray
and to know the Faith. They did much good; for many
resorted to them, and even to this day can be seen in these
the good habits which they learned when they were little.
But it did not last long; for the devil, being annoyed by the
good work, made the parents consider it mean to allow their
daughters to be taught gratis[1]. This together with the infirmities which began to oppress her, brought the work to an
end.

---

[1] This touch is expressive and hits off the stupidly quixotic character
of Spaniards then and now. It is unlikely that there was any teacher of
little girls there. But the gentry, rather than that their children should
take their turn with the children of the poor or be taught gratis, preferred
that they should grow up ignorant.

Five years after the death of the girls' father, their mother died. And, as it had always been Doña Catalina's vocation to be a nun, only that she had not been able to persuade them of it, she immediately sought to go and be a nun. Since there was no convent at Veas, her relations advised her, as the sisters had fairly sufficient to found a convent, to try to found one in her own town; for that this would be more to our Lord's service. As the town was under the Order of St James, the licence of the Council of Orders was requisite, and so she began diligently to set to work to get it. It was so hard to obtain that four years passed, during which they went to much expense and trouble, and until they presented a petition beseeching it of the King himself, nothing was of any avail: so much so that, seeing how great was the difficulty, her relations told her it was folly and she should let it alone. And, since she was almost always in bed, with such great infirmities, as I have said, they told her that no convent would admit her as a nun. She answered that if our Lord gave her good health within one month, they should recognize that the foundation would be to His pleasure, and she herself would go to Court to obtain it.

When she said this, it was more than six months since she had got out of bed and about eight since she had been able to move without help. At that time she had had continual fever for eight years, wasting and consumption, dropsy, with inflammation of the liver which burnt her up in such sort that even through her clothes the heat could be felt, and it singed her shift—a thing which seems incredible, but I myself heard from the doctor about the sicknesses which she had at that time; and I was greatly astonished. She had also arthritic gout and sciatica.

On the Eve of one St Sebastian's Day, a Saturday, our Lord gave her such perfect health that she did not know how to conceal it so that the miracle should not be known. She says that when the Lord was about to heal her, He sent her an interior trembling such that her sister thought her life was coming to a close; but she perceived in herself a complete change, and she says that in her soul she felt the difference, so much better was she. And she was much more pleased at having the health to be able to carry out the affair of the convent than she was to have her sufferings cease: because from the first moment when God called her, He had given her such self-abhorrence that for suffering she cared nothing. She says she had so strong a desire to suffer that she used to pray to God from her heart to exercise her in it in every way. His Majesty did not fail to accomplish this desire: for in those eight years she was bled more than five hundred times, besides so many cuppings as can be seen by the scars. Sometimes they rubbed salt into them, because a physician said it was good for drawing the poison out of a pain in the side; so this was done more than twenty times. What is most wonderful is that, when the doctor prescribed one of these remedies, she was eager for the moment when it should be carried out, without any dread; and she encouraged the doctors to the cauteries which were frequent for the cancer and on other such occasions. She says that what made her desire it was to prove the sincerity of her desire for martyrdom.

When she found herself suddenly well, she spoke to her confessor and doctor about moving her to another town, so that it might be said that the change of air had done it. They were not willing: rather the doctors told it abroad, because she was already considered incurable on account of a hemorrhage through the mouth so bad that they said it was the lungs themselves. She stayed in bed three days, not daring to get up, lest her good health should be known: but as that could no more be concealed than had been her sickness, it was of little use.

She told me that in the previous August, one day when she was imploring our Lord either to take from her the great desire she had to be a nun and found the convent, or else to grant her the means of doing so, she was assured with great certainty that she would be well in time to go in Lent to obtain the licence. And so she says, that during that period, although her infirmities oppressed her much more, she never lost hope that the Lord would do her that favour. And although she received unction twice: once so much *in extremis* that the doctor said it was no good going for the oil, for she would be dead before it came, she never lost her confidence in the Lord that she would die a nun. I do not mean to say that it was in that time between August and St Sebastian's Day that she twice received unction, but before.

When her brothers and relations saw the mercy and the miracle which the Lord had done in giving her health so suddenly, they dared not hinder her going, although it seemed folly. She spent three months at Court, and in the end the licence was not given her. But when that petition was presented to the King, and he heard it was for Barefoot Carmelites, he ordered it to be given at once. When it came to founding the convent, it was well seen that she had obtained its acceptance with God, by the Superiors' being willing to accept it, even though it was so far off, and the endowment very small. That which His Majesty desires cannot fail to be accomplished.

So the nuns arrived at the beginning of Lent, 1575. The people went forth in procession to receive them with great solemnity and rejoicing. The satisfaction was universal: even the very children shewed it to be a work with which the Lord was pleased. The convent was founded that same Lent, on St Matthias' Day, and called St Joseph's of the Saviour[1]. The two sisters took the habit in the same day, to their great joy. The health of Doña Catalina improved. Her humility, obedience, and desire to be thought little of shew clearly that her desires for the service of our Lord were genuine. May He be glorified for evermore!

This Sister told me among other things that, about twenty years ago, she lay down one night desiring to find the most perfect religious Order in the world, to become a nun in it. And she began to dream that she was walking along a way very strait and narrow, and dangerous for fear of falling into great ravines which she could see. And she saw a Barefoot friar such that, when afterwards she saw Brother Juan de la Miseria, a poor little Lay Brother of our Order who came to Veas while I was there, she thought he was the one she had seen. He said to her, Come with me, Sister. And he led her to a house where were a great number of nuns, and there was no other light in the house but that of the lighted candles which they were holding in their hands. She asked what Order it was; but they all kept silence, and lifted up their veils, and their faces were happy and smiling. And she declares that the faces she saw were those of the same Sisters whom she has now seen. And the Prioress took her by the hand, and said, Daughter, I want you here; and she shewed her the Constitutions and Rule. And when she awoke from this dream, it was with such content that she felt as if she had been in heaven: and she wrote down what she remembered of the Rule.

[1] This convent no longer exists. The Community was dispersed during the civil war, several of the nuns going to the convent at Jaen. The chapel is used for public worship, serving as a parish church.

A long time passed before she told her confessor or any-one; and nobody could tell her about that Order.

There came to Veas a Father of the Company [of Jesus] who knew her desires, and she shewed him the paper and said that if she could find that Order, she would be happy; for she would enter it at once. He knew of our monasteries and told her that that was the Rule of the Order of our Lady of Carmel—although he did not clearly make her understand this, but only told her about the monasteries which I was founding: and so she arranged to send me a messenger, as I have said. When the answer was brought her, she was so ill that her confessor told her she might make herself easy: for even if she were in the convent, they would turn her out; much less would they take her now. She was greatly distressed, and turned to our Lord with earnest longing and said, "My Lord and my God, I know by the Faith that Thou art He Who can do all things; then, O Life of my soul, do Thou take from me these desires, or give me the means of accomplishing them!"

This she said with exceeding confidence, imploring our Lady by the grief she felt when she saw her Son dead in her arms, to intercede for her. She heard a voice within her saying, Believe and hope; for I am He Who can do all things: Thou shalt have health. For to Him Who has had power to keep thee from dying of so many sicknesses, all mortal in their nature, and has forbidden them to work their natural effect, it will be more easy to take them away. She says that these words were said with such force and assurance that she could not doubt but that her desire would be accomplished, although many more infirmities weighed upon her, until our Lord gave her the health of which I have spoken. What has taken place certainly seems something incredible:

and if I had not myself gained my information from the doctor and from the women who lived in the house and from other people, it would have been little wonder, wicked as I am, if I had thought that it was somewhat exaggerated.

Although she is not strong, she has health enough to keep the Rule, and looks well, and is very cheerful and so humble in every way, as I have said, that she makes us all praise our Lord. The sisters gave to the Order all they had, without any reservation; for their only condition was that we should be willing to receive them as nuns. Her detachment from friends and country is great, and she always greatly desired to go far away, so she earnestly begged it of the Superiors; although she is so obedient that she remains there contentedly. Just in the same way, when she took the veil[1] she would not hear of being a choir Sister but a lay, until I wrote to her, saying many things and rebuking her for desiring anything but the will of the Father Provincial, saying that that was not the way to greater merit, and other such things, speaking harshly to her. And it is her greatest satisfaction when she is so treated. By this means I prevailed with her, much against her will.

Of this soul I know nothing which is not such as to please God: and this is the experience of us all. May it please His Majesty to keep her in His hand and increase her virtues and the grace which He has given, to His greater service and honour. Amen.

[1] [In Profession. Tr.]

CHAPTER XXIII

Of the Foundation of the Carmelite Convent of the glorious St
  Joseph in the city of Seville. The first mass was said on the
  Feast of the Blessed Trinity, 1575.

WELL, while I was at the town of Veas, waiting for the
licence of the Council of Orders for the foundation at Caravaca,
there came to see me a Barefoot Father of our Order, called
Master Fray Gerónimo of the Mother of God, Gracian, who
had taken our habit a few years before, at Alcalá. He was
a man of great learning, understanding, and modesty, together with great virtues practised through all his life: so
that our Lady seems to have chosen him out for the good of
the Primitive Order, when he was at Alcalá, very far from
taking our habit, although not from joining an Order. For
though his parents had other views for him on account of his
great ability and their being in high favour with the King, he
himself was far from being of their mind.

As soon as he became a student, his father wished to set
him to study law; but he, although he was very young,
minded this so much that by force of weeping he prevailed
upon him to let him attend the courses of theology. As soon
as he had taken his Master's degree, he treated with the
Jesuits[1] about entering the Company, and they had accepted

---

[1] In point of fact, the character of Father Gracian was rather that of
a Jesuit than of a Barefoot Carmelite. His great liking for the pulpit
and the confessional, his erudition, ability, and other qualifications for
the active life, seem to belong more to a Jesuit than to a member of a
religious Order given almost exclusively to the contemplative life. For
all that, the reform of the Carmelite Order required a man of great
activity, intelligence, and readiness; and Providence gave this to St
Theresa in the person of Father Gracian. On the other hand, St Theresa,

him, but for certain reasons they said he should wait some time. He has told me that every pleasure he had was a torment to him, because he felt that that was not a good way to heaven: and he always kept hours of prayer and his recollection and purity of thought with extreme care.

At that time a great friend of his, Fray Juan of Jesus, who likewise had a Master's degree, entered our Order as a lay Brother at the monastery of Pastrana. I do not know whether it was through a letter which he wrote to him about the greatness and antiquity of our Order, or what the beginning was: but something gave him such a great taste for reading everything about it and verifying it by the writings of great authors, that he says he often had an uneasy conscience, feeling that he was neglecting the study of other things because he could not tear himself away from these; and his hours of recreation he employed in these.

O wisdom and power of God! how little can we escape from what He wills! Well did our Lord see the great need there was of a person such as him for the work which His Majesty had commenced. I often give Him praises for the favour He has done us in this: for if I had taken great pains to request of His Majesty such a person as could set in order all the affairs of the Order in these their beginnings, I could not have succeeded in asking so much as His Majesty gave us in him. Blessed be He for ever!

Well, while it was very far from his mind to take our habit, he was asked to go to Pastrana to speak to the Prioress

accustomed as she was to be directed by Jesuits, found within her young Order a priest with such qualities as theirs, and at once made a vow of obedience to him. When the reform was accomplished and St Theresa was dead, Gracian seemed to be out of place, and he was expelled from the Order. He wished to join the Jesuits; but they would not accept him.

of the convent of our Order there (for it had not yet been removed thence) about receiving a nun. What means does not the Divine Majesty employ! For if he had meant to go there to take the habit, probably there would have been so many people to oppose it that he would never have done it. But our Lady the Virgin, to whom he is extremely devoted, desired to reward him by giving him her habit, and so I think it was through her intercession that God did him this favour. And indeed the cause of his having conceived such affection to the Order and taken the habit, was this glorious Virgin, who would not leave one so desirous of serving her without the opportunity of carrying it into effect: for it is her wont to favour those who seek her protection.

When he was a boy at Madrid he used often to go to an image of our Lady to which he had a special devotion. I forget where it was. He called it his lady-love, and visited it constantly. It must have been she who obtained from her Son the purity in which he has always lived. He says that sometimes the image seemed to him to have its eyes swollen with weeping for the many offences done against her Son. Thence there sprang up in him a great desire driving him to the cure of souls, and a very great distress when he witnessed offences against God. He is so strongly bent on this desire for the good of souls that any trouble whatever seems little to him if he thinks it can bear some fruit. This I have found by experience in many troubles which he has undergone.

Well, the Virgin led him to Pastrana as one caught with guile, he thinking that he was going in order to obtain the habit for a nun, and God was leading him there to give it to him himself. Oh secrets of God! And how, without our seeking, does He keep disposing our ways to shew us loving-kindness: and how thus did He reward this soul for the good works he had done and the good example he had always given and his earnest desire to serve His glorious Mother; for His Majesty must always repay this with great rewards.

So, when he got to Pastrana, he went to speak to the Prioress in order to get her to receive this nun; and it would seem as though he spoke in order that she might gain from our Lord his own reception. For when she saw him, his conversation is so agreeable that, for the most part, all who have to do with him love him—it is our Lord's grace—and thus he is loved extremely by all the monks and nuns who are under him. For though he overlooks no fault, for he is extremely particular about this, his way of seeing to the good of the Order is so mild and agreeable that no one is able to complain of him.

Well, it happened to the Prioress as to others; and it gave her the strongest wish that he should enter the Order. She told the Sisters to consider how important it was for them, because at that time there were in the Order very few or, one might say, nobody like him: and so they should all beseech our Lord not to let him go, but that he might take the habit. This Prioress is a very great servant of God, so that I think her petition alone would have been heard by His Majesty, how much more that of souls so good as the Sisters who were there.

All took it much to heart, and with fasting, discipline, and prayer they continually besought it of His Majesty: and so He was pleased to do us this loving kindness. For when Father Gracian went to the Brothers' monastery and saw so much religion and such good arrangements for the service of our Lord, and above all, knew it was the Order of His glorious Mother, whom he so desired to serve, his heart began to be moved not to return to the world. The devil set before him plenty of difficulties, especially the distress it would be to his parents, who loved him greatly, and who built their hopes on his helping the fortunes of their children[1]: for they had many sons and daughters. But he, leaving this charge to God, for Whom he was giving up everything, determined to become one of the Virgin's subjects and take her habit. So they gave it him, to the great joy of all, especially the nuns and Prioress, who gave great praises to our Lord, deeming that it was through their prayers that God had done them this favour.

He went through his year of probation with the humility of the most insignificant novices. His virtue was specially tried during a time when, the Prior being away, there was left as Senior a very young and ignorant Brother, who had not the least ability or sense for ruling: and as for experience, he had none, because he had only entered the monastery a short time before. The way he led them and the mortifications he made them do were something quite excessive, so that whenever I think of it I wonder how they could stand it, particularly people such as Fray Gerónimo. He had need, to bear it, of the enthusiasm which God gave him. And it has since been seen that that Brother is afflicted with melancholia, and wherever he has been there have been difficulties with him, even when under obedience; how much more when he had to rule! For his moods are master of him, although he is a good monk. And God sometimes permits such mistakes as that of putting people like him in office, in order to perfect the virtue of obedience in those whom He loves. So it must have been in

---

[1] Considering that Gracian's father was secretary to Philip II and that the king was very fond of him, he was by no means well off. Several of his daughters, for want of money, had to enter convents which accepted them without dowry, as a charity.

this case.   And by virtue of this trial, God has given Father
Fray Jerónimo of the Mother of God the greatest light in
matters of obedience, to teach those who are under him, as
one who had such good practice in it at the beginning.   And
in order that he might not lack experience in anything which
is needful for us, he had great temptations three months
before his Profession; but, like the good captain he was to
be of the Sons of the Virgin, he defended himself well against
them: and when the devil more strongly urged him to give
up the habit, he defended himself by promising not to give it
up and promising to make his vows.   He gave me a certain
work[1] which he had written during those great temptations,
which edified me greatly, and shews well what strength the
Lord gave him.

It may appear unsuitable that he should have communicated to me so many particulars about his soul.   It may be
that the Lord willed it in order that I might set it down here,
for praised be He in His creatures: for I know that he has
not opened himself so freely to his confessor nor to anyone
else.   The reason why he sometimes did so was that he had
reason to think that, from my age and from what he had
heard of me, I must have some experience.   *A propos* of
other things of which we happened to be speaking, he told
me these things and others which are not for writing down,
or I could say much more.   I have indeed restrained myself
lest it might pain him if this ever came into his hands.

I have not been able to write more, nor have I thought it
necessary; because this writing will not, if ever, be seen for a
long time; and it will be long before the memory is forgotten
of one who has worked so well for the reformation of the

---

[1] What this work was, is not known.

primitive Rule. For, although he was not the first to begin it, he came at the right moment; for sometimes I should have been sorry that it had begun before if I had not such great trust in God's mercy. I am speaking of the monks' Houses: for the nuns' Houses, through His goodness, have always done well up to the present. And those of the Brothers had not done badly: only they carried in them seeds of quick decay; because, as they had no separate Province, they were governed by the unreformed Carmelites. To those who might have governed—that is, Father Fray Antonio of Jesus, who began the reform—was not given this power; no more had they Constitutions given by our Most Reverend Father General. In each House they did as seemed good to them. Until the Constitutions came, or they were governed by the reformed Order, there was continual trouble: for to some one thing seemed good and to others another. It sometimes distressed me sorely.

Our Lord set it right by the hand of Father Master Fray Jerónimo of the Mother of God: because he was made Apostolic Commissary, and was given authority and rule over the Discalced monks and nuns, and made Constitutions for the Brothers. For we nuns had them already from our Most Reverend Father General: so he did not make them for us, but for them; through the Apostolic authority which he held, and through the good abilities which, as I have said, the Lord had given him. The first time he visited them he set everything in such order and reasonable ways, that it plainly shewed him to be aided by the Divine Majesty, and to have been chosen by our Lady for the good of her Order. Of whom I earnestly entreat that she would prevail with her Son to favour him continually and give him grace to advance in His service. Amen.

CHAPTER XXIV

Continuation of the Foundation at Seville.

WHEN, as I have said, Father Master Fray Jerónimo Gracian came to see me at Veas, we had never met, although I had greatly desired it; sometimes written, however. It gave me great pleasure when I heard he was there, for I greatly desired to see him on account of the good which had been told me of him. But very much more was I delighted when I began to talk with him: for he pleased me so much that I felt as if those who had extolled him to me had not really known him. I had been so sorrowful; but when I saw him it seemed as if the Lord were making me see the good which was to come to us by means of him. And so during those days I went about in such exceeding joy and satisfaction that truly I myself was surprised at myself. At that time he only held a commission for Andalusia; but while he was at Veas, the Nuncio sent for him to see him, and then he gave it to him for the Barefoot monks and nuns of the Province of Castille[1].

[1] [The circumstances were as follows. The battle between the Observant Carmelites and the Reformed Descalzos had just begun. Gracian was selected by the latter as the best man to lead them. Vargas, the Dominican, had at the request of Philip II been appointed by the Pope Apostolic Visitor of the Order in Andalusia with very wide authority. He was in favour of reform and had transferred his powers to Gracian late in 1573, whereby the latter *secretly* was invested with authority over the Order in the Province even greater than that of the General and the Provincial. As soon as this was discovered by the latter they obtained from the new Pope Gregory XIII a revocation of Vargas' powers (though the revocation was not made public at the time). The reform party with the aid of Philip II obtained from the Nuncio, Ormaneto, in the meanwhile a confirmation of Vargas' powers (22 Sept. 1574). So that when Gracian went to Veas in the spring of 1575, after Lent, he was, by Apostolic authority and the transference of Vargas'

Chapter XXIV

My spirit was so full of joy that, during those days, I could not give thanks enough to our Lord, nor did I want to do anything else.

At that time the licence to found at Caravaca was brought

Commission, supreme in the Order in Andalusia ; and as such—and also because of her admiration and affection for him—was the recipient of Sta Teresa's obedience. He was summoned to Madrid by the Nuncio whilst he was at Veas to take possession of the new brief that had been made out for him investing him direct with the powers formerly held by Vargas (April 1575). A month afterwards the General Chapter of the Order by virtue of the Pope's revocation denounced Vargas' Commission, and that held by his colleague Fernandez for Castile, and fulminated their edicts against the reformers. The issue was thus joined. On the one hand was the King, the Nuncio, Sta Teresa, Gracian, the Court and the Reformers ; on the other the Pope, the General and Provincial of the Carmelites and the old Observants. The next move (a disastrous one for Gracian) was for the King and the Nuncio to invest Gracian with full powers as "Visitor over the Descalzos Houses of Castile and Andalusia, and Apostolic Commissary over the Observant Houses of Andalusia." This was in the autumn of 1575. When Sta Teresa says that she was brought under his obedience by reason of his Apostolic Commission for Castile she meant that this was in regard of her foundations in Castile (Avila, Salamanca, Valladolid, etc.) as she had already been under his obedience in respect to her foundation in Veas, by reason of his Apostolic Commission for Andalusia. Teresa, writing her *Fundaciones* some time afterwards, rather confused matters. Gracian was summoned from Veas by the Nuncio not primarily to be made Commissary for Castile : that appointment was made some months afterwards as a retort to the action of the Carmelite Chapter, but to receive the direct brief from the Nuncio appointing him Visitor of Andalusia, in order that the Papal revocation of the powers held by Vargas might in no case divest Gracian of his authority there. Gracian thenceforward therefore held the authority by a double tenure : i.e. by Vargas' transfer and by the direct brief of the Nuncio. The authority over Castile was given to him four months later for the reasons stated above.

It is curious that Sta Teresa herself did not know until a few months before she saw Gracian that Veas was for ecclesiastical purposes in Andalusia. She first learnt it from her Prioress at Valladolid, Maria Bautista. MARTIN HUME.]

me, but different from what was necessary for my purpose, and so it had to be sent back to the Court again. For I had written to the foundresses saying that in no wise could it be founded unless permission were obtained for a certain particular thing which was here lacking; so it had to go back to the Court. I myself did not at all like waiting at Veas so long, and I wanted to go back to Castille. But, as Father Fray Jerónimo was there, to whom that convent was already subject, he being Commissary of all the Province of Castille[1], I could do nothing without his will; so I communicated with him. He thought that, once I was gone, the foundation at Caravaca would drop through. Also that it would be greatly to the service of God to found a convent at Seville: which seemed to him very easy, because certain people had asked him for it who were very well able to give a house at once; and the Archbishop of Seville was so much in favour of the Order that he felt certain it would be doing him a great pleasure. So it was agreed that the Prioress and nuns whom I was taking for Caravaca should go to Seville.

For certain reasons I had always greatly resisted the foundation of convents in Andalusia. (For when I went to Veas, if I had known that it was in the Province of Andalusia, I should never have gone: but the mistake was that, although it is not in the country of Andalusia, but, I think, about four or five leagues before that begins, it is in that [ecclesiastical] Province.) Yet, when I found that that was the mind of the Superior, I immediately fell in with it: for our Lord gives me grace to think that they are right in everything. Although I had settled to found elsewhere, and although I had certain very serious reasons against going to

[1] [A slip for *Andalusia*. Tr.]

Seville, I began to prepare for the journey quickly, because it was beginning to be very hot.

Father Gracian, the Apostolic Commissary, being sent for by the Nuncio, went off by himself, and we to Seville with my good escort, Father Julian of Avila and Antonio Gaytan and a Barefoot Brother. We went well covered up in carts, which was always our manner of travelling, and when we went into the inn we took an apartment good or bad as there might be, and a Sister took in at the door whatever we needed; for not even those who travelled with us came in. We made such haste that, although we did not travel on feast days, we got to Seville on the Thursday before the Feast of the Blessed Trinity, having endured the greatest heat on the journey. For I can tell you, Sisters, that when the whole force of the sun was beating down on the carts, going into them was like going into a purgatory. What with sometimes thinking on hell, at other times feeling that they were doing and suffering something for God, the Sisters travelled very contentedly and cheerfully: for six of those who went with me were souls such that I think I could have ventured to go with them into the land of the Turks and they would have had courage, or more properly speaking, the Lord would have given it them to suffer for Him. For such were their desires and their conversation, well trained as they were in prayer and mortification. Because, as they had to remain so far away, I had arranged that they should be of those who seemed to me most fitted for the purpose. And they needed it all, they had to go through such troubles: some of which, and the greatest, I will not relate, because a certain person might be concerned.

One day before Whitsuntide, God gave them a grievous trouble, which was the giving me a very bad fever. I believe that it was their crying to God which availed to arrest the

sickness: for never in my life have I had a fever of that kind
which did not go on to worse. It was of such a sort that
I seemed like one asleep, I was so light-headed. They took
to throwing water on my face, but so hot from the sun that it
gave but little refreshment. I will not omit to tell you what
a bad lodging we had in this extremity: that is, they gave us
a little room with an unceiled roof. It had no window; and
if the door was opened, the full sun poured in. You must
remember that the sun there is not like the sun of Castille,
but much more harassing. They had me laid in a bed, but
I thought it better to lie on the floor, because the bed was so
uneven that I did not know how to lie in it, for it seemed to
be made of sharp stones. What a thing is sickness! for in
health everything is easy to bear. At last I thought it best
to get up and go on: for the sun seemed more bearable in the
open air than in that little room. What must it be for the
wretched people in hell, who can never make a change, for ever!
For although it be from hardship to hardship, a change seems
some alleviation. I have sometimes happened to have a severe
pain somewhere, and if I got one somewhere else, although
quite as painful, the change seemed an alleviation. So it was
in this case. It gave me no distress that I can remember to
find myself ill: the Sisters suffered much more than I did.
It pleased the Lord that the worst of it did not last more
than that day.

A little before that—it may have been two days—something else happened which put us in a little difficulty while
we were crossing the Guadalquivir in a ferryboat. At the
time when the carts crossed, it was not possible to go straight
across where the rope was, but slanting down the stream,
although the rope partly helped us, slanting it also. But
those who were holding it chanced to let it go, or somehow

it happened that the ferryboat floated away with the cart
without rope or oars. Seeing the ferryman's distress I
minded very much more than the danger. We fell to
prayer, all aloud. There was a gentleman watching us
from a castle near at hand, and, moved with pity, he sent
someone to help us, while we still had the rope, and our
brethren were holding on to it with all their might; but the
force of the current carried them all away, so that some of
them tumbled down. A son of the ferryman caused me such
edification that indeed I shall never forget it—he looked about
ten or eleven—he was so unhappy at seeing his father in trouble
that it made me give praise to our Lord. But as His Majesty
always tempers afflictions with mercy, so it was here; for the
boat happened to ground on a sandbank, and there was not
much water between it and the bank, and so all came right.
We should have had difficulty in finding our way out to the
road, for it was already dark, if the men from the castle had
not guided us. I did not mean to speak of these things, which
are of little importance, or I might have told of plenty of
misadventures by the way: I have been begged to narrate
this one at some length.

A far greater trouble to me than the above was what
befell us on the last day of Whitsuntide. We had made
great haste to arrive early at Cordova, so as to hear mass
without anyone's seeing us, and we were directed to a church
across the river, for greater retirement. When we came to
cross, we had no licence for carts to cross, for the mayor has
to give it: and more than two hours passed before it came,
because they were not up; and many people kept coming to
find out who was travelling there. This we did not much mind,
because they could not; for we travelled very closely shut in.
When at last the licence came, the carts could not get through

CORDOVA BRIDGE

from photograph by Messrs W. M. Spooner & Co.

the door of the bridge, and had to be cut smaller or something in which more time was spent.

When at last we arrived at the church where Father Julian of Avila was to say mass, it was full of people, because it was the Feast of its dedication to the Holy Spirit, of which we did not know; and there was a great festival and a sermon. When I saw this, I was greatly concerned; and to my thinking it would have been better to go away without hearing mass than to go down into such a hurly-burly. Father Julian thought not; and as he is a theologian, we Sisters all had to bow to his judgement; for the rest of our escort perhaps would have followed mine, which would have been very improper: although I do not know that I should have trusted my judgement alone. We alighted close to the church. And although nobody could see our faces, for we always wore long veils over them, it was enough to see us in them and the white serge cloaks which we always wear, and sandals, to stir them all up: and so it did. The shock of this it must have been—for assuredly it was a severe one to me and to us all— that quite drove away my fever.

As soon as we entered the church, a good man came up to me to keep off the people. I earnestly begged him to take us into some chapel. He did so, and locked it, and did not leave us until we started again to get out of the church. A few days after this he came to Seville, and he told a Father of our Order that he thought God had done him a favour on account of that good deed of his; for he had been given a large property of which he had no expectation.

I can tell you, daughters, that although this may seem nothing to you, it was for me one of the worst moments that I have passed; for the uproar among the people was as if bulls had come into the church. So I was longing to get out of the place. Although there was no place near at hand wherein to spend the festival, we kept it under a bridge[1].

When we had arrived at Seville at a house which Father Mariano had hired for us, for he had been told beforehand to do so, I thought everything was accomplished. For, as I have said, the Archbishop was greatly in favour of the Barefoot Carmelites; and he had sometimes written to me, shewing me great affection. This did not suffice to shield me from much trouble; for God so willed it. The Archbishop is much against convents of nuns without endowment; and he has good grounds for his view. That was the mischief—or rather the good, that this work might be accomplished—for if they had told him of it before I set out, I am certain he would never have agreed to it. But the Father Commissary and Father Mariano, being perfectly certain that my going would give him the greatest satisfaction, and that they were doing him the greatest service through my going, did not tell him beforehand. And, as I say, it might have been a great mistake, they thinking that they were right. For, in the rest of the convents, the first thing which I sought to obtain was the licence of the Ordinary, as the Holy Council[2] [of Trent] commands. In this case we not only took it as given, but, as I say, thought we were doing him a great service, as indeed it was, and he has since seen it. But it has been the Lord's pleasure that no foundation should be made without much trouble to me, some in one way, some in another.

Well, when we arrived at the house which, as I have said, had been hired for us, I thought to take possession immediately,

---

[1] And to get possession of even this they had to turn out some pigs, as the Venerable Julian of Avila relates in his *Life* of the Saint.

[2] The Council ordered that the Ordinary's leave was to be *prius obtenta*—obtained beforehand.

as we were used to do, in order to say the Divine Office. But Father Mariano—for it was he who was on the spot—began to put me off; for he did not like to tell me the whole truth, not to distress me. But as his reasons were insufficient, I saw what the difficulty was—that we had not got the licence. Thus he told me he thought it had better be an endowed convent, or other things of that kind; I forget what. At last he told me that the Archbishop did not like a convent for nuns to be established by his leave, nor since he had been Archbishop had he ever given leave for any. (He had been many years there and at Cordova, and he is a great servant of God[1].) Particularly for a convent without endowment: and he would not give it. This was as much as to say that the convent would not be founded. For one thing, its being in the city of Seville would have gone much against the grain with me: because the places where I have founded endowed Houses are little villages, where they must either be founded in this way or not at all, because there is no means of supporting them. For another thing, we had only one half-penny left over from the cost of the journey, nor had we brought any goods with us except the clothes we wore, and some tunics and hoods, and what was necessary for travelling hidden up and comfortably in the carts: and for the return journey of those who had come with us we had to try to borrow money. A friend of Antonio Gaytan's lent him this; and Father Mariano tried to borrow some for fitting up the house; nor had we a house of our own. So it was an impossibility.

[1] The Archbishop was the celebrated Don Cristobal de Rojas y Sandoval, formerly Bishop of Oviedo and of Cordova. He was promoted to Seville in 1571, and died in 1580. He was present at the Council of Trent, and he was distinguished by his strictness in matters of ecclesiastical order and discipline and his charity to the poor.

It must have been for the aforesaid Fathers' great importunity that the Archbishop allowed us to hear mass for the Day of the Blessed Trinity, which was our first day there. He sent to say that no bell was to be rung; nor even put up, he said, unless it was put up already. In this way we went on more than a fortnight; and I know my mind was, that if it had not been for the Father Commissary and Father Mariano, I should have returned with my nuns to Veas for the foundation of Caravaca, with small sorrow. Much more did I endure during that time—as my memory is bad, I do not remember how long it was, but I think over a month. For the going away in the end would have been worse to bear than going right away at once; because people had heard about the convent. Father Mariano would never let me write to the Archbishop, but little by little he kept getting him to relent, being aided in this by letters from the Father Commissary from Madrid.

One thing relieved me myself from much doubt: and that was our having had mass said with his leave; and we always said the Divine Office in Choir. He did not omit to send people to visit me, and to say that he would soon see me; and it was one of his own servants he sent about saying the first mass. Whence I saw clearly that all this served no purpose but to keep me in distress; although my distress was not for myself, nor for my nuns, but for the Father Commissary's distress; for it was great, as it was he who had commanded me to go: and it would have been very great if any disaster had taken place, for which there were abundant occasions.

During that time the Calced Fathers also came, to know by what authority we were founding. I shewed them the patents I had from our Most Reverend Father General; and with this they were satisfied: but I think this would not have sufficed, if they had known about the Archbishop. But nobody thought of this; for everyone believed that it was much to his liking and satisfaction. At last it pleased God that he should come to see us; and I told him what harm he was doing us. In the end he said that what I wished should be done, and as I wished: and from that time forward he has always favoured us and done us kindnesses at every opportunity.

CHAPTER XXV

Continues the account of the Foundation at Seville, and what took place in moving into a house of the nuns' own.

NOBODY could have supposed that in so chief a city as Seville, and with such rich inhabitants, there would be less of the wherewithal for founding than in any other place where I had been. So much less was there that I sometimes thought it would be better for us not to have a convent in that town. I do not know whether it is the climate of the country, but I have always heard say that the devils have a freer hand to tempt us there; which must be given them by God: and thus they set upon me, for I never in my life felt myself more pusillanimous and cowardly than I found myself there; indeed I hardly recognized myself. The trust, indeed, which I am accustomed to put in our Lord did not fail me; but my natural self was so different from what I usually am since I have been occupied in these matters, that I could see that the Lord was partly withdrawing His hand, to remain in His own Being, and that I might see that, if I had possessed courage, it was not my own.

Well, we had been there from the time that I said until

a little before Lent, and there was not the slightest prospect
of buying a house: neither wherewithal; nor anyone who
would be surety for us, as elsewhere.   For those who had said
so much to the Father, the Apostolic Visitor, about entering
the Order, and had begged him to bring nuns, must afterwards
have thought our strictness excessive, and more than they
could stand: and only one entered, as I shall presently tell.
It was already time to send for me to come from Andalusia,
because other affairs were presenting themselves here[1].   It
caused me the greatest distress to leave the nuns without
a house; although I saw very well that I was of no use there;
for the favour which God shews me here, of having someone
to help me in these works, was not shewn me there.

It pleased God that at that moment there came from the
Indies one of my brothers, Lorencio de Cepeda, who had been
out there thirty-four years: and he took it to heart even
more than I that the nuns should remain without a house of
their own.   He helped us a great deal, particularly in man-
aging to get the house in which they now are.   I also at that
time urged it much more earnestly on our Lord, beseeching
Him not to let me go away without leaving them a house;
and I made the Sisters pray for it, and ask it of the glorious
St Joseph, and we made many processions and prayers to our
Lady.   And what with this and with seeing my brother bent
on helping us, I began to negotiate about buying certain
houses.   But when, it seemed, it was just going to be settled,
it was all unsettled again.

One day when I was in prayer, beseeching of God that,
since they were His spouses and so greatly desired to serve

---

[1] [At Toledo. She had been ordered to leave Andalusia and to remain,
as she says, "as a sort of prisoner," in any convent she chose, in
Castille, until further orders. Tr.]

Him, He would give them a house, He said, Let me be;
I have heard thee. This left me well content, feeling I
had the house already. So it was. His Majesty saved us
from buying one with which everybody was satisfied because
it was in a good situation: but it was so old and so badly
arranged that we should have been buying nothing but the site,
and for little less money than the house which they now have.
And when it was already settled, and nothing to be done but
sign the papers, I was not at all satisfied, feeling that this did
not agree with the last words which I had heard in my prayer;
because I thought those words meant that we were to be given
a good house. And so it proved; for the seller himself,
though he was to get a good price for it, made difficulties
about signing the papers, although he had promised to do so ;
and we were able, without any wrong-doing, to get out of the
agreement. This was a great mercy; for they would not have
finished working at the house during the life time of the
Sisters who are there; and they would have had a great deal
to do and little wherewithal.

This was greatly due to a servant of God who, almost
from the time we first got there, when he heard that we had
no mass, came every day to say it for us, although his house
was a long way off, and the sun tremendous. His name was
Garci Alvarez. He was a very good man, esteemed in the
city for his good works, which were the only thing he ever
occupied himself with: and if he had been well off, we should
have lacked nothing.

As he knew the house well, it seemed to him folly to give
so much for it, and so he kept telling us every day, until he
succeeded and there was no more talk of it. He and my
brother went to see the one in which the nuns now live.
They came back saying they liked it very much, and with

good reason; and our Lord desired it: and in two or three days the papers were signed.

A good deal happened before we got into it: for the tenant was not willing to quit: and the Franciscan friars[1] living close at hand came at once to require us not on any account to move into it. And if the deeds had not been so securely made, I should have thanked God that they could be annulled; for we found ourselves in peril of paying the price of the house, six thousand ducats, without being able to go into it. The Prioress[2] would not have desired this, but rather she thanked God that they could not be annulled: for His Majesty gave to her much more faith and courage than to me, in all that concerned that house. So indeed she has in everything, for she is a great deal better than me.

We were more than a month in this hard case. At last it pleased God that the Prioress and I and two other nuns went in with great fear, one night, so that the friars should not know of it until we had taken possession. The men who went with us said that every shadow they saw they thought was a friar. At daybreak, the good Garci Alvarez, who went with us, said the first mass in it; and so we were left without fear.

O Jesus, what fears I have been through while taking possession! I reflect that if such great dread is experienced in going not to do harm, but in the service of God, what must it be for those who go to do harm, against God and against their neighbour. I cannot think what profit they can have or what pleasure they can seek, with such a counterpoise.

---

[1] The Canon law forbids the establishing of new monasteries close to old ones, for very good reasons.

[2] Maria de San José of Molina. She was a very able woman. St Theresa had a very high opinion of her: and from this year onwards she carried on a copious correspondence with her.

I had not even my brother there: for he had taken sanctuary,
on account of a certain mistake which had been made in the
papers, they having been drawn up in such haste, and the
convent stood to lose much by it: and as he was surety, they
sought to take him to prison; and as he was not a native of
the place, it would have given us a great deal of trouble. And
so it did even as it was: for he was in difficulties until he had
given them a property on which they took security. Afterwards the business went on smoothly: although there was some
time wasted in the legal proceedings, that I might have more
troubles.

We were enclosed in some rooms on the ground floor: and
he spent all the day there with the workmen, and he gave us
our food, and so indeed he had done for some time: because,
since everyone did not know that it was a convent, as we were
in a private house, there was but little alms, except from a
saintly old man, a great servant of God, who was Prior of
the Carthusian monastery of Las Cuevas. He was one of the
Pantojas of Avila. God put into his heart a great affection for
us from the time we went there; and I believe he will go on
doing us good in every possible way so long as his life lasts.
Because it is right, my daughters, that you should commend
to God anyone who has so greatly helped us, if you should
read this, be they living or dead, I set it down here. We owe
much to that saintly man.

This went on, I think, more than a month: but my
memory is bad in the matter of time, so I may be wrong:
always understand that it may be a little more or less; for it
is of no importance. During this month my brother worked
hard in making a chapel out of some rooms, and in so fitting
it all up that after he had finished we had nothing more to do.
I wanted to have the Blessed Sacrament reserved very quietly,

because I do not at all like giving trouble when it can be
helped; and so I told Father Garci Alvarez. He talked it
over with the Prior of Las Cuevas,—for they were quite as
anxious about our affairs as if they had been their own; and
they thought that this could not be allowed, but that it must
be done solemnly, in order that the convent might become
known in Seville. So they went to the Archbishop. Between
them all they agreed that the Blessed Sacrament should be
brought from a parish church with great solemnity; and
the Archbishop ordered the clergy to take part in it, and
some Confraternities, and the streets to be decorated.

The good Garci Alvarez decorated our cloister, which, as
I have said, served at that time as a passage, and the chapel
most elaborately, with very fine altars and devices. Among
them was a fountain of orange-flower-water. This he made
without our seeking or even liking it, although afterwards we
were much edified. And we were rejoiced to see our festival
ordered with such solemnity, and the streets so decorated and
so many instruments of music and minstrels that the saintly
Prior of Las Cuevas told me that he had never seen the like at
Seville; and it was clearly seen to be the work of God. He
himself went in the procession, contrary to his custom[1]. The
Archbishop set the Blessed Sacrament in its place. You see
here, my daughters, the poor Barefoot Carmelites honoured
by everyone, when a little time before it would have seemed
there was not even water for them—although there is plenty
in that river. It was quite extraordinary, the number of
people who came.

One thing happened which all who saw it say is worth
noting. Although there had been so many salvoes of artillery

---

[1] Carthusians, being bound to a solitary and retired life, do not take
part in processions.

and rockets, yet after the procession was over, which was about
dusk, it came into their heads to let off more, or somehow it
happened that a little powder took fire—and they think it a
great wonder that it did not kill the man who was holding it.
A great flame rose up to the roof of the cloister, the arches of
which were covered with silks, which they thought must have
been burnt to ashes; but though they were yellow and crim-
son, it did them no damage whatever. And the wonderful
thing which I have to tell you is that the stone of the arches,
underneath the silk, was blackened by the smoke, while the
silk which was over it was just as if the fire had not been near
it. Everyone was astonished when they saw it : and the nuns
thanked the Lord, for we had no money to pay for more silk.
The devil must have been so enraged at the solemn festival which
had taken place, and at seeing another house of God, that he
must have wanted to revenge himself somehow ; but His
Majesty did not give place to him. May He be blessed for
ever and ever ! Amen.

CHAPTER XXVI

Continues the account of the Foundation at Seville. Of the first
nun who joined the Convent, and of her remarkable history.

You may well imagine, my daughters, the joy we felt that
day. My own, I can tell you, was very great, especially in
seeing that I was leaving the Sisters in so good a house in so
good a situation, and that the monastery was known; and
that there were nuns in the house who had money enough to
pay the greater part of the price of the house, so that with
those who should be received to make up the number[1], if they

[1] [i.e., thirteen. Tr.]

brought in only a little, they would be left free of debt. And above all, it cheered me to have enjoyed the fruit of our labours. But, when I ought to have taken some rest, I went off. For this festival was the Sunday before Whitsunday, 1576, and I started immediately on the following Monday, because the heat was becoming great, and in order, if possible, not to travel at Whitsuntide, but to spend it at Malagon; for I had desired to stay there some day: and therefore I hastened my movements. I should have liked to hear mass once in the chapel, but this was not the Lord's will.

The Sisters' joy was tempered by my departure; for they felt it much, as we had been together that year and gone through so many troubles. As I have said, the worst troubles I do not set down here. For I think (except the foundation at Avila, for with that there is no comparison) that no foundation has cost me so much as this one, because my trials were mostly interior. May it please the Divine Majesty that He may always be served therein, for then the troubles are as nothing. And so I hope He will be; for His Majesty began to draw good souls to that house: and about those who remained there of the nuns whom I took with me, which was five, I have already told you what can be told —which is the least part—of how good they were.

Of the first who entered there I wish to speak, because it will give you pleasure. She is a girl who was the daughter of very good Christian parents. Her father came from the mountains. When she was very young, about seven, an aunt of her's who was childless begged her of her mother to live with her. She took her home, and made much of her, shewing her all due affection. Some of her women must have been in hopes that she would leave them her property; and it was clear that, if she cared for the child, she would wish it rather to go to her. So they agreed to avert that contingency by a devil's deed. They accused the child of wishing to kill her aunt: and said that for this purpose she had given one of them I do not know how many maravedis to get her some corrosive sublimate. When they told the aunt, as they all three said the same thing, she at once believed them: and so did the child's mother, who is a most virtuous woman.

She took the child and brought her home, thinking she was bringing up a girl who would be a very wicked woman. Beatrice of the Mother of God—for that is her name—told me that every day for more than a year she beat and punished her, and made her sleep on the floor, to make her confess such a great sin. As the little girl said she had not done it, and did not know what corrosive sublimate was, she thought much worse of her, seeing her obstinate enough to deny it. The poor woman was miserable at seeing her so stubborn in denying it, thinking that she could never amend. It was a wonder that the little girl did not accuse herself in order to escape such torments; but as she was innocent, God enabled her always to speak the truth. And as His Majesty always protects those who are not to blame, He sent two of these women such a grievous sickness that it seemed as if they had raging madness. They sent secretly for the little girl to come to her aunt, and begged her pardon; and, seeing themselves at the point of death, they retracted their charge: and the third, who died in childbirth, did the same. Finally all three died in torments, in requital of what they had made that innocent child suffer. This I have heard not only from herself: for her mother, when she saw her a nun, being distressed to think of all her illtreatment of her, told it me together with other things—for great were the girl's sufferings. Though she was a very good Christian, God permitted her, knowing no better,

to be so cruel to her daughter, though she greatly loved her.
She is a very truthful and religious woman.

When the child was perhaps just over twelve, she conceived a great devotion towards the Saints of Mount Carmel,
from reading a book about the life of St Anne: for it says there
that St Anne's mother (I think her name was Merenciana)
often went to speak with them; and hence she conceived such
a great devotion to the Order of our Lady that she immediately vowed chastity and to be a nun in that Order.   She
observed many times of solitude and prayer, when she could.
God gave her great graces in her prayer, and so did our Lady,
and very special ones.   She would have liked to become a nun
without delay, but dared not because of her parents: no more
did she know where to find this Order; for it was a curious
thing that, though there was at Seville a convent of the
Mitigated Rule, she never knew of it until she heard of our
convents, which was many years later.

When she came to the age for marrying her, her parents
arranged a marriage for her, though she was full young for
her age; but she was the only child they had. (For though
they had had others, they all had died; and this one, who was
the least beloved, remained to them.   For when there befell
her what I have narrated, she had one brother living, who took
her part and said they ought not to believe it.)   They had
already completely arranged the marriage, never thinking that
she would do anything else: and when they came to tell her,
she told them of the vow she had made not to marry, and
that she would not do it for anything they could do to her, not
if they killed her.

The devil blinded them, or God permitted it, that she
might suffer as a martyr, but they thought she must have
misbehaved herself in some way, and therefore was unwilling

to marry. And as they had already given their word, and they felt what an affront it was to the other party, they gave her so many beatings and inflicted such tortures, even to hanging her up and throttling her, that it was only a chance they did not kill her. God Who had need of her for other things preserved her life. She told me that towards the end she hardly felt anything, because she called to mind what St Agnes had suffered, for the Lord brought it to her memory, and it was a happiness to her to suffer something for Him, and she kept offering it up to Him. They thought she would die; for she was three months in bed, unable to move.

It seems a very strange thing how her parents could have thought such evil of a girl who never left her mother's side, and whose father, as I heard, lived very quietly. For she was always religious and virtuous, and so charitable that she gave away everything she could get. If our Lord wills to bestow the favour of suffering on any one, His means are many. However, for some years God had kept shewing them the virtues of their daughter, so that they gave her whatever she wanted to give in alms; and their persecutions were turned into kindnesses. Nevertheless, all was wearisome to her, for the mind she had to be a nun: and so, as she told me, she lived dissatisfied and sad.

Thirteen or fourteen years before Father Gracian went to Seville, when there was no thought of Barefoot Carmelites, something happened. She was with her father and mother and two other neighbours, and a Brother of our Order, habited in serge, as they now are, and barefoot, entered the room. They say his countenance was ruddy and venerable, but he was so ancient that his long beard was like threads of silver[1]. He placed himself close to her, and began to say a few words in a language which neither she nor anyone else understood; and, when he had done

---

[1] Thus the Prophet Elijah was usually represented.

speaking, he made the sign of the cross over her thrice, saying, "Beatriz, God make thee strong," and departed. Nobody stirred while he was there, but were as in a maze. Then her father asked her who it was. She supposed that her father knew him. In great haste they arose to seek for him, but he was seen no more. She was left greatly comforted, and all were amazed: for they saw that the thing was from God; and so they began, as I have said, to think great things of her. After this, all those years went by, I think fourteen, in which she continued steadfast in serving our Lord and praying that He would accomplish her desire.

She was in great sadness, when Father Master Fray Gerónimo Gracian went to Seville. One day she went to hear a sermon at a church at Triana, where her father lived, not knowing who would be the preacher. It was the Father Master Gracian. She saw him come out to receive the benediction: and when she saw the habit and the bare feet, at once it recalled the monk whom she had seen; for the habit was the same, though the countenance and the age were different, for Father Gracian was not yet thirty. She told me that she almost fainted with the excess of joy. For though she had heard that a monastery had been founded at Triana, she did not know that it was of the Carmelite Order.

From that day she set to work at once to get Father Gracian to hear her Confessions: and it pleased God that this also should cost her much; for she went about a dozen times, more or less, and he would never hear her. She was young and good looking, for she was not then seven and twenty; and he, being very reserved, kept off from any communications with people like her. At last one day when she was in the church crying—for she too was very shy—a woman asked her what was the matter, and she said that for so long she had been wanting to speak to the Father who was then hearing Confessions, and could not tell how. The woman took her to him and begged that he would hear this girl. And so he came to be her ordinary confessor. When he saw a soul so richly endowed, he was glad; and he comforted her by telling her that possibly Barefoot nuns might be coming there, and he would see that they received her at once. And so it was : for the first thing he bade me was that she should be the first we received, for he was satisfied with the state of her soul; and so he told her.

When we went there, she made a great point of her parents' not hearing of it, because if they did, she would not succeed in coming to us. And so on that very day, Trinity Sunday, she left the women who went with her (for her mother did not go to Confession with her, and it was a long way to the Barefoot monastery, where she always went to Confession, and gave away much in alms, and her parents through her). She had arranged with a lady, a great servant of God, to fetch her to us. This lady was well known in Seville as a servant of God, occupied in good works. So the women who went with her let her go, on her saying that she would soon come back. She took her habit and her serge cloak, so heavy that I do not know how she could move ; but it was nothing to her for the joy she felt. Her only fear was lest it might be noticed how loaded she was, and she might be stopped : for it was very different from her usual way of going about. What will not the love of God effect ! And since she already had given up human respect[1] nor thought of anything but the fear

---

[1] [*Honra.* Often wrongly translated *honour*, whereby St Theresa has been made to teach that religion and honour are opposed. Honour, as an inner principle, is *honor*. There is the same sort of distinction between our English *honour*, the inward, and *honours*, the outward dignity. Tr.]

lest her desire should be baulked, we opened the door to her without delay. I sent to tell her mother. She came as one beside herself, but she said that she already saw what a favour God was doing to her daughter. And, although sorrowfully, she accepted it without taking to extreme courses such as refusing to speak to her daughter, as some others do: on the contrary she continually gave us large alms. The spouse of Jesus Christ began to enjoy the fruition of her great desire. She was so lowly and such a lover of work that we had enough ado to get the broom away from her: though she had been so waited upon at home, all her pleasure was in hard work. Her happiness quickly made her grow much fatter; and her father thought a great deal of this, so that her parents soon were pleased at her being with us.

That she might not have such complete rejoicing without sufferings, some two or three months before the time for her Profession, she experienced great temptations : not that she determined to give up her Profession, but it seemed to her a very dreadful thing. All the years of her suffering for the sake of what she now enjoyed were forgotten : the devil so fiercely beset her that she could do nothing with herself; but in spite of all, doing the greatest violence to herself, she so overcame him that in the midst of the storm she covenanted to be professed. Three days before her Profession, our Lord, Who must have been only waiting to prove her constancy the more, visited her and put the devil to flight and comforted her very specially. This left her so happy that those three days she seemed beside herself with joy, and with great cause, for it was a great mercy. Not many days after her Profession, her father died, and her mother took the habit in the same convent, and bestowed on it everything she possessed : and mother and daughter are living in the greatest happiness, to the edification of all the nuns, and serving Him Who had shewn them such great mercy. Before another year had gone by, another girl also came, greatly against the will of her parents. And thus the Lord keeps peopling His house with souls so desirous of pleasing Him that no rigour nor enclosure puts them from it. May He be for ever blessed and praised for ever. Amen.

CHAPTER XXVII

Of the Foundation at Caravaca, on the first of January 1576. The Convent was dedicated to St Joseph.

WHEN I was at St Joseph's of Avila, prepared to start for the foundation at Veas of which I have spoken, and ready all but putting on the clothes we were going in, there arrived a special messenger, sent by a lady of Caravaca named Doña Catalina[1] because there had come to her house, after a sermon they had heard preached by a Father of the Company of Jesus, three young ladies, resolved not to leave the house until a convent should be founded in the town. It must have been arranged beforehand between them and the lady, for she it was who helped them towards the foundation. They were daughters of the foremost gentlemen of the town. The father of one of them was Rodrigo de Moya[2], a very great servant of God, and of excellent judgement. Between them all they had enough money to attempt such an undertaking. They had

[1] In St Theresa's MS. there is a blank left for the surname [de Otalora], which she could not remember.

[2] His daughter's name (for daughters did not always bear the same name as their father) was Francisca de Cuellar, afterwards Sister Francisca of the Cross.

heard of the work which our Lord was doing in the founding of our convents, for they had been told by Fathers of the Company of Jesus, who always have helped and furthered it.

When I saw the fervent desire of these souls, and that they were coming from so far to seek the Order of our Lady, it stirred me and made me wish to further their good intention. And hearing that Caravaca was near Veas, I took with me more nuns than I had been about to take, intending to go on there, when the foundation of Veas was accomplished ; for, from the letters, I thought this other foundation could not fail to be arranged.

But as the Lord had appointed otherwise, my plans were of little avail, as I have said in my account of the foundation at Seville : for when the licence of the Council of Orders was brought, it was so made out that, although I had already settled to go, I did not.   It is true that when, at Veas, I found out where Caravaca was : and found that it was so out of the way and such a bad road from one place to the other that those who had to visit the nuns would have trouble in doing so, and that the superiors would not be best pleased, I felt very little inclination to go and found there.   But, as I had given them good hopes of it, I begged Father Julian of Avila and Antonio Gaytan to go there and see how matters stood, and to break it off, if they thought fit.

They found the affair very lukewarm, not on the part of the intending nuns, but on that of Doña Catalina, on whom the whole thing turned.   She was keeping them in an apartment by themselves as being already enclosed.

The nuns were so resolute—I mean those who purposed to be nuns—and knew so well how to gain over Father Julian of Avila and Antonio Gaytan, that before they came away they left the papers signed, and came away leaving the nuns well contented : and they came back so full of the country and of the nuns and of the mishaps of their journey [1] that they could not stop talking about it.

When I saw that it was already settled, but the licence was long in coming, I sent the good Antonio Gaytan back again ; and he took all this trouble with a very good will, out of affection for me. Besides, those two had a mind that the convent should be founded : for indeed, it is they who are to be thanked for this foundation ; for if they had not gone and arranged for it, I should not have cared to make it. I told him to go and put up a turn [2] and gratings wherever they were going to take possession ; and that the nuns should stay there until a suitable house could be found. So he stayed there some time : and Rodrigo Moya, who, as I have said, was the father of one of the girls, gave them part of his own house. And Antonio Gaytan stayed there some time arranging this with a very good will.

When they brought the licence and I was upon the point of starting, I found that the licence provided that the house should be subject to the Knights Commanders, and the nuns be under their obedience : a thing which was not in my power to do, since it was to be a house of the Order of our Lady of Carmel. So they went back to petition afresh for a licence : for otherwise there was no means of having a house either there or at Veas. But the King was so gracious to me that, on my writing to him, he ordered the licence to be given. For the King, who

[1] In his *Life* of St Theresa, Father Julian of Avila describes at great length their misfortunes on the journey. Their guide was drunk, and Father Julian tried to instruct him in Christian doctrine, which muddled him the more, and he led them wrong.

[2] [*Torno.* A revolving shutter with a floor on which things could be placed and conveyed from without to within and within to without, while those who thus delivered them could not see each other. Tr.]

is Don Felipe, takes pleasure in doing benefits to members of
Religious Orders, and understands that they ought to keep
their Rule; and as he had heard of the customs of our
monasteries and that they kept the primitive Rule, he has
shewn us favour in every matter. Therefore, daughters, I
earnestly beseech you always to make special supplications
for his Majesty, as we do now.

Well, as they had to go back again for the licence, I started
for Seville by command of the Father Provincial, who, as I
have said, was then and still is Father Master Fray Jerónimo
Gracian of the Mother of God. And there were the poor
damsels shut up until the New Year's Day following: and it
was February when they sent to Avila. Shortly after my
departure the licence came: but I was so far away and with so
much to do, that I could not help them. I was very sorry for
them: for they often wrote to me mournfully; and so at last
I could not bear to make them wait longer. Since it was
impossible for me to go, being so far away, and the foundation
at Seville not being completed, Father Master Fray Jerónimo
Gracian, who, as I have said, was the Apostolic Visitor, agreed
that, although I could not go, the nuns should go who
were destined for that foundation, and had been staying at
St Joseph's at Malagon.

I had arranged that one should be prioress whom I could
trust to do very well, for she is much better than me; and
they started, taking every precaution, with two of our Discalced
Fathers: for Father Julian of Avila and Antonio Gaytan had
returned to their own places some time ago; and I did not
want them to go, because it was so far and such a bad time of
year, being the end of December.

When the nuns arrived, they were received with great joy
by the people, especially by the girls who were shut up. They

founded the Convent, bringing in the Blessed Sacrament, on the Day of the Name of Jesus[1], 1576. Two of the girls took the habit immediately. The other had a very melancholic temperament, and it must have been bad for her to be shut up at all, how much more in such great strictness and austerity. She agreed to go home again with a sister of hers.

Consider, my daughters, the judgements of God, and under what obligation we are to serve Him, when He has allowed us to persevere up to our Profession and to remain ever in the house of God and as daughters of the Virgin. For His Majesty made use of this girl's good will and of her wealth ; and just at the moment when she should have entered into the enjoyment of what she had so greatly desired, her courage failed her and she was overcome by her natural disposition— on which, daughters, we often put the fault of our failings and ficklenesses. May it please His Majesty to grant us the abundance of His grace : for with this, there will be nothing which can hinder our steps in advancing continually in His service. And may He defend us all and be favourable to us, lest through our weakness might be wasted a beginning so great as He has been pleased should be initiated by such a poor sort of women as we. In His Name I entreat you, my sisters and daughters, always to entreat this of our Lord ; and so let each do of those who come hereafter, for each is making a new beginning of keeping this primitive Rule of the Order of our Lady the Virgin : and in no wise consent to any relaxation. Consider that by very small things the door is opened to very great ones, and that, without your observing it, the world will be coming in upon you.

Call to mind in what poverty and trouble has been established that which you now enjoy at your ease. And if you take

[1] [The Circumcision. Tr.]

notice, you will see that most of these houses have been founded, not so much by man as by the mighty hand of God : and that His Majesty takes pleasure in carrying forward His own works, if they are not hindered by us. Whence think you that an insignificant woman like me could have had power to do such great works, being under obedience and without so much as a maravedi or any one who could help me with anything ? (For that brother of mine who helped in the foundation at Seville, having some money and a good heart and a mind to give some help, was in the Indies.) Behold, behold, my daughters, the hand of God. And then the favour shewn me has not been on account of illustrious birth : in every way, however you please to look at it, you will see that it is His work. It is not right that we should in any way lower it, even if it cost us our life, esteem, or peace. How much more when here we possess all these together ! For life is to live in such wise that neither death is feared nor any chances of this life, and to abide in the habitual joy which now is common to you all, and a prosperity than which none can be greater, which is, to desire poverty instead of fearing it. Then what can be compared to the inward and outward peace in which you live? In your own hands it is to live and die in it, as you see those nuns die whom we have seen dying in these houses. Wherefore if you always pray to God to further the work and in no wise trust in yourselves, He will not deny you His mercy, if you have confidence in Him, and courageous souls : for His Majesty loveth such.

Fear not that you will lack anything. If you are satisfied with the motives and abilities of those who come to be nuns, and that they are coming not for their own advantage, but in order to serve God more perfectly, and if they are endowed with virtues, never hold back from receiving them because they are not endowed with this world's goods. For from some other quarter God will send you double what you would have received from them. I have great experience in this. Well does His Majesty know that, so far as I can remember, I have never held back from receiving anyone for want of money, if otherwise I was satisfied with her. Witness the many who have been received for God's sake alone, as you know. And I can assure you that it has not given me so much pleasure when I have received one who has brought in much as when I have taken them for God's sake alone: on the contrary, I have been in fear about those; but the poor ones have cheered my heart, and it has given me a rejoicing so great that it has made me weep with joy. This is the truth. And then if when the houses had to be bought or built, God helped us even to do this, how should He not afterwards do so, giving us the means of living in them? Believe me, daughters, that whereby you might think to gain, you would lose. When one who comes has money, not having other obligations, as of giving it away to others, because there happens to be no one who needs it, it is well that she should give it you as alms, and I confess that I should think it lack of affection if she did not. But always see that one who enters the convent acts according to the advice of learned men, telling her what will be to the greater service of God: for it would be quite wrong that we should accept the property of anyone who entered, if she did not come for that end. We gain much more by her doing her duty towards God—I mean, doing it more perfectly, than by whatever she might bring in; since we all seek nothing, and may God never give us the opportunity of seeking anything but that His Majesty's will may be done in all and through all.

And although I am wretched and bad, yet for God's

honour and glory I say it, and that you may take pleasure in thinking of how these houses were founded—that never in my dealings about them nor in any matter concerning them which presented itself, even if I expected not to succeed at all unless I deviated somewhat from my principle—never would I, nor have I done anything whatsoever (I mean to say in these foundations) which I understood to deviate by one point from the Lord's will, as I understood it from my confessors, (who, ever since I have been engaged in this, have been, as you know, very learned and servants of God) : nor that I can remember did it ever come into my mind to do otherwise. Perhaps I am deceiving myself : and I may have done many things which I am not aware of, and my failures doubtless are beyond number. This is known to our Lord, for He is the true judge : I speak of myself so far as I have been able to see. And moreover I see very well that this did not spring from myself, but of God's desiring that this work should be done ; and as being His undertaking He was favourable to me and shewed me this mercy. And I say it, daughters, for this purpose—that you may understand your greater obligation, and may know that up to the present these things have been done without doing any wrong to anyone[1]. Blessed be He Who has done it all, and has aroused the charity of the people who have helped us ! May it please His Majesty ever to protect us and give us grace, that we may not be ungrateful for so many and great mercies ! Amen.

You have already seen, daughters, that some troubles have been gone through, although I think I have only written down

[1] [It may be worth reminding ourselves that current morality in Spain in the 16th century differed considerably from ours now. And, as St Theresa says above, in doubtful matters she left decisions to whatever "learned servant of God," secular, Jesuit, Dominican, or Carmelite, happened to be her confessor at the time. Tr.]

the smallest part of them : for if they had to be narrated in detail, it would be a great labour, both the journeys as well as the floods and snow and losing the way, and above all my often being so unwell. Something once befell me—I do not know whether I have mentioned it[1]—in the first day's journey when we set out from Malagon to Veas. I had fever and so many sicknesses all together that, considering the long distance I had to go and seeing myself so ill, it seemed to remind me of our father Elijah when he was fleeing from Jezebel, and I said, Lord, consider ; how can I possibly bear this ? And true it is then when His Majesty saw me so weak, suddenly He took from me the fever and the sickness ; so much so that until later when I understood it, I thought it must have been because a servant of God, an ecclesiastic, had entered the place : and perhaps it was that ; anyhow He took away from me both the outward and inward ills.

In time of health, I went through the bodily labours cheerfully. Then again, it was no little difficulty to accommodate oneself to the dispositions of many people, which had to be done in every place. And I can tell you that, loving my daughters so dearly, it has not been my smallest cross to have to quit them when I went away from one place to another : especially when I thought that I should not return to see them, and I saw their great emotion and weeping : for though they are detached from other things, this detachment God has not given them, may be in order to give me the keener pain. For no more am I detached from them, although I used to find fault with them and put all the force I could on myself not to shew it : but little did it avail me ; for the love we bear each other is great, and by many proofs can well be seen to be sincere.

[1] It is not mentioned in ch. xxii, where it belongs. This shews how rapidly and simply St Theresa wrote : for she did not revise her writing.

You have also heard how it was not only with the leave of our Most Reverend Father General but under his instructions or command subsequently laid down that these foundations were made : and not only this, but on the foundation of each house he wrote to me that it gave him the greatest satisfaction that such and such a house was founded. And certainly my greatest comfort in these labours was to see the satisfaction it gave him, because I thought that our Lord must be pleased with this, he being my Superior : and I greatly love him, into the bargain.

Whether His Majesty was pleased to give me some repose, or whether the devil was annoyed at so many houses being founded in which our Lord was served.—It could very well be seen not to have been by the wish of our Father General: for when I had besought him, and that, not many years before, not to order me to found any more houses, he had written to me refusing, because, he said, he wished me to found as many as I had hairs on my head.—But before I came away from Seville, there was brought me from a General Chapter which had been held, where one would have thought that what had brought credit to the Order would have been reckoned a service—there was brought me an order made in Chapter, not only that I was to make no more foundations, but also that I was by no means to quit the house which I might choose to live in. Which was a kind of imprisonment : for there are no nuns whom the Provincial cannot order to go from one place to another—I mean from one convent to another, for reasons expedient for the good of the Order. But the worst, and the thing which distressed me, was that our Father General was displeased with me, entirely without cause, but on the reports of prejudiced people. Together with this I was told of two other matters, two very serious accusations which were brought against me.

I tell you, sisters, that you may see the mercy of our Lord,
and how His Majesty does not forsake those who desire to serve
Him, that this not only did not give me pain, but a joy so
unexpected that I could not contain myself; so that I do not
wonder at what King David did when he went before the ark
of the Lord, for I at that time should have liked to do nothing
less, for joy; for I did not know how to keep it in.   I do not
know why this was; for in great obloquy and opposition in
which I have found myself at other times, it has not been so.
Moreover, at least one[1] of the accusations they brought against
me was most serious. As for the making no more foundations,
if it had not been for the displeasure of the Most Reverend
General, it would have been great peace for me, and a thing
which I often desired, to end my days in quiet : although
those who brought this about did not think this, but imagined
that they were causing me the greatest distress in the world.
And perhaps they had other good intentions.

At other times also I have received pleasure from the great
oppositions and gainsayings which I have met with in going
to make foundations, some with a good intention, some with
other aims.   But such great gladness as I felt in this, I never
remember to have felt in any other trouble that has come
upon me : for I confess that, at some other time, any one of
the three things which came upon me all together would have
been trouble enough for me.   I believe my chief joy was
in thinking that, since creatures rewarded me thus, the
Creator was pleased with me.   For I do understand that
anyone who finds his happiness in earthly things or the
sayings and praises of men is greatly deceived, let alone the

[1] One was the manner of her return journey from Seville. Her
brother Lorenzo took her, and the comfort and state in which he
caused her to travel was made a reproach against her. [She was also
accused of heresy. Tr.]

little profit there is in them : to-day they think one thing, to-morrow another ; what they speak well of at one time, they quickly change and speak evil of. Blessed be Thou, my God and Lord, Who art for ever immutable! Amen. He who will serve Thee to the end shall live without end in Thine eternity.

———————

As I said at the beginning, I began to write the account of these foundations by order of the Father Master Ripalda of the Company of Jesus, who was at that time Rector of the College at Salamanca and heard my Confessions. While I was in the Convent of the glorious St Joseph at Salamanca, I wrote some of them. Then with my many occupations I had let it drop, and did not want to go on with it : because, being away in different places, I was no longer making my Confessions to Father Ripalda, and also because of the great toil and trouble which what I have written costs me ; although I consider that well bestowed, as it has always been commanded me under obedience. When I had quite determined not to go on, Master Fray Gerónimo Gracian of the Mother of God, who is at this present time Father Apostolic Commissary, ordered me to finish them.

I told him how little leisure I had, and other things which came into my mind to say—for I spoke as one shockingly poor in obedience : because this writing fatigued me greatly on the top of other things which I had to do. For all that, he told me to finish them little by little, or as best I could. So I have done it, submitting it entirely to those who are of understanding, that they may cross out what is wrongly said. For it may be that what seems to me the best may be wrong. I have finished to-day, the Eve of Saint Eugenius, the fourteenth of November, 1576, in the Convent of St Joseph at Toledo, where I now am living by order of Master Fray Gerónimo

Gracian of the Mother of God, Father Apostolic Commissary, whom we now have as Superior of the Barefoot monks and nuns of the primitive Rule, being also Visitor of the monks of the mitigated Rule in Andalusia, to the glory and honour of our Lord Jesus Christ, who reigns and shall reign for ever. Amen.

For the love of the Lord I beseech the Brothers and Sisters who shall read this to commend me to our Lord, that He may have mercy on me and deliver me from the torments of purgatory, and may permit me to enjoy Him, if I may attain to dwell in Him : that, since during my lifetime you are not to see this, after my death I may in some way profit by the toil this has given me, and by my great desire in writing it to succeed in saying something which may help you, if it is thought fit that you should read it.

CHAPTER XXVIII

JESUS

The Foundation of Villanueva de la Jara[1].

WHEN the foundation at Seville was completed, the foundations ceased for more than four years. The reason was that great persecutions arose all of a sudden against the Discalced monks and nuns. For although there had been plenty of such before, they were not so severe as now, when they almost made an end of us. It shewed very plainly what the devil felt about this holy beginning which our Lord had initiated ; and also that it was His work, since it did continue. The Barefoot Brothers suffered greatly, especially the chief of

[1] The following forms as it were a second part of the book written after the interruption mentioned in the text.

them, from serious accusations, and from the opposition of almost all the Fathers of the mitigated Rule. They so represented matters to our Most Reverend Father General that he insisted on the foundations of Discalced Brothers being discontinued. (He was always friendly to those of the Sisters.) This was in spite of his being very saintly and of its being by his own licence that all the monasteries had been founded except the first, that of St Joseph of Avila; for that was done by the Pope's licence. And because I had helped in this, he was put against me, which was the greatest trouble I have suffered in these foundations, though I have been through plenty. For the men of great learning who heard my Confession and advised me would not allow me to cease helping forward a work which I clearly saw was to the service of our Lord and the increase of our Order: yet to go against what I saw my Superior wished was like death to me; for, let alone my duty to him as Superior, I loved him very tenderly, and of good right I owed him affection. It is true that, even if I had thought well to give him satisfaction in this matter, I could not; because of having Apostolic Visitors, whom I had perforce to obey. The Nuncio died, a saintly man[1], who shewed favour to virtue, and therefore appreciated the Barefoot friars. Another[2] came who seemed to have been sent by God to exercise us in suffering. He was

---

[1] Monseñor Nicolás Ormaneto, one of the most zealous Bishops of the 16th century. He spent some time in England with Cardinal Pole, and was afterwards present at the Council of Trent. St Charles Borromeo made him his Vicar-General, and he afterwards became Bishop of Padua. He came to Spain as Nuncio in 1572. He died in June 1577, in such poverty, through his abundant almsgiving, that Philip II had to defray his funeral expenses.

[2] Monseñor Filipo Sega. He had been in Belgium with Don John of Austria, and thence came to Spain. Before he left Italy for Belgium, the Italian [unreformed] Carmelites ingratiated themselves with him

some connection of the Pope, and must have been a servant of God, only that he had begun to have it much at heart to shew favour to the Fathers of the Mitigation : and agreeably to their reports of us, he quite made up his mind that it was not a good thing that our beginnings should go forward. So he began to carry this out with the greatest rigour, censuring those who he thought might be able to resist him, imprisoning and banishing them.

Those who suffered most severely were Father Fray Antonio of Jesus, the one who began the first monastery of Barefoot Carmelites, and Father Fray Gerónimo Gracian, whom the late Nuncio had made Apostolic Visitor of the Fathers of the Mitigation. He was greatly displeased with him and with Father Mariano de San Benito. These Fathers I have described in the account of the former foundations. Others of the more considerable Fathers he punished, but not so severely. These he bound under heavy penalties not to take any part in the affairs of the Order. It can be well seen that all this came from God, and that His Majesty permitted it for the best and that the virtue of these Fathers might be better known ; as in fact it has been. He appointed one of the mitigated Rule as Superior, to visit our monasteries of nuns and friars : and a grievous trouble it would have been if all that he proposed had come to pass. And so we suffered exceedingly, as will be told by someone who knows how to say it better than I.

I am only touching on it, so that nuns to come may understand how great is their obligation to keep up their perfection, since they find smooth and easy what has cost

through his relation, Cardinal Boncompagni, a patron of theirs, nephew of Pope Gregory XIII. Thence the prejudice of the Nuncio against St Theresa and her reform.

the present nuns so dear: for some of them suffered greatly during that time from serious accusations, for which I was much more sorry than for what I myself suffered : for my own sufferings were a great happiness to me. It seemed to me that I was the cause of all this storm ; and that if they threw me into the sea like Jonas, the tempest would cease.

Praised be God Who defends the truth! He did so now : for when our Catholic King Don Felipe heard what was taking place, and was told of the life and Rule of the Barefoot Carmelites, he took up our cause in this way, that he would not allow the Nuncio alone to decide our case, but gave him four assistants, men of weight, three of them members of Religious Orders, in order that our right might be fairly considered. One of them was Father Master Friar Pedro Fernandez, a man of very holy life and of great learning and understanding. He had been Apostolic Commissary and Visitor of the Friars of the Mitigation in Castille. To him we Barefoot Carmelites also were subject, and he very well knew the truth as to how each sort lived : and all of us desired nothing but that this should be known[1]. Therefore when I heard that the King had appointed him, I reckoned the affair as settled, as indeed by the mercy of God it is. May it please His Majesty that it may be to His honour and glory. Although there were many Lords of the realm and Bishops who hastened to tell the Nuncio the truth, little would it all have availed if God had not made employment of the King.

We all, sisters, are under a great obligation to commend

[1] He was appointed by St Pius V, at the request of Philip II, who was not altogether satisfied with the work of Father Rossi. Father Fernandez made his visitation on foot, with a companion. While he was at Pastrana he lived like the Barefoot friars, following all their Rule. No wonder therefore that St Theresa put such confidence in him.

him continually to our Lord in our prayers, and the others, too, who have helped forward the cause of our Lord and of our Lady the Virgin : therefore I earnestly commend it to you.   You can well see, sisters, what opportunity there was for making new foundations !   We all occupied ourselves without ceasing in prayers and penances that God would preserve and continue the already existing foundations, if they were to be to His service.

These great troubles, narrated so briefly, will seem small to you ; but having been endured such a long time, they really were very great.

At the time of their beginning I was at Toledo, for I had come from the foundation at Seville, in the year 1576.   There a cleric of Villanueva de la Jara brought me letters from the Corporation of that town, and came to negotiate with me about accepting as a Convent nine women who, some years before, had entered all together into a hermitage of the glorious St Anna in that place, which had a little house next door.   They lived there with retirement and sanctity so great that it made the whole town wish to obtain the accomplishment of their desire ; which was, to become nuns.   There wrote to me also the parish priest, Doctor Augustin Ervias, a learned and virtuous man.   His virtue made him help as much as he could in this holy undertaking.

To me it seemed not by any means fitting to accept the Convent, for the following reasons.   The first, that there were so many of them, and it seemed to me very difficult for them, when they were fashioned to their own way of living, to accommodate themselves to ours.   The second, that they possessed hardly any means of subsistence, and the town had little more than a thousand inhabitants, which is little to reckon on for living on alms ; and although the Corporation

offered to maintain them, that did not seem to me a lasting
security. The third, that they had no house. The fourth,
that it was a long way from the other convents. And
although I was told that they were very good, yet as I had
not seen them, I could not tell whether they possessed the
qualifications which we require in our convents. So I
resolved to decline altogether. With this view I sought first
to speak to my confessor, who was Dr Velasquez, a Canon and
Professor at Toledo, a very learned and good man, now Bishop
of Osma; for my custom always is to do things not according
to my own judgement, but that of people such as he. When
he saw the letters and understood the affair, he told me not
to decline, but to give a favourable answer; because when
God united so many hearts in one purpose, it was clear
that it was to be to His service. So I did; for I neither
altogether accepted nor declined. They went on asking
for the foundation and getting people to persuade me to
make it; and so the time went by until the year 1580, I all
the time thinking it would be foolish to accept. When I answered them, I never could answer altogether unfavourably.

It happened that Father Fray Antonio of Jesus, in
fulfilment of his sentence of banishment, went to the
Monastery of our Lady of Succour, which is three leagues from
the town of Villanueva; and he used to preach at Villanueva,
and the Prior of the Monastery, Father Fray Gabriel of the
Assumption, a very clear-sighted man and a servant of God,
also went a great deal to Villanueva; for they were friends of
Dr Ervias. They began to speak with those saintly Sisters:
and being much taken with their goodness, and being persuaded
by the townspeople and by the Doctor, they made the affair
their own, and began persuading me very vigorously by letter.
And when I was at St Joseph's at Malagon, which is twenty-

six leagues or more from Villanueva, the Father Prior himself came over to speak to me about it, telling me in detail what could be done, and how, after it was done, Dr Ervias would give three hundred ducats a year out of what he got from his benefice : and that leave could be got from Rome. This seemed to me very doubtful, as there might be slackness in payment after the Convent was made : for it was quite enough together with the little the Sisters possessed. Therefore I gave the Father Prior many and to my mind sufficient reasons for him to see that it was not fitting to make the foundation. I told him to consider it well, together with Father Antonio ; and that I left it to their conscience. For I thought that what I had said was sufficient to prevent them. After he was gone, I considered how much he was taken with the idea, and I felt almost sure he would persuade our present Superior, Master Fray Angel de Salazar, to accept the foundation. So I made great haste to write to the Superior, begging him not to give the licence, and telling him my reasons. And as he has since told me in writing, he would not have given it, except with my approval.

About six weeks passed, or it may have been a little more. When I fairly thought I had got it stopped, a messenger was sent me with letters from the Corporation, formally undertaking that the Sisters should not lack necessaries ; from Dr Ervias, promising what I have mentioned ; and most urgent letters from the two Reverend Fathers. I greatly dreaded accepting so many Sisters, thinking there would be sure to be some party, as usually happens, against the Sisters who went from us. Also I did not see sufficient security for their maintenance ; for what they offered was not entirely secure. So I was greatly perplexed. Afterwards I saw that it was the devil : for, although the Lord has given me courage, I was at that time so pusillanimous that I seemed not to have any confidence in God. But the prayers of those saintly souls at last prevailed.

One day I had made my Communion, and was commending the thing to God, as I often did. (For what had made me answer favourably at first was my fear of hindering some good to any souls ; for my desire always is for any means whereby our Lord may be praised and may have someone more to serve Him.) Then His Majesty gave me a severe rebuke, asking, With what riches had all been accomplished which had been accomplished so far ? And that I was not to hesitate to accept this house ; for it would be greatly to His service and the benefit of souls.

The words of God are so powerful that not only does the understanding understand them, but they also enlighten it to understand the truth, and they dispose the will to desire to practise it. Thus was it with me : for not only did I think with pleasure of accepting the Convent, but I felt I had been to blame in delaying so long, and being so wedded to human reasonings, since that which I have seen of His Majesty's work for our holy Rule has been so much above reason. Having determined to accept this foundation, I thought I would go with the nuns who were to live there. This was for many reasons which came into my mind, although it was much against the grain ; for I had come from Malagon very unwell, and was so still. But, thinking it would be to our Lord's service, I wrote to the Superior to order me to do whatever he thought best. He sent the licence for the foundation and instructions to me to go in person, and to take whichever nuns I thought best. This was a serious anxiety to me, because of their having to live with those who were there already. Earnestly commending it to our Lord, I took two from the Convent of St Joseph at Toledo, one of them as

Prioress ; and two from that of Malagon, one as Sub-Prioress. And, having been the subject of so many prayers to His Majesty, it all turned out well, which I thought no small matter—for in foundations begun with our own Sisters alone, they all fit in well together.

There came for us Father Fray Antonio of Jesus and the Father Prior, Fray Gabriel of the Assumption. Having obtained all necessary securities from the town of Villanueva, we started from Malagon on the Saturday before Lent, February 13th, 1580. It pleased God to give us such fine weather, and to me such good health, that I seemed never to have been ill. And I was amazed, and considered of what great moment it is, in any matter which we see is to the Lord's service, not to pay attention to our own weakness and the difficulty which that opposes to us : since He has power to make the weak strong and the sick whole. And should He not do so, it will be better for our soul to suffer and to forget ourselves, fixing our eyes on His honour and glory. What is life and health for, but to lose it for so great a King and Lord ? Believe me, Sisters, that if you go by that way it will never go ill with you. I confess that my badness and weakness have often made me fear and hesitate : but I cannot remember a single time, since the Lord gave me the Barefoot habit, nor for some years before that, that He has not, of His sole mercy, given me grace to overcome such temptations and to throw myself into what I saw was to His greater service, however difficult it might be. I quite clearly understand how little was what I on my part did: but God requires nothing beyond such a resolve in order to do everything Himself. May He be for ever blessed and praised ! Amen.

We had to go to the monastery of our Lady of Succour, which, as I have said, is three leagues from Villanueva, and to wait there to give notice of our arrival : for so they had arranged, and it was right that I should obey the Fathers with whom we were going in every particular. This monastery is situated in a most delightfully wild uninhabited country. And when we came near, the friars came out in very orderly array to receive their Prior. As they advanced barefooted and in their poor serge cloaks, they touched the hearts of us all, and me they moved deeply, making me feel as though we were in the spring time of our holy forefathers. They looked like so many white fragrant flowers in that field ; and so I believe they are in God's sight, for I think He is served there with genuine sincerity. They entered the chapel with a *Te Deum*, sung with very subdued voices. The entrance is underground as through a cave, representing that of our father Elias. I entered in a state of such inward rejoicing that indeed I should have thought it well worth a longer journey : although I felt deep regret that the saint through whom our Lord had founded this house was already dead. It had not been vouchsafed me to see her, though I greatly desired it.

I think it will not be idle to relate something of her life and under what conditions our Lord was pleased to have the monastery founded there, which, as I am told, has been so profitable to many souls in the neighbouring villages. And I tell it that, hearing of that saint's penance, you, my Sisters, may see how far behind we lag, and may make efforts to serve our Lord anew. For we have no excuse for doing less than she, since we are not sprung of a race so gentle and noble as hers : for, although this is of no importance in itself, I say it because she had led a luxurious life, agreeably to her estate, for she was of the family of the Duke of Cardona : thus her name was Doña Catalina de Cardona. After she had written me a few letters, she used to sign herself only *The Sinner*. Of her

life before the Lord gave her such graces, those who write her
Life will speak, and will relate in greater detail all that there is
to be told of her.   In case that should not come into your
hands, I will here set down what I have been told by various
trustworthy people who had dealings with her.

While this saint was living among people and ladies of high
rank, she always was very careful of her soul, and did penance.
The desire for penance increased greatly in her, and for going
away by herself where she could enjoy communion with God and
be occupied in doing penance, without anyone to hinder her.
She spoke of this to her confessors, and they would not
consent.   And, as the world is now so very prudent and we
have all but forgotten the great graces which God has bestowed
on holy men and women who served Him in the deserts, I do
not wonder at their thinking it folly.   But, as His Majesty
never fails so to assist sincere desires that they may be carried
into effect, He appointed that she should go to confession to
a Franciscan Father, Fray Francisco de Torres, a man whom I
used to know well, and I consider him a saint.   He has lived
these many years in great fervour of penance and prayer, and
in abundant persecutions.   He must have known very well
what grace God gives to those who will do themselves violence
to receive it : so he told her not to delay, but to follow His
Majesty's call.   I do not know that those were his exact words ;
but that was what she understood, for she put it in practice
immediately.   She told her secret to a hermit who lived at
Alcalá, and begged him to go with her, and never to tell
anyone : and they arrived at the place where the monastery
now stands.   There she found a little cave which hardly gave
her shelter ; and there he left her.   But what love must have
borne her there ! for she felt no anxiety about what she would
have to eat, nor about the dangers that might befall her, nor

about the evil that might be said about her when she was found
to be missing. How inebriated that saintly soul must have
been, engrossed with the desire of enjoying undisturbed
communion with her Spouse, and resolved to care no more for
the world, since she thus fled from all its pleasures! Let
us think well over this, Sisters, and consider how she overcame
all at one blow. For, although what you do is no less than
what she did when you enter our holy Order, and offer to God
your will, and vow such constant enclosure, yet I could not
say that in some of us our first fervour does not pass away, so
that in some points we fall back under the sway of our own
self-love. May it please the Divine Majesty that thus it may
not be, but that as we have imitated this saint in choosing to
flee from the world, we may live in every way very far from it
in spirit.

I have heard a good many details of the great severity of
her life, and what is known of it can only be a small part : for,
living so many years as she did in that solitude, and having
no one to restrain her, and with such strong desires for
penance, she must have illtreated her body terribly. I will
relate what she herself told various people, especially the
nuns of St Joseph of Toledo, into which she went to see the
nuns, and talked to them as to sisters, with all openness.
So she did to other people ; for her simplicity was great, and
so must have been her humility. And as one who knew as a
matter of course that she had nothing of herself, she was very
far from vainglory, but delighted in telling of the graces
which God bestowed on her, that through them His Name
might be praised and glorified : a dangerous thing for those
who have not attained to her condition, because it may at
least seem to be to their own praise. That openness and holy
simplicity of hers must have kept her free from this ; for I
have never heard her charged with this fault.

She said she had spent eight years in that cave.   For many days she lived on wild herbs and roots.   The hermit who went with her left her three loaves ; but when those were finished, she had no more until a shepherd lad passed that way, who from that time provided her with bread and flour. This was what she had to eat, little cakes baked on the ashes, and nothing else ; this every third day.   And it is certainly true, for the friars who live there are also witnesses thereof : for although when she went about to try to found a monastery, when she was already much worn out, they sometimes made her eat a sardine or something, it did her more harm than good.   She never drank wine that I heard of.   Her disciplines were taken with a sort of thick chain, and she often went on with them two hours or an hour and a half.   Her hair shirts terribly sharp.   For a certain person, a woman, told me that once, on her return from a pilgrimage, she had stayed for the night with her, and had pretended to be asleep, and saw her take off her hair shirt soaked with blood, and wash it. According to what she told the St Joseph's nuns, the worst she went through was from the evil spirits ; for they appeared to her like so many great mastiffs and jumped on her shoulders, and sometimes like snakes : but she was not in the least afraid of them.   After she had founded the monastery, she went just the same to her cave to live and sleep, except for attending the Divine Office.   Before it was founded, she used to go to mass at a monastery of the Ransomers, a quarter of a league off, and sometimes went there on her knees.   Her dress was of coarse cloth with a tunic of serge, and was so fashioned that she was taken for a man.   After those years during which she lived there so lonely, it pleased the Lord that it should be made known and people began to honour her so highly that she did not know what to do, for the crowds they came in. She spoke to all with great charity and kindness. The longer this went on, the greater the concourse of people who resorted to her ; and anyone who succeeded in getting speech of her thought no little of it. She got so tired with it, she said they were killing her. The time came when all the plain was full of carriages. Just after the friars were settled there, there was nothing else to be done but to lift· her up on high to give the people the blessing, and so dismiss them.

After the eight years when she was living in the cave (which now was larger, because those who resorted there had made it so) she had a very serious illness of which she thought she should die ; and she went through it all in that cave. She began to entertain desires for a monastery of friars in that place ; and this continued for some time, she not knowing of what Order to make it. But one day while she was reciting her prayers before a crucifix which she always carried with her, our Lord shewed her a white cloak, and she understood that it was the cloak of the Discalced Carmelites ; and yet she had never heard that there were such Brothers in the world : and at that time there were only two monasteries founded, those of Mancera and Pastrana. After this, she must have got information about them. She heard that there was one at Pastrana : and as the Princess of Eboli, Prince Ruy Gomez' wife, to whom Pastrana belonged, was a very old friend of hers, she started for Pastrana to see how to found this monastery which she so greatly desired. There in the chapel of St Peter—for so it was called—in the monastery of Pastrana, she took the habit of our Lady, although not with the intention of being a professed nun. For as the Lord was guiding her by another way, she never was inclined to be a nun, but thought it would mean her having to give up on obedience her purposes of mortification and solitude. In the presence of all the Brothers, she received the habit of our Lady of Carmel. Father Mariano, of whom I have before spoken in my account of these foundations, happened to be there : and he told me myself that it put him into a trance or suspension so that his senses were quite gone. And that, in this state, he saw many friars and nuns dead, some decapitated, others with their legs and arms cut off, as martyrs : for so in this vision he understood they were. And he is not a man who would say it if he had not really seen it ; no more is he accustomed to such suspensions : for God does not lead him by that way. Ask of God, Sisters, that it may come true, and that in our time we may be worthy to see so great a good, and have part in it ourselves.

From that time at Pastrana the saintly Cardona began to work towards founding her monastery, and for that purpose she returned to the Court whence she had so gladly departed. This can have been no slight torment to her. Nor were there lacking slanders and troubles ; for whenever she went out of the house, she did not know what to do for the mob that followed her. This was the case wherever she went. Some cut off pieces from her habit, some from her cloak. After that, she went to Toledo, where she stayed with our nuns. They all have assured me that there was about her so strong an odour as of relics that, even after she left them there, the habit and cincture retained it very strongly, moving the nuns to praise the Lord. And the nearer the nuns came to her, the better the odour ; when naturally the odour of such garments, with the heat, which was great, would rather have been unpleasant. (The nuns took her habit from her, and gave her another.) I know that they would not say anything that was not quite true. Thus she left them greatly edified.

At the Court and elsewhere she was given the means to make her monastery, and when she had obtained the licence, it was founded. The chapel was built where her cave had been, and they made another cave for her in a retired spot, where she had a stone tomb, and there she spent most of the day and night. This did not last long; for she only lived about five and a half years after she had the monastery there. And indeed, that she should have lived even so long seems a supernatural thing, considering the austerity of her life. Her death took place in 1577, if I remember rightly. Her last honours were performed with great solemnity; for there was a gentleman named Fray Juan de Leon who was greatly devoted to her, who made a great point of this. She is now buried temporarily in a chapel of our Lady, to whom she had a great devotion, until a larger chapel than they now possess shall be built to receive her blessed corpse, as is fitting. Great is the devotion of the monastery and of the whole neighbourhood to her memory; especially because of her solitude and the cave where she lived before she resolved to found the monastery; and therefore her body has rightly been left there.

The monks assured me that she was so wearied and distressed at finding what a number of people came to see her that she wanted to go somewhere else where nobody had heard of her : and she sent for the hermit who had brought her there to come and fetch her; but he was dead. And our Lord, having purposed that this house of our Lady should be established there, gave her no chance of departing; for, as I have said, I know that He is greatly served there. They are very careful in their observance, and it can well be seen that they like being withdrawn from human habitation, particularly the Prior. For God brought him out from a life of great enjoyment to take the habit, and so He has well rewarded him with spiritual joys. He was very kind to me there. They gave us some of their chapel furniture for the chapel which we were going to found : for, as that saintly woman was beloved by many great people, the chapel was well provided with fittings.

I was very happy while I stayed there, although filled with shame—and it has not left me. For I saw that she who there had done such sharp penance was a woman like myself, but more delicate, being of such high estate, and not a great sinner as I am ; and that in this there is no comparison between us : and I have received of our Lord much greater favours in many ways ; and my not being already in hell, by reason of my great sins, is a very great one. The thought of imitating her, if I could, was the only thing which comforted me, but not much : because all my life has gone by in desires, but the works I do not. May God's mercy help me, in Whom I have always trusted through His Most Blessed Son, and the Virgin our Lady, whose habit I wear through the goodness of the Lord !

One day when I had made my Communion in that hallowed chapel, I fell into a deep abstraction and a sus-pension which took away my senses. During this state, that saintly woman appeared to me in an intellectual vision as a glorified body, and some angels with her. She told me not to be discouraged, but to endeavour to go forward with these foundations. I know, although she did not expressly say so, that she was aiding me before God. She said something else as well, which I need not write down.

This left me greatly consoled and with a desire for work ; and I hope in the goodness of the Lord, that with such good aid as her prayers, I may be able in some degree to serve Him.

You see hereby, my Sisters, how her troubles were already

ended, and the glory which is now hers will be without end. Let us, for the love of our Lord, make an effort to follow this our Sister, hating ourselves as she hated herself; let us accomplish our day's work, since it is so short, and all will be at an end.

On the first Sunday of Lent, which was St Barbacian's Day, the Eve of the Festival of the Chair of St Peter, 1580, we arrived at Villanueva de la Jara. That same day the Blessed Sacrament was brought into the chapel of St Anne, at the time of High Mass. All the Corporation came out to meet us, and Dr Ervias and some others, and we went and alighted at the parish church, which is a long way from St Anne's.

All the people were rejoicing greatly, and it made me happy indeed to see the joy with which they received the Order of the Blessed Virgin our Lady. From afar off we could hear the pealing of the bells. As we entered the church, they began singing the *Te Deum*, the choir chanting one verse and the organ the next. When that was over, they carried the Blessed Sacrament shoulder high on a bier, and an image of our Lady in like manner, with crosses and banners. The procession travelled with great pomp. We in our white cloaks and our veils over our faces walked in the middle, next to the Blessed Sacrament, and next to us our Barefoot Brothers—for a great many came from the monastery. The Franciscans—for there is a Franciscan monastery in the town—went in the procession, and a Dominican Brother who happened to be in the place; and although he was alone, it gave me pleasure to see that habit there. As it was a long distance, there were many altars on the way: and they stopped from time to time, reciting poems about our Order. We were greatly touched by this and by seeing that all the poems were in praise of the great God

Whom we were bearing with us, and that for His sake so much
was made of us seven poor insignificant Barefoot nuns who
were walking along there.   It filled me with confusion when I
considered all this, seeing that I was walking among them,
and that if I had what I deserved, everyone would be turning
against me.

I have given you a long account of these honours done
to the habit of the Virgin, that you may praise our Lord
and pray that He may make use of this foundation.   For I
am happier when a foundation is begun amidst persecution
and troubles, and I narrate those with a better will.

It is true that the Sisters who were living there had been
through many during those six years—or at least five and a
half—since they entered that house of the glorious St Anne ;
besides their deep poverty and their toil in earning their living.
For they never liked to ask for alms, because they did not wish
people to think they had gone there that they might feed them.
They lived very austerely, fasting much, eating little, with
uncomfortable beds, and in a very tiny house, which last was a
real hardship for people so strictly enclosed as they always were.
They told me that the hardest thing to bear was their sore desire
to see themselves in the habit : for day and night this troubled
them sorely, fearing it would never come to pass.   So their
constant prayer to God, with frequent tears, was that He would
bestow that favour upon them.   And when they saw that there
was some hitch, they were in great affliction and redoubled
their penances.   They went without food in order to save from
their earnings the pay of the messengers whom they sent to
me, and to make such presents as their poverty permitted to
those who could in any way help forward their cause.   I see
very well, since I have spoken with them and seen their
saintliness, that it was their prayers and tears which effected

their reception into the Order. Therefore I hold it a greater treasure to have such souls within the Order than if they had possessed an ample endowment; and I hope the house will advance greatly.

Well, when we entered the house, they were all at the inner door, each in her own costume: they had gone on dressing just as when they came in; for they had never chosen to adopt the dress of *beatas*[1], but were waiting in hopes of our habit. However, their apparel was very sober : and the little care they took of themselves was shewn by their being so badly dressed; and most of them were so weakly that it shewed how severe a life they had led. They received us with abundant tears of joy. These were obviously genuine, and so was their goodness, their cheerfulness and humility and obedience to the Prioress : and they did not know how to do enough to please the nuns who had come for the foundation. All their fear was lest, when they saw their little house and their poverty, they might go away again. None of them was head; but with great Community spirit each worked as hard as she could. Two who were older than the others, transacted any necessary business : the others never spoke to anyone, nor wished to do so. They had no lock to the door, but only a bolt ; and no one ventured to go to the door but the eldest, who answered. They slept very little in order to work for their food and not to lose their prayer time : for they kept long hours, on Festivals the whole day. They guided themselves by the books of Fray Luis of Granada and Fray Pedro of Alcántara. Most of their time they spent in reciting the Divine Office, though they could read but little—for there was only one of them who could read well—and had not Breviaries alike.

---

[1] [*Dévotes*; women who lived at home but spent their time at church and among the poor. Tr.]

Some they had of the old Roman[1] Use, given them by priests
because they were of no use to themselves, others they had
got as they might : and, as they could not read, they spent
many hours at it. They did not recite it where anyone from
outside could hear them. God no doubt accepted their good
intention and laborious effort ; for they can have said very
little sense.

When Father Fray Antonio of Jesus began to have
dealings with them, he made them recite only the Office of
our Lady.

They had an oven in which they baked their bread :
and they did everything in as orderly a way as if they had
had someone over them. It made me give praise to our
Lord : and the more I saw of them, the more glad I was to
have come. I feel that I would not have failed to satisfy the
desire of such souls, whatever troubles I might have had to
endure. Those of my companions who remained there told
me that just the first few days they felt some repugnance,
but when they got to know them and realized their goodness,
they felt great affection for them and were delighted to be
remaining with them. Saintliness and goodness accomplish
much. It is true that our Sisters were of such a sort that,
even if they had met with many difficulties and troubles,
they would have borne it well, by the Lord's grace, because
they desire to suffer in His service. And any Sister who
should not feel in herself this desire, let her not reckon herself a true Barefoot ; seeing that our desires are not to be for

[1] At that time a reform of Missals and Breviaries was taking place,
conformably with the decisions of the Council of Trent ; and the clergy
had to do away with their old Breviaries of any diocesan Use. St Theresa
calls them " old Roman " because they were of the Roman or secular
type, not of the monastic type, and were unreformed.

repose but for suffering, that we may in some wise follow our true Spouse. May it please His Majesty to give us the grace for it! Amen.

This hermitage of St Anne had its origin as follows. There was living in the town of Villanueva de la Jara an ecclesiastic named Diego de Guadalajara, a native of Zamora, who had been a Carmelite Brother. He had a devotion to the glorious St Anne; so he built this hermitage adjoining his own house, and kept it up for hearing mass in: and, moved by his great devotion, he went to Rome and brought back a Bull with many indulgences for this chapel or hermitage. He was a virtuous and unworldly man. When he died, he directed in his will that the house and all he possessed should be for a convent of Carmelite nuns; and that, if this could not be carried into effect, there should be a chaplain to say so many masses a week; and that if and whenever a convent was established, the obligation of saying mass should cease. So it went on more than twenty years, with a chaplain who let the property fall into decay. For though those girls went to live in the house, they had only the house. The chaplain lived in another house belonging to the same chapelry, which he now will give up with the rest, and very little that is: but the mercy of God is so great that He cannot fail to shew favour to the house of the glorious mother of His Mother. May it please His Majesty that He may be always served therein, and may all creatures praise Him for ever and ever! Amen.

CHAPTER XXIX

Of the Foundation of St Joseph's of our Lady of the Street,
at Palencia, on King David's Day, 1580.

WHEN I came away from making the foundation of
Villanueva de la Jara, I was ordered by the Superior to go
to Valladolid. This was at the request of the Bishop of
Palencia, Don Alvaro de Mendoza, who had accepted and
always befriended our first convent, St Joseph's, at Avila,
and who always befriends the Order in all its concerns. He
had now resigned the See of Avila and been translated to
Palencia, and our Lord put it into his heart to have another
convent of this holy Order founded there. When I got to
Valladolid, I became so ill that they thought I should die ;
and the illness left me with so little energy, and feeling it so
impossible to do anything that, although the Prioress of
our convent at Valladolid, who was anxious the foundation
should be made, urged me to it, she could not persuade me,
nor did I think it reasonable ; for the convent was to be
founded without endowment, and I was told that the place
was too poor to support it.

This foundation, together with one at Burgos, had been
under consideration for about a year : and formerly I had not
been so averse to it ; but now, although I had gone to
Valladolid for that very purpose, many were the difficulties I
found. I do not know whether it was my severe illness and
the weakness it had left, or whether it was the devil, seeking
to hinder the good which has since been done. Indeed, it
frightens and grieves me—and I often complain of it to our
Lord—to see what a great share the poor soul has in the

weakness of the body; so that it appears to have nothing to do but observe its rules, laid down according to its needs and sufferings. This seems to me one of the greatest troubles and miseries of this life, when the spirit is not so high as to master it. For I reckoned nothing to be ill and suffer great pain— though it is a trial—if the soul is vigorous; for the soul knows that this comes from the hand of God and continues to praise Him. But to be on the one hand suffering and on the other inactive is a fearful state, especially for a soul which has experienced strong desires never to rest inwardly or outwardly, but wholly to employ itself in the service of its great God. There is no help for it in this state but in patience and the confession of its own wretchedness, and in resigning itself to God's will, to be made use of as He pleases and for what ends He pleases. This was my condition at that time: for although I was already convalescent, yet I was so weak that I had lost even the confidence which God is wont to give me when I have to begin any of these foundations. Everything seemed impossible to me. If at that time I had happened to meet with anyone to encourage me, it would have done me much good; but some only encouraged my fears, and others, though they gave me some hope, yet could not overcome my pusillanimity[1].

There happened to come that way a Father of the Company, Doctor Ripalda, a great servant of God, who at one time used to hear my confession. I told him how it stood with me, and asked him to tell me what he thought, for that I wished him to stand towards me in the place of God. He

---

[1] [In that year, 1580, there swept through Europe a disease very much like the present influenza: and it was this which St Theresa caught at Valladolid. It seems to have been like influenza, at any rate in her case, in its peculiar sequelae of depression and lack of energy. Tr.]

PALENCIA

from photograph by Messrs Laurent & Co.

began to urge me on; and he told me that my cowardice came just from old age. But I saw very well that this was not the case; for I am older now and not cowardly : and he too must have known this quite well, but said it to rebuke me and to shew me that it was not of God's sending. At that time the foundations of Palencia and of Burgos were being prepared for together, and I had nothing to make either with; but this had nothing to do with it, for I am used to beginning with less. Doctor Ripalda told me on no account to give it up. So had Baltasar Alvarez, a Provincial of the Company, told me, at Toledo; but at that time I was in good health. This was enough to have decided me : but, although it made a great difference, it did not altogether decide me ; because, as I have said, either the devil or my sickness held me bound : still, I was the better for it. The Prioress of Valladolid helped me as well as she could, because she strongly desired the foundation at Palencia; yet she also had her fears when she saw me so lukewarm.

Now let the true fire come; for no human beings, not even servants of God, will do the work! Hence it may be seen over and over that it is not I who effected anything in these foundations, but He alone Who is Almighty.

One day, while in doubt and not resolved to make either foundation, I besought our Lord, just after I had made my Communion, to give me light, that I might do His will in everything : for my lukewarmness was not such as to make me falter one hair's breadth in this desire. Our Lord said to me, as it were reproaching me, What dost thou fear ? When have I ever failed thee ? What I have always been, that same am I now. Thou must not fail to make these two foundations. O Great God, how different are Thy words from human words ! These words left me with such resolution and spirit that the whole world would not have been strong enough to oppose me; and I began at once to set to work, and the Lord to give me the means. I received two nuns, that we might have money to buy a house. And, although people told me it was impossible to live on alms in Palencia, it was as though they had not told me: because, as to founding the house with an endowment, I saw that at that time it could not be done; and, since God commanded it to be founded, His Majesty would provide. Accordingly, although my health was not quite restored, I determined to go: in an inclement season too, for I left Valladolid on Holy Innocents' Day in the aforesaid year[1]. For a nobleman of Palencia, who had gone to live elsewhere, had said he would lend us until Midsummer Day a house at Palencia which he had rented. I wrote to a Canon in the city, although I did not know him: but a friend of his had told me that he was a servant of God, and I had a presentiment that he would be of great assistance to us. For our Lord Himself, as has been seen in the accounts of other foundations, selects in every place some one to help us, because His Majesty sees how little I can do. I wrote to beg him to get the house left free for us—for it was tenanted—as quietly as he could, and without saying who it was for: because; although some of the chief people there had shewn goodwill towards us, and the Bishop's goodwill was so great, yet I knew it was on the safe side to let nobody know.

Canon Reinoso—for this was his name—did it so well that he not only had the house cleared for us, but we also found beds and many comforts abundantly provided; and indeed we needed them, for it was bitterly cold, and the preceding day had been difficult, with a fog so thick that we could hardly see one another. It is true, we rested but little until we had got

[1 1580. Tr.]

the place ready for saying mass next day, before anyone knew we were there; because this is what I have found to be the best plan in making these foundations: for if things begin to be left to discussion, the devil disturbs everything; and although he cannot succeed in anything, he causes anxiety. So it was done; for early, just about dawn, an ecclesiastic named Porras, a great servant of God, who went with us, said mass, and also another priest, Agustin de Vitoria, a friend of the nuns at Valladolid, who had lent me money to furnish the house, and given us many comforts for the journey.

There went, counting myself, five choir nuns, and one who has been my companion this long time, a lay Sister, but such a true servant of God and so sensible that she can help me more than other Sisters can[1]. That night we slept but little, although, as I say, the journey had been tiring because of the wet. I was much pleased at having the foundation made on that day, because it was the day on which King David is commemorated[2], and I have a special devotion to him. That morning I at once sent to tell the Most Illustrious Bishop; for not even he knew that I had come that day. He came at once, with that great kindness which he has always shewn towards us. He said he would give us all the bread we wanted, and he told his steward to supply us with many things. The Order owes him so much that whoever reads the

[1] The Venerable Anna of St Bartholomew, who went about with her until her death and acted as her secretary. It is told of her that she did not know how to write, and St Theresa happened to say that if she did, she could be of use to her. She begged the Saint to write out some lines for her; and by tracing them over and over, she taught herself to write in one night. There are preserved several letters in her writing signed by St Theresa.

[2] [Dec. 29, kept as the Feast of St Thomas of Canterbury, with a commemoration of King David. Tr.]

history of these foundations is bound to pray to our Lord for him, living or dead, and so I beg them to do of their charity.

The satisfaction shewn by the people was so great and so general as to be quite remarkable; for there was no one who was dissatisfied. The knowledge that it was the wish of the Bishop went a long way towards this, he being greatly beloved there: but the whole population is the most generous and of the best stuff that I have ever seen; and so I am more and more glad every day to have made a foundation there.

As the house was not our own, we began at once to see about buying another: for although that house was for sale, it was in a very bad situation. And, with what I had received from the nuns who were to go there, we seemed to have something to bargain with; for, though it was but little, it would go far at Palencia. However, if God had not given us the good friends He had sent us, nothing would have been of any use. The good Canon Reinoso brought us another, Canon Salinas, a friend of his, a man of great charity and good sense; and between them both, they took upon themselves the charge of the affair as if it had been their own, or even, I believe, more earnestly. And they have always continued to look after the interests of the house.

There was in the town a house held in great devotion, a sort of hermitage, dedicated to our Lady and called Our Lady of the Street. It was resorted to by a great many people, and held in reverence through all the town and the surrounding country. To his Lordship and to us all, it seemed that we should be well placed close to this chapel. There was no house belonging to it; but there were two next door which, if we bought them, would be large enough for us, together with the chapel. This the Chapter and a certain Confraternity would have to give up to us: and this we began to arrange

for. The Chapter at once made us a present of it, and although
I had some difficulty in coming to an understanding with the
people of the Confraternity, they also willingly did so : for, as
I have said, if I have ever seen good people in my life, it is
the people of Palencia. When the owners of the houses saw
that we were disposed to buy them, they raised the price, very
naturally. I thought well to go and see them : and to me and
to those who went with us they seemed so poor that I would
not on any account have them. Afterwards it was clearly
seen that a good deal of this was the devil's doing, because
it annoyed him that we should go there. To the two Canons
who were acting for us it seemed too far from the cathedral ;
and so it is, but it is in the most thickly peopled part of the
city. Finally we all agreed that that house would not do, and
we must look for another.

This the two Canons began to do with a care and diligence
which made me give thanks to the Lord, not letting anything
go by which might chance to suit us. They came at last to be
satisfied with one belonging to a man called Tamayo. Some
parts of it were particularly well suited to our needs, and it
was close to the house of one of the first gentlemen, Suero de
Vega, who was very well disposed towards us, and who,
together with others in that quarter, very much wished us to
settle there. The house itself was not large enough, but with
it he offered us another, although not such that we could very
well join both together.

Any way, from the account they gave me of it, I wished the
purchase to be effected ; but the two men would not buy the
house, unless I saw it first. I so much disliked going out in
the town, and I so thoroughly trusted them, that they could
hardly persuade me. At last I went, and also to the houses
of our Lady ; not, however, with any intention of buying them,

but lest the owner of the other house should think that we had no choice but to buy his. They appeared, as I have said, to me and to the Sisters who went, so poor that now we cannot understand how they can have appeared so poor. In this mind we went to the other house, quite determined to have it and no other: and, although we found serious drawbacks, we passed over them, notwithstanding that it would be very difficult to overcome them; for in order to make the chapel—and a poor one too—we should have to lose all of the house that was well fitted to live in. What a strange thing it is to go into a matter with one's mind already made up! Indeed it taught me the lesson of how little I could trust to my own judgement—though on this occasion it was not I alone who was under a delusion. Any way, we came away determined to buy no other than that house, and to give the owner what he had asked, which was a great deal, and to write to him; (for he lived not in the town, but near it).

It may seem irrelevant to have given such a long account of the purchase of the house, until it is seen what the devil must have had in view, in hindering us from going to the house of our Lady. It frightens me every time I think of it. We all having made up our minds, as I have said, to buy no other house but that one, next morning at mass I began to be extremely anxious as to whether I had done right, and the disquiet hardly let me remain tranquil during the whole of mass. I went to receive the Blessed Sacrament, and just as I received It, I heard these words, This is the right house for thee, in such a way that I quite determined not to buy the one I was thinking of, but the house of our Lady. I began to consider what a bad thing it would be to draw back in a negotiation which had gone so far, and which our zealous helpers had so much at heart. Our Lord answered me, They

do not know how grievously I am offended in that place : and
this will put it right.

It came into my mind to wonder whether this might be a
delusion, but not to believe it so : for I well knew by the effect
it worked in me that it was the Spirit of God. He said to me
at once, It is I. These words left me quite calm, and rid
of the commotion I had been in. Yet I did not know how to
undo what had been done, and the bad account I had given
my Sisters of that house ; for I had made the most of its
badness, and said that I would not for anything in the world
have had them go there, without seeing it first.   This,
however, I did not so much concern myself about, because I
knew that whatever I did they would think right : but I was
concerned about the others who wished to buy Tamayo's
house.   I thought they would consider me light and change-
able, since I had so quickly altered my mind—a thing which I
greatly abhor.

These were not the sort of considerations to move me
much or little to give up going to the house of our Lady ;
nor did I even remember that it was not a good one : for
if the nuns could put a stop to one venial sin, all the rest
was trifling in comparison ; and any of them who knew what I
knew, would have been of my mind.

The means I took was this : I was at that time going to
confession to Canon Reinoso, one of our two helpers ; but I
had not hitherto spoken to him of spiritual matters of this sort,
because there had been no occasion to do so. But, as I have
been accustomed in these matters always to do what my
confessor advises, as being the safest way, I determined to tell
him this in great secrecy : although I could not feel sure that
I should give up doing what I had been told without great
heaviness of heart. But any way I should have done so :

because I trusted in our Lord to do what in my experience He has often done—to change the confessor's mind, so that he may do what He desires, although his own judgement might be opposed. I told him first about the many times that our Lord had been used to teach me in this way, and that up to that time many things had happened which proved it to have been the work of His Spirit. Then I told him what had taken place; but said I would do what he thought right, although it would give me pain.

He is very discreet and religious, and of good judgement in all sorts of matters, though he is young: and although he saw there would be remarks about the affair, he did not decide that I must give up doing what I had been told. I told him that we had better wait for our messenger's return, and he agreed: for I indeed trusted in God that He would set it right. And so it was: for the owner of the house, when we had consented to give him all he wanted and asked for, now asked three hundred ducats more, which was absurd, for it was excessive. So we saw that this was God's doing: for it was much to the man's interest to sell; and to ask more when the bargain was made was not the way to do so. This was a great help, for we told him that we should never come to terms with him: yet it did not altogether settle the matter, because it was clear that for a matter of three hundred ducats we ought not to give up a house which appeared suitable for a convent.

I told my confessor not to concern himself about my credit, since in his opinion we should buy this house; but to tell his friend that, good or bad, cheap or dear, I was determined to buy the house of our Lady. His friend is of an exceedingly quick understanding; and, seeing so sudden a change, I feel sure that, although nothing was said to him, he guessed the cause; and so he pressed me no further in the matter.

Well have we all since seen the great mistake we should have made if we had bought the other : for now we are surprised to see the superior advantages of our present house. Let alone the greatest of all, which is easy to see—that there our Lord and His glorious Mother are served, and many occasions of sin removed : for as many nightly vigils were kept there, and as the chapel was only a hermitage[1], many things might be done there which the devil was not pleased to have stopped ; and we ourselves have the joy of being able to do some service to our Mother and Lady and Patroness. And very ill we should have acted if we had not gone there ; for this was all we needed to take into account. It shews clearly how the devil blinds us in many matters ; for in that house there are many conveniences which we should not have found elsewhere. Also it is the greatest satisfaction to all the inhabitants, who wanted us to go there : even some who did wish us to go to the other house afterwards quite approved of it. Blessed for ever be He Who gave me light therein ! And if in any matter I happen to do well, it is He Who gives the light. For every day I am more astonished at the little ability I have for anything. And this must not be supposed to be humility ; for every day I keep seeing it more plainly. For our Lord would seem to desire that I and everyone else should have to acknowledge that it is His Majesty alone Who does these works ; but that, as He with clay gave sight to the blind man, so to so blind a creature as I He will find means of giving sight. Certainly in this matter I was, as I have said, very blind indeed ; and every time I think of it, it makes me desire to thank our Lord afresh. But even this I cannot do; and I do not know how He can bear me. Blessed be His mercy ! Amen.

[1] [Being in the midst of a town, it was not, properly speaking, a hermitage, but it was on the footing of one. The abuses of such chapels hinted at in the text caused them to be suppressed from time to time. Tr.]

Well then, those saintly friends of the Virgin at once made haste to buy the houses; and, in my opinion, they got them cheap. They worked hard. For in each one of these foundations it pleases God that there shall be some who do well in helping us; and I am the one who do nothing, as I have said elsewhere —and I never mean to leave off saying it, for it is the truth. They did a great deal, then, in getting the house ready, and in giving money towards it, because I had not enough; and also in becoming sureties for it. For in other places, until I can find a surety—and not for so large a sum either—I am always harassed: and it is very reasonable: for if they do not trust to our Lord for it, I myself have not a penny. But His Majesty has always been so gracious to me that no one has ever lost anything by trusting me, nor failed to be paid liberally: and I count that as a very great favour done me.

As the owners of the houses were not satisfied with those two as sureties, the Canons went to find the Vicar-general, whose name was Prudencio—at least so they tell me now, but I am not sure that I remember it; for, as we used to speak of him as *the Vicar-general*, I did not hear his name. He has been so good to us that we owed and still owe him much. He asked them where they were going; and they said, To find him, that he might sign the bond. He laughed and said, "Well, so this is the way you ask me to become surety for so large a sum?" And without getting off his mule, he signed it on the spot: a notable thing for such times as these. I cannot help speaking in great praise of the kindness I met with in Palencia, in general and in particular. Indeed it seemed to me just like the ways of the primitive Church—at any rate not at all usual now-a-days—that when we had no endowment and they had to provide us with food, they not only permitted us to come, but said that God was giving them the greatest privilege. And, looked at in the right light, that was true:

for, if it were only the having one church more wherein is the Blessed Sacrament, it is a great thing.

May He be for ever blessed! Amen. For it is shewn more and more that it is His good pleasure to be there : and that unseemlinesses must have taken place, which have now been put a stop to : for as many people kept night-vigils there, and the hermitage was lonely, not all of them went out of devotion [1]. This is coming right. The image of our Lady was in a very unfitting place. The Bishop, Don Alvaro de Mendoza, built a chapel for it ; and, little by little, things are coming to be done to the honour and glory of the glorious Virgin and of her Son. May He be praised for ever ! Amen, Amen.

Then when the fitting up of the house was finished, ready for the nuns to go in, the Bishop wished their entry to be made with great solemnity, and so it was done on the Octave of Corpus Christi. He himself came from Valladolid, and he was attended by the Chapter and the Religious Orders and almost all the people of the place, with a great deal of music. We all went in procession from the house where we were, in our white cloaks, with our veils over our faces, to a parish church close to the house of our Lady. There her image itself met us, and thence we took the Blessed Sacrament and set It in our chapel with great ceremony and solemnity, which stirred up much devotion. Some more nuns went with us who had gone there to make the foundation at Soria ; and we all had candles in our hands. I believe our Lord was greatly

[1] Probably these abuses did not completely cease even after the nuns were settled there : for they left the house ten years later, but this may have been partly on account of some difficulty with the Confraternity. The Jesuits took the chapel and enlarged the church, and it continued to be a much frequented place of worship.

praised that day at Palencia.   May He grant that all creatures may so praise Him for ever !   Amen.

While I was at Palencia, it pleased God that the separation of the Barefoot Carmelites from the Carmelites of the Mitigated Rule should take place, making them a separate province, which was all that we desired for our peace and quiet.   At the request of our Catholic king, Don Philip, a very ample Brief was brought from Rome to effect this : and his Majesty helped us very greatly, as he had done from the beginning.   A Chapter was held at Alcalá by mandate of a Reverend Father, Fray Juan de las Cuevas [1], a Dominican, who was at that time Prior at Talavera.   He was appointed from Rome on the King's nomination.   He was a saintly and wise person, as was fitting for such an office.   The King bore the cost of the Chapter, and at his command the whole University shewed kindness to the friars.

The Chapter was held at St Cyril's, our College of Barefoot friars at Alcalá, and in great peace and concord.   They elected as Provincial Father Master Fray Jerónimo Gracian of the Mother of God.   Those Fathers will narrate elsewhere what took place there ; so I need not speak of it here.   I have mentioned it because it was while I was founding the house at Palencia that our Lord brought to pass an event so closely concerning the honour and glory of His glorious Mother, as it concerned her Order, she being our Lady and Patroness. And it gave me one of the greatest happinesses and satisfactions I could have in this life.   For the troubles and persecutions

---

[1] His real name was Juan Velasquez de las Cuevas, but he was usually called by his mother's surname, Juan de las Cuevas. His family was of Coca. He was a Brother of the Monastery of St Stephen at Salamanca. He was made Bishop of Avila in 1596, and died ten years later.

and distresses which I had gone through for more than twenty-five years would take too long to tell ; and our Lord alone can enter into them. And now to see the end of them all, no one who did not know the troubles I had undergone could understand the joy which filled my heart, or the desire which possessed me that all the world should praise our Lord, and that we should pray for our saintly king Don Philip, through whose instrumentality God had brought our affairs to so good an end. But for him, all would have been ruined, so cunningly had the devil gone to work.

Now we are all in peace, Mitigated and Reformed : no one hinders us in the service of our Lord. Therefore, my Brothers and Sisters, since His Majesty has so graciously heard your prayers, up and haste to serve Him ! Let the present generation, who are eyewitnesses of it, consider the mercies He has done us and the troubles and disquiet from which He has delivered us : and those who are to come after, since they find the way made plain, let them, for the love of our Lord, never suffer a single thing which belongs to perfection to slip away. Let it not be said by their fault as is said of some Orders, that their beginning was praiseworthy[1]. Now we are beginning : but let them try to keep on beginning to go on from good to better continually. Let them remember that the devil keeps using very small faults with which to bore holes through which the very greatest may find entrance. Let them never catch themselves saying, "This does not matter : they are over particular." Oh my daughters, everything matters which hinders our progress. For the love of our Lord I entreat them to remember how soon all will be over, and what a mercy our Lord has done us in leading us into this Order, and what a heavy penalty will be incurred by anyone who initiates any relaxation. Nay, let them keep their eyes ever fixed on the

---

[1] A euphemism, implying that later the developments are not so.

race of holy prophets from which we are sprung. What Saints
have we in heaven who wore this habit ! Let us aspire with a
holy audacity, by the grace of God, to be ourselves like unto
them. Short will be the battle, my Sisters; the issue is
eternal. Let us put aside those things which are really
nothings, for only those are realities which lead us to our
true end, to serve and love Him more, seeing He liveth for
evermore. Amen. Amen. To God be thanksgivings !

JESUS

CHAPTER XXX

The Foundation of the Convent of the Blessed Trinity at Soria,
in 1581. The first mass was said on the Day of our Father
Saint Elisha.

WHILE I was at Palencia, making the above-mentioned
foundation, a letter was brought me from Doctor Velasquez,
Bishop of Osma. With him, at the time when he was Professor
and Canon of the Cathedral at Toledo, and when I was troubled
by certain fears, I had sought communication, because I knew
him to be a most learned man and a great servant of God.
So I besought him to hear my confession and take upon
him the care of my soul. Although he was a very busy man,
yet when I begged this for the love of our Lord and he saw my
necessity, he did it so willingly that I was surprised; and he
was my confessor and director all the time I was at Toledo,
which was a long while. I told him of the state of my soul
quite plainly, as I always do. He did me so much good that
from that time I began to suffer less from those fears. It is

true that there was another cause for this, not to be told here.
Still he did me a great and real good, because he reassured me
by means of passages from Holy Scripture, which is the thing
that has most weight with me, when I am certain that he who
makes use of them thoroughly understands them.   I well knew
this of him ; and knew his good life too.

He wrote me this letter from Soria, where he was staying.
He told me that a lady whose confession he heard there had
spoken to him about founding a convent of our nuns, and that
he approved of it : that he had promised to persuade me to go
and make the foundation there, and that I must not leave him
in the lurch : that if I thought it suitable I must let him
know, and he would send for me.   I was much pleased : for,
let alone its being a good foundation to make, I wanted to tell
him some matters concerning my soul, and to see him ; for I
bore him a great affection for the good he had done me.

The lady foundress' name was Doña Beatriz de Veamonte
and Navarre, for she was sprung from the Kings of Navarre.
She was the daughter of Don Francés de Veamonte, of illustrious and high descent.   She had been married some years,
and was left with no children and great wealth, and had an
ardent desire to found a convent of nuns.   When she mentioned
this to the Bishop and he told her of the Order of our Lady,
the Barefoot Carmelites, it was so exactly what she wanted
that she was in great haste to carry it out.   She is a person
of gentle disposition, generous and lowly ; in a word, a true
servant of God.   She owned at Soria a good solidly built house
in a very good situation ; and she said she would give us that
together with whatever might be needed for the foundation :
and with this she gave a sum of money which at two per cent.
would bring in five hundred ducats a year.   The Bishop
offered to give a very good parish church all built of hewn

stone, close at hand, which we could make use of with a covered way. He could rightly do this because there were many churches in the town, and this one was poor, so that he could join the parish to another church. In his letter he set forth all this. I discussed it all with the Father Provincial, who was there at the time; and he and all my friends there decided to write by a special messenger to say they might come to fetch me, because the foundation at Palencia was accomplished. And I was much pleased about this, for the reasons I have given.

I began to collect the nuns whom I was to take with me. There were seven, because the foundress wished to have more rather than fewer, and a lay sister, and my companion and myself. A very suitable person came for us without delay. I told him that I would take with me two Barefoot Fathers: so I took Father Fray Nicolas of Jesus Maria[1], a Genoese, a man of great discretion and perfection. He was over forty when he took the habit, I think: at any rate he is so now, and that was not long ago. But the progress he has made in this short time shews clearly that our Lord chose him to come to the aid of the Order in those troublous times of persecution. He was a great help: for of the others who could have helped, some were banished, some in prison. Having been, as I have said, such a short time in the Order, he held no office, and so less notice was taken of him; this was the work of God's providence, that such valuable help might be left me[2]. He is so discreet that he was able to stay in the monastery of the

---

[1] The celebrated Father Doria, afterwards first Vicar-general of the Order in Spain.

[2] The Dorias were bankers and contractors, and the King of Spain had borrowed heavily of them: so Nicholas Doria had considerable influence at court.

Mitigation at Madrid, as it were for other businesses, and hid ours so well that they never found out what he was there for, and so let him stay. We wrote to each other continually, for I was in the monastery of St Joseph at Avila, and discussed what was to be done ; for this was a relief to him. It shews how badly off our Order was, that so much was made of me, as the saying is, "For want of better people[1]." In all those vicissitudes I made proof of his discretion and perfection ; so he is one of those whom I greatly love in the Lord and highly esteem in our Order.

Well, he and a companion went with us at once. I had little difficulty on this journey, because the Bishop's envoy caused us to travel in great comfort, and helped us to obtain good lodgings : for when once we were within the diocese of Osma, the Bishop is so much beloved that people gave us good lodgings on hearing that it was his errand we were on. The weather was fine, and our stages were short : so there was no toilsomeness, but only pleasure ; for it gave me the greatest pleasure to hear what people said of the Bishop's sanctity. We arrived at Burgo[2] the day before the Octave of Corpus Christi. We made our Communion there next day, Thursday, the Octave Day, and we dined there, because we could not reach Soria next day. That night we spent in a church, because there was no other lodging, but we were none the worse for it. Next day we heard mass there, and we arrived at Soria about five in the evening. The saintly Bishop was at a window of his house when we passed by : and thence he gave us his

---

[1] St Theresa is referring to the old proverb, "For want of a better, my husband is mayor."

[2] Burgo de Osma, the seat of the Episcopal palace and Cathedral of the diocese to which Soria belongs, Soria having only a Collegiate church.

blessing, which was a great comfort to us ; for the blessing of
a Bishop and a saint is not to be lightly esteemed.

Our lady foundress was waiting for us at the door of her
house, for it was there that the monastery was to be established.
We did not see how to get in, the crowd was so great.   This
was nothing new ; for the world is so fond of novelties that,
wherever we go, there are such crowds that, if we did not wear
veils over our faces, it would be a great annoyance : with our
veils, it is not unbearable.   Doña Beatriz had had a large hall
very well fitted up for saying mass, because the covered way
to the church which the Bishop had given us had yet to be
made : and without delay it was said next day, the festival of
our father Saint Eliseus.   The foundress provided us most
amply with all that we needed, and settled us in those quarters,
where we were enclosed, until the passage was made ; that is,
until the Transfiguration.   On that day the first mass was
said in the church, with great solemnity and with a large
congregation.   A father of the Company of Jesus preached,
the Bishop having already gone to Burgo—for in his work he
never loses a day nor an hour—although he was not in good
health, for he had lost the sight of one eye.   This sorrow I
had there : for I felt it such a grievous pity that eyesight so
valuable in the service of our Lord should be lost.   The Lord's
judgements are His own.   This must have been allowed in
order to give His servant more to gain ; for he ceased not to
labour as before : and in order to try his submission to His
will.   He told me that it gave him no more concern than if it
had befallen his neighbour : and that he sometimes felt he
would not be sorry if he lost the sight of the other ; for then
he would go and serve God in a hermitage with no more
responsibility[1].

[1] In the end Señor Velasquez' desire was accomplished. Having been

This had always been what he felt himself called to before
he was made Bishop ; and he sometimes spoke to me of it,
having almost made up his mind to give up everything and be
gone. I could not bear him to do this, because I thought he
would be of great use in the Church of God, and so I wished
him to be what he is now. For all that, on the day when he
was offered the bishopric, when he sent to tell me, it at once
put me into great perturbation, imagining I saw him under a
heavy burden, and I did not know what to do with myself or
how to keep quiet. I went into the choir to commend him to
our Lord. His Majesty calmed me at once, telling me that it
would be greatly to His service ; and so indeed it is continually
shewn to be. In spite of the disease of the eye and other
painful infirmities, and his round of work, he fasts four days
in the week and does other penances ; his food is by no means
luxurious. When he visits the diocese, he goes on foot : his
servants cannot bear it, and have complained to me. The
servants must lead a good life or not remain in his service.
He does not entrust important affairs to his Vicars-general,
but they go through his own hands : and so I think do all.
During the first two years he was at Osma he underwent a
fierce persecution of false accusations, which amazed me, for
he is upright and just in administering justice. This has now
been coming to an end : for although they have been to court
and to wherever they thought they could do him injury, they
have little power to harm him, because the good he is doing in
all the diocese is getting to be well known. And he has borne it

promoted in 1583 to the metropolitan see of Santiago, and being in very
bad health, he obtained permission to resign. The King wished to
assign him a pension of 12,000 ducats, but 6,000 was all he could be
made to accept. He died in 1587, and his body was taken to his native
place, Tudela de Duero.

all so perfectly that he has put them to shame, doing good to those who he knew were doing evil to him[1]. For all that he has to do, he does not fail to find time for prayer.

I seem to have been carried away in speaking the praises of this saintly man—and I have said but a small part—but that it may be known who it was that began the foundation of the Convent of the Blessed Trinity at Soria, and that its future nuns may take comfort from that, it has been no waste of time. The nuns who are there now know it well. Although he did not give the endowment, he gave the church; and, as I say, it was he who put it into the heart of our foundress, who was, as I have said, a very good Christian, virtuous and humble.

Well, when we had made the passage to the church and arranged everything needful for our enclosure, it became necessary for me to go to the Convent of St Joseph at Avila : so I started at once in the great heat, and such road as there was, was very bad for wheeled conveyances. There went with me a prebendary of Palencia, named Ribera. He had been extremely helpful to me in the work of making the covered way, and in everything else ; Father Nicolas of Jesus Maria having departed as soon as the papers relating to the foundation were done with, because he was greatly needed elsewhere. Ribera had business to transact at Soria when we went there, and he went with us. From that time forth God gave him such an effectual desire to do us good that we may well commend him to God amongst the benefactors of the Order. I did not want anyone else to go with me and my companion, because he was so careful that he sufficed, and the quieter the better for me in travelling.

---

[1] The proceedings were largely on account of the attempts made to have a cathedral at Soria. See Loperaez, *History of the Diocese of Osma.*

In this journey I paid for the comfort in which I had travelled to Soria; for although our driver knew his way to Segovia, he did not know the carriage road, and so the youth took us into places where we often had to alight, and led the cart along deep precipices where it almost went over. If we engaged guides, they took us just so far as where they knew there was a plain road; and left us, saying they had another engagement, just before the way became difficult. Before reaching any lodging place, as we did not know the country, we had to endure the sun for long hours, and often the danger of the cart's overturning. I was sorry for our escort: for sometimes when we had been told we were on the right way, we had to turn and retrace our steps. But his goodness was so deeply rooted that I do not think I ever saw him out of temper: which made me marvel and thank God that temptations have so little power where anyone is radically good. I thank God that He was pleased to deliver us from the dangers of that journey.

On the eve of St Bartholomew we arrived at Segovia, where our nuns were in anxiety because of the delay; which indeed was great, the journey having been what it was. There they made much of us; for God never sends me trouble but He repays me at once. I rested there a week or more. But this foundation was made with so little trouble that the journey back is not worth thinking of, for it was nothing.

I came away well content, because it seemed to me a neighbourhood where, by God's mercy, the foundation will be to His service, as indeed is being shewn already. May He be praised and blessed for ages upon ages. Amen. Deo gracias[1].

---

[1] From this conclusion it is apparent that she wrote the two preceding chapters soon after making the foundations at Palencia and Soria; and thought to have ended the book with them, having made her last Foundation.

CHAPTER XXXI

Of the Foundation of the glorious St Joseph of St Anne's, at Burgos.
The first mass was said on April 19th within the Octave of Easter
Day, 1582.

MORE than six years before this time, certain people who
had long been professed in the Company of Jesus, very
religious, learned and spiritual, had said to me that it would
be greatly to the service of our Lord if there were a house of
our holy Order at Burgos ; and they gave me certain reasons
which moved me to desire it. What with the many troubles
of the Order and with other foundations, I had had no
opportunity of carrying it out. While I was at Valladolid in
the year 1580, the Archbishop of Burgos[1] passed that way.
He had been Bishop of the Canaries, and now had been given
this archbishopric, and was on his way to it.

I have before spoken of the Bishop of Palencia, Don Alvaro
de Mendoza, and all he has done for our Order : that he was
the first to accept the Convent of St Joseph at Avila, he
being Bishop then ; and that ever since then, he has shewn us
great kindness, making the interests of the Order his own,
especially those which I have commended to him. I begged
him to ask the Archbishop's leave to make a foundation at
Burgos, and he very willingly consented ; because, as he believes
that our Lord is served in our houses, he is much pleased
when any is founded. The Archbishop would not come into
Valladolid, but lodged at the monastery of San Geronimo,
where the Bishop of Palencia entertained him sumptuously,

---

[1] Don Cristóbal Vela, son of Don Blasco Nuñez Vela, Viceroy of
Peru. He was appointed Bishop of the Canaries in 1575.

TORRE DE LA VELA, GRANADA

and went to dine with him and give him a girdle[1] or some
such ceremony, which was to make him Bishop. There he
asked him for the licence to found the convent. He said
he would grant it most willingly; for indeed he would have
liked to have one in the Canaries, and he was wanting to get
one founded, because he knew how well our Lord was served
in them, for he came from a place where there was one, and
he knew me well[2]. So the Bishop told me that as he was so
delighted to have the foundation, we were not to wait for the
licence : this could be considered as already granted, since the
Council[3] did not specify that it was to be in writing, but only
that it was to be with the Bishop's consent.

In my account of the previous foundation at Palencia I
have spoken of the great repugnance I had at that time for
making foundations, because I had been so ill that I was not
thought likely to live, and was not yet recovered. This,
however, is not my wont when I see that something is to the
service of God : so I do not understand the reason of such
unwillingness as I then felt. If it had been for want of
means, I have had less in making other foundations. To my
thinking, now that I have seen the sequel, it was the devil's
doing. And so it has regularly happened that every time
I was to have difficulties in making a foundation, our Lord,
knowing what a poor creature I am, has helped me by words
and by deeds. I sometimes think over it—how in some
foundations in which there were no difficulties, His Majesty
apprised me of nothing. So it was in this one, that, as He
knew what I should have to go through, He began to inspirit

---

[1] The Metropolitan's pallium.

[2] For he was of a family of Avila.

[3] The Council of Trent, Cap. 3. § 25, de Reform. Regul. "licentia prius
obtenta."

me from the first. May He be praised for all! So it was here—as I have said in my account of the foundation at Palencia, which was arranged at the same time—for as though reproving me, He said, What was I afraid of? When had He ever failed me? "I am the same : do not fail to make these two foundations." I have before spoken of the courage which such words infused into me, so I need not speak of it again. All my sloth at once vanished : which shewed that the cause of it was not infirmity or old age ; so I set about making both, as I have said.

It seemed better to make the foundation at Palencia first, as it was nearer, and because the weather was so severe and Burgos so cold, and also to please the good Bishop of Palencia ; and so this was done, as I have said. And since, while I was there, the opportunity for founding a convent at Soria presented itself, it seemed best to go there first, as everything was made ready for us ; and thence to go on to Burgos.

I begged the Bishop of Palencia, and he thought it right, to keep the Archbishop informed of what was going on ; so after I had gone to Soria, he sent a Canon, Juan Alonso, to the Archbishop, for this and no other purpose. The Archbishop wrote to me that he was affectionately desirous of my coming, and had talked over it with the Canon and was writing to his Lordship, putting himself into his hands ; that he was acting in this way because he knew Burgos, and that I should need the town's consent to come in. The practical outcome was that I was to go there and treat first with the city ; and if the city refused leave, that should not tie his hands to hinder him from giving it ; that he was there at the first foundation at Avila and remembered the great commotion and opposition there had been, and so he wished to prevent the like here : that it would not be fitting to found the convent except with the consent of the city, unless it were endowed— a condition which he mentioned because it was not one which I liked[1].

The Bishop naturally considered the thing settled when the Archbishop said I was to go there, so he sent to tell me to go. But to me there seemed a certain lack of courage in the Archbishop ; and I wrote thanking him for his kindness to me, but saying that it seemed to me worse to make the foundation against the will of the city than to do so without telling them, and would bring more trouble upon his Lordship. I seem to have divined how little we could expect from him if there should be any opposition to my getting the licence: and I thought there would be difficulty in getting it because of the contrary opinions there usually are in such matters. I wrote also to the Bishop of Palencia begging him to let the matter stand over for the present, there being so little of the summer left, and I being too unwell to stay in so cold a part of the country. I did not mention my doubts of the Archbishop, because he was already vexed at his having made difficulties after having shewed such eagerness for it ; and I did not want to sow discord, as they were friends. So I went off from Soria to Avila, without any idea at the time that I should have to go so soon to Burgos. And for certain reasons it was very necessary that I should go to St Joseph's[2].

There was at Burgos a saintly widow, Catalina de Tolosa,

---

[1] There is something of ambiguity in these provisions of the Archbishop. They seem to shew that he wished for the foundation, but was not resolutely determined to have it made.

[2] [The convent had grown slack, and alms had fallen off. The Provincial, Fray Jerome, had just been to visit the convent: the Prioress resigned at once, and the nuns elected St Theresa in her place, " through sheer hunger," she says. Tr.]

a Biscayan by birth, whose virtues would take me a long time to tell, so great were her austerities and her devotions, her alms and charity, so good her understanding and courage. She had placed two daughters as nuns in the Convent of Our Lady of the Conception at Valladolid, I think four years before this, and had just placed two more at Palencia; for she was waiting until that house was founded, and brought them there before I departed. All four have turned out as children brought up by such a mother, like angels. She gave them good dowries and everything very perfect, for she herself is so, and all that she does is handsomely done, and she can make it so, for she is rich.

When I went to Palencia, we considered the Archbishop's licence so certain that there seemed no need for cautious delay: so I asked her to get me a hired house to take possession of, and to put up some gratings and a turn, and put it to my account. It never entered my head that she would spend money of her own, but I meant her to lend it. She so much desired the foundation that she was distressed at its standing over; and so, after I had gone to Avila, as I have said, without any thought of making the foundation then, she did not let it rest; but, thinking there was nothing needed but the city's permission, she began, without telling me, to set to work to get it.

Doña Catalina had two neighbours, mother and daughter, great people, and good servants of God, who earnestly desired the foundation. The mother was Doña Maria Manrique. She had a son, Don Alonso de Santo Domingo Manrique, who was a town councillor. Her daughter was called Doña Catalina. These two ladies talked to him about his asking the council's leave. He spoke to Catalina de Tolosa, asking, What means of subsistence should he say we possessed? For

CARMELITE CONVENT AT GRANADA

if we had none, the council would not consent. She told him that she would pledge herself (and so she did) to give us a house if we needed one, and our food, and thereupon she gave in a petition signed with her name. Don Alonso went so prudently to work that he got the leave of all the councillors, and went to the Archbishop taking him the written licence.

Directly Doña Catalina had set to work, she wrote to me, saying that she was in treaty about it. I did not take it seriously, knowing how unwilling people are to permit convents founded without endowment; and as I did not know, nor did it enter my head, that she was so binding herself, I thought that much more had to be done. However, one day within the Octave of Martinmas, while I was commending the matter to our Lord, I considered what was to be done if the licence were given. As for going to Burgos myself, that seemed out of the question, considering my infirmities; for, being so chilly as I am, cold is very bad for me: and it seemed rash to set out on so long a journey when I had only just made a journey so trying as that from Soria, of which I have spoken: nor would the Father Provincial allow me to go. I thought the Prioress of Palencia might well go; for, everything being plain and easy, there would be nothing to do.

While I was considering this, and quite decided not to go myself, our Lord said to me the following words, from which I saw that the licence was already granted: Pay no regard to the cold, for I am the true warmth. The devil is putting out all his strength to hinder this foundation; put out all thine on My side, that it may be made; and fail not to go thyself, for great fruit will come of it. This made me change my mind. Although nature sometimes hangs back in laborious undertakings, yet my resolution to suffer for our great God never flags: and so I pray Him not to regard the feelings which come from my weakness, but to bid me do whatsoever may please Him, for with His help I shall not fail to carry it out.

There was snow at the time: but what made me most cowardly was my poor health; for, with good health, I think I should have made nothing of it. This was what all along weighed me down in making this foundation: the cold was so little, at least I felt it so little, that I really think I felt it no more than I did at Toledo. Well did our Lord fulfil His word in this.

Only a few days later the licence was brought me, with letters from Catalina de Tolosa and her friend Doña Catalina, bidding me make great haste, because she was afraid there might be some mischance: for at that very time the Order of the Vitorinos[1] had come to make a foundation, and the Carmelites of the Mitigation had been there a long time also trying to make a foundation. The monks of St Basil had come since. And this made a great difficulty; and it was a remarkable thing that so many of us should have come all together at the same time: and yet one could only thank God for the great liberality of the place; for the city gave its consent most willingly, although it was not so prosperous as it was wont. I have always heard the city well spoken of for its liberality; but I did not suppose it would come to so much as this. Some were in favour of one Order, some of another. But the Archbishop, considering all the difficulties it might

---

[1] The Minims of St Francis de Paula, who in Spain are commonly called *Frailes Vitorios* or *Frailes de la Victoria*, because their coming into Spain coincided with the taking of Granada.

CARMELITE CONVENT AT GRANADA

cause, hindered it[1], thinking that it might be doing a wrong to the existing Houses which were without endowment, taking away their means of support. Perhaps these themselves had made representations to him, or it may have been suggested by the devil in order to prevent the great good which God works in places to which He brings many monasteries: for He is able to maintain many as easily as few.

This, then, was the reason why those saintly women hurried me on: and, if I had done as I pleased, I should have started immediately, only I had other business to do: for I considered how much more I was bound not to miss an opportunity for myself than those whom I saw to be so zealous.

The words which I had heard apprised me that there would be great opposition. I could not tell from whom, nor wherefore: for Catalina de Tolosa had already written to me that she had secured the house in which she was living for us to take possession of; the city had agreed, and the Archbishop also. I could not imagine from whom the opposition was to come which the demons were going to raise: yet I did not doubt that the words I had heard were from God. But God gives more light to Superiors: for when I wrote to the Father Provincial about going to Burgos on account of what had been said to me, he did not forbid me, but he asked whether I had the Archbishop's licence in writing. I answered that they had written to me from Burgos saying that they had arranged with him; and that the city's licence had been obtained and the Archbishop was satisfied with it: this together with all that he had said about the affair, seemed to leave no doubt.

---

[1] The Canon law prescribes that monasteries which live by alms are not to be founded without consultation with the Mendicants and other Regulars in the place, to see whether the new foundation would be likely to injure their welfare.

The Father Provincial was pleased to go with us to this foundation. This must have been partly because he was disengaged at the time; for he had just finished preaching in Advent, and he had to visit the Convent at Soria, which he had not seen since its foundation, and this was not much out of his way. Partly it was to look after my health on the journey, the weather being so bad, and I so old and infirm, and my life seeming to them of some consequence. And this was certainly God's ordering: for they were such roads, with a great deal of water out, that it was quite necessary that he and his companions should go on ahead to see where we could pass, and to help to get the carts out of bogs, especially on the way from Palencia to Burgos. It was really foolhardy to set out from Palencia when we did. It is true that our Lord had said to me that we could very well go, that I need not fear, for He would be with us. I did not tell this to the Father Provincial at the time; but to me it gave assurance in the great difficulties and dangers which we met with. Especially at a certain crossing near Burgos called The Pontoons, where, on account of the frequent floods, the water was out so high that the passage could not be seen nor guessed at: nothing but water; and on either side of the road it was very deep. Indeed it is very rash to go that way, especially with carts, with which, if they go but a little to one side, it is all over with them; and accordingly one of ours did get into danger. From a wayside inn before we came to this place we took a guide who knew the passage; but it certainly is very dangerous.

Then the inns![1] For we could not go a full day's journey

---

[1] "They at least are in no way altered—this link, at all events, between now and then is not missing. You can see it any day, the wretched wayside venta, dark as a cave inside, its mud floor trodden into a puddle

because of the bad state of the roads. It was a quite common thing for the carts to sink into the mud so that they had to take the mules from one cart to help to drag out another.

The Fathers who went with us had a great deal to go through, for we happened to have got drivers who were young and careless. To be travelling with the Father Provincial was a great comfort, for he took care of everything, and was so even tempered that no difficulties seemed to put him out, but what was really serious he made nothing of, so that it seemed of no account. Not at The Pontoons, however: there he was in considerable fear. For to see ourselves go into a world of water without a way or a boat, even though our Lord had given me an assurance, I was not without fear, what then must my companions have felt!

There were eight of us travelling, two who were to return with me, and five who were to remain at Burgos, four choir Sisters and one lay. I do not think I have said who the Father Provincial was: it was Fray Gerónimo Gracian of the Mother of God, whom I have mentioned elsewhere. I myself was suffering from a very bad sore throat, which I got on the journey to Valladolid, and from continued fever: the pain was so severe that it prevented me from entering as I otherwise should into the amusement of the adventures of the journey. I have the sore throat still; (that is, at the end of June,) not nearly so severe as it was, but still extremely painful. All the nuns enjoyed the journey; because when any danger was past, it was a pleasure to talk over it. It is a great thing to

by the passage in and out of men and beasts. A little straw or dried dung, perhaps, if a little better-to-do, some dried vine-shoots, burn in the midst of the floor, the smoke going out through a hole in the roof. The misery of the roads and weather nothing to the intolerable misery, fleas, and dirt within." Cunninghame Graham, *Santa Teresa*, vol. ii. p. 349.

suffer for obedience' sake when anyone, like those nuns, lives under it continually.

In spite of this bad road we arrived at Burgos, passing through a great deal of water which was out near the town. The Father would have us first go to visit the Holy Crucifix[1], to commend our undertaking to Him, and to wait for nightfall; for it was early. It was a Thursday, January 26th, the day after the Conversion of St Paul, when we arrived. We came determined to make the foundation immediately, and I took with me several letters from Canon Salinas, of whom I have spoken in my account of the foundation at Palencia— and this foundation cost him no less trouble—and from influential people, earnestly requesting their relations and other friends to help on our undertaking. This they did; for at once, next day, they came to see me, and came as delegates from the City Council, saying that they did not repent of what they had said, but were glad that I had come, and I must see what they could help me in. If we had had any fears, it was about the city's mind, so we thought all was now made smooth: and indeed we had intended before anyone else could know of our coming (but because of the floods no one could well get to the house of the good Catalina de Tolosa) to inform the Archbishop, so that the first mass might be said without delay, as is my practice almost everywhere; but because of this it was left undone. We rested that night in great comfort, by the kindness of that saintly woman. But it brought me some suffering: for a great fire was made for us to dry our things; and although it was in a chimney, it did me so much harm that next day I could not raise my head, so that I had to talk lying down to those

[1] The celebrated *Christ of Burgos*, which was at that time in the Convent of St Augustine.

who came to see me. I spoke through a grated window, over
which we stretched a curtain. As it was a day when I was
absolutely obliged to transact business, it was very uncomfortable for me.

Early next morning the Father Provincial went to the
Most Illustrious to ask his blessing; for we thought that was
all there was to be done. He found him perturbed and
angry at my having come without his licence, as if he had
never told me to come nor had anything to do with the
matter. So he spoke to the Father Provincial very angrily
about me. He admitted indeed that he had bid me come,
but said that he only meant me to come alone to make
arrangements; but to come with so many nuns, God deliver
us from the annoyance it gave him! It was of no use telling
him that the matter was already arranged with the city, as he
had required; that there was nothing left to be done but make
the foundation; nor that, when I had asked the Bishop of
Palencia whether it would be right to come without first
informing his Lordship, he had said there was no need, as he
had already said he wished it. It had taken place thus,
because God willed that the house should be founded: and so
the Archbishop himself has since said; because if we had
plainly told him we were coming, he would have forbidden it.
Thereupon he dismissed the Father Provincial, saying that
unless we had an endowment and a house of our own he would
on no account give the licence, and we might as well go back.
Pretty roads indeed, and lovely weather for it!

O my Lord, when anyone has done Thee some service,
how certain it is to be at once repaid with a heavy cross!
And what a precious reward it is to those who truly love
Thee, if at once it is given us to realise its value! But at
that time we did not welcome our gain, because it seemed to

make everything impossible; for the Archbishop said besides
that the endowment and purchase-money were not to be
drawn from any dowry the nuns might bring us. Then, as
such a thing was not to be thought of in these present days,
there was clearly nothing to be done. I however did not
think so: because I remained assured that all was for the best,
and only devices of the devil to hinder us, but that God would
make His work succeed.

Upon this the Provincial came away in very good spirits,
and not discomposed. God so ordained it, causing him not
to be angry with me for not having obtained the licence in
writing, as he had asked.

There had been with me some of the friends to whom, as
I have said, Canon Salinas had written. They and his
relations came at once, and they resolved that the Archbishop's leave should be asked to have mass said in our house,
so that we need not go through the streets, for they were deep
in mud, and it was not fitting for Barefoot nuns to go. In our
house, too, there was a suitable room, which had been the
chapel of the Company of Jesus when first they came to
Burgos, where they had been more than ten years; and this
being the case, we thought there was nothing against our
taking possession there until we had a house of our own.
Never could the Archbishop be prevailed upon to let us hear
mass there, although two Canons went to beg it of him. All
that we obtained from him was that, when we had got the endowment, we might make the foundation there until we had
bought a house; and for the purchase of the house we were
to give sureties, and that we were not to move from where we
were.

The sureties we found at once: for Canon Salinas' friends
volunteered that; and Catalina de Tolosa to give the

endowment. In the discussion of ways and means, more than three weeks must have gone by, and there were we not hearing mass except very early on festivals, and I with a fever and very unwell. However, Catalina de Tolosa took such care of us that I was in great comfort; and she gave all of us our meals during that month, in an apartment which we had to ourselves, with as good a will as if she had been the mother of every one of us. The Father Provincial and his companions stayed in the house of a college friend of his, Doctor Manso, who was a Canon preacher of the Cathedral. It was a great annoyance to him to be detained there so long, yet he did not see how he could leave us.

Well, when the sureties and the endowment had been arranged for, the Archbishop told us to put it into the hands of his Vicar-general, that it might be settled at once. The devil must have got at him: for when all had been thoroughly gone into, and we thought there could be no further cause of delay, having spent about a month in getting the Archbishop to be satisfied with what we were doing, the Vicar-general sent me a memorandum saying that the licence would not be given until we had a house of our own; that the Archbishop did not like us to make the foundation in the house we were in, because it was damp and in a noisy street; and all sorts of rigmaroles about the securities of the property and other such things, just as if the negotiations were only just beginning: there was to be no more discussion; and the house must be to the satisfaction of the Archbishop.

Strongly roused was the Father Provincial's feeling when he heard this, and so with us all : for everyone knows that it must be a long business to buy a place for a convent; and it distressed him to see us going out to hear mass. For, though the church was not far off, and we heard mass in a chapel where nobody could see us, yet to His Reverence and to us the turn things had taken was a great distress.

Indeed at that time, I think, he came to the conclusion that we must go away. I could not bear to do this, when I remembered what our Lord had said to me, that I was to do my best to make this foundation for His sake; and I was so confident that it would be accomplished that these things hardly distressed me, only I was grieved for the distress of the Father Provincial, and very sorry that he had come with us, not knowing how much his friends would help us, as I shall soon relate. While I was in this trouble (and my companions also were in great trouble; but I did not mind theirs, but only the Provincial's) our Lord, without my being in prayer, said to me these words, Now, Theresa, stand firm. Upon this, I more earnestly pressed the Father Provincial to go away and leave us: (and His Majesty must have brought this home to him) for it was already near Lent, when he was bound to go and preach.

He and his friends arranged that we should be given certain rooms in the Hospital of the Conception; for the Blessed Sacrament was there, and daily mass: and with this arrangement he was fairly satisfied. However, there was not a little to be gone through in getting this: for a widow in the town had hired one of the best apartments; and although she was not going into it until the half-year, she not only refused to lend it to us, but also was angry because we were given some attic rooms, one of which opened into her quarters. She was not satisfied with locking it from outside, but also had bars put across on the inside. Besides this, the Confraternity imagined that we were going to appropriate the hospital: an absurdity; but God would have us merit more thereby. They made the Father Provincial and me promise before a notary

that when we were given notice to quit, we would do so
immediately. This I thought the greatest difficulty, because
I was afraid of the widow, who was rich and had relations
there; lest whenever the fancy took her, she would make us
go. The Father Provincial, however, being wiser than I,
would have us do whatever they wished, to get in quickly.
They only gave us two rooms and a kitchen. But the
superintendent of the hospital, Hernando de Matanza, was a
great servant of God; and he gave us two more for a parlour,
and was most kind to us, as indeed he is to everyone, and he
does a great deal for the poor. So also was Francisco de
Cuevas, who has a great deal to do with the hospital, and is
postmaster of Burgos: he always has shewed us kindness at
every opportunity.

I am naming our benefactors in these beginnings, because
our nuns present and to come ought to remember them in
their prayers. This they owe still more to founders. And,
although I never meant Catalina de Tolosa to be one, nor did
it enter my head; yet her good life obtained this from our
Lord, Who so ordered matters that she is undeniably our
foundress. For, let alone paying for the house, which we
could not have done, no words can say what the shifts of the
Archbishop cost her. For it was a terrible distress to her to
think that the foundation might not be made. And she was
never weary of doing us good. The hospital was a long way
from her house, but almost every day she came to see us most
willingly, and sent us all we needed. And because of this
people kept continually saying disagreeable things to her,
enough to make her give it all up, if she had not been the
courageous woman she is. It was a sore grief to me to see all
that she went through; for, although she mostly concealed it,
she could not always hide it, especially when they appealed to

her conscience; for she had so delicate a conscience that, amidst all the great provocations she received from certain people, I never heard from her a word which could offend God. They told her that she was on the way to hell, for how could she, when she had children of her own, act as she was doing? All that she did was with the approval of learned men: for, even if she had wished it, I would not for anything in the world have consented to her doing what she ought not, not for a thousand convents, much less one. But, as the plan we were discussing was kept secret, I am not surprised that people's imagination was the more active. She answered with a prudence which she possesses abundantly, and bore it so well that it shewed God was teaching her the art of pleasing some and putting up with others, and was giving her courage to bear it all. How much more courage for great things have the servants of God than the highborn people who are not His servants!—Not but that Catalina herself was of the purest descent; for she is very much of a hidalgo[1].

Well, to return to what I was saying, when the Father Provincial had found us a place where we could hear mass and be enclosed, he took heart, and went off to Valladolid, where he had to preach, although very unhappy at not seeing in the Archbishop any sign from which we might hope he would give the licence. And though I always maintained he would, he could not believe it, and indeed he had great reasons which I need not tell for thinking as he did: and if he had little hope, his friends had less, and made him still more disheartened. It was a real relief to me to see him gone, because, as I have said, my greatest trouble was his.

He left instructions to get a house to have for our own; a very difficult matter, for up to that time we had not found one

[1] [*Hijadalgo* : daughter of a somebody; lit. *daughter of something.* Tr.]

which could be bought. Our friends, especially the Father Provincial's, now felt themselves more responsible for our affairs; and they all agreed not to say a word to the Archbishop until we had got a house. The Archbishop always said that he desired the foundation more than anyone; and I believe it: for he is such a good Christian that he would not say it if it were not true. His conduct did not shew it; for he imposed conditions which, to all appearance, we could not possibly fulfil: this was the devil's device to prevent the foundation. But, O Lord, how well is it shewn that Thou art mighty! For the very means which he devised to stop it, Thou didst adopt for making it better. Blessed be Thou for ever!

From the Eve of St Matthias, when we went into the hospital, until the Eve of St Joseph, we kept inquiring about this and that house. They all had so many drawbacks that none which was for sale would do for us to buy. I had been told of one belonging to a gentleman which had been for some time for sale: and though so many Orders had been looking for houses, it pleased God that none of them liked it—at which they all are now astonished, and some indeed greatly regret it. One of the two people had mentioned it to me; but so many people had described it as bad that I had quite put it out of my thoughts as unsuitable.

One day when the licentiate Aguiar, one of our Father's friends, was with me, and was telling me about some houses he had seen,—for he was making a careful search for us—and saying there was not one suitable in all the place,—nor did it seem possible to find one, from what they told me—I remembered this one which, as I have said, we had given up thinking of; and it occurred to me that, even if it was as bad as they said, it might serve as a refuge in our need, and we might afterwards sell it; so I asked the licentiate Aguiar if he would do me the kindness of looking at it. He thought this not a bad plan. He had not seen the house; and he chose to go at once, although it was a rough stormy day.

There was a tenant in it who was unwilling that it should be sold and would not shew it him; but he was much pleased with the site and what could be seen of the house, and so we resolved to see about buying it. The gentleman who owned it was not at Burgos, but he had given authority to sell it to an ecclesiastic, a servant of God, into whose heart God put the desire to sell it us, and to deal quite fairly with us. It was agreed that I should go to see it. I was so extremely pleased with it that if they had asked twice as much as what we understood they did, I should have considered it cheap: and that is not saying much, for, two years before, that sum had been offered to the owner, and he would not sell. Immediately on the next day the ecclesiastic came, and the licentiate, who, when he saw what the ecclesiastic was satisfied with, would have wished to conclude the bargain at once. I had told some friends about it, and they had said that, if I gave that, I should be giving five hundred ducats too much. I told him this; but he thought the house was cheap even if I gave as much as was asked. So did I, and that I need not delay, because the house seemed to be almost given away: yet as the money belonged to the Order, I felt some scruple. This meeting took place on the Eve of the glorious St Joseph, before mass: I said we would meet again after mass and settle it. The licentiate is a man of very clear understanding, and he saw plainly that if the thing got abroad, we should find we had to pay much more or not get the house. So he pushed the matter on, and made the ecclesiastic promise to come back after mass.

We nuns went to commend the matter to God; and He said to me, Art thou holding back for money? giving me to understand that it was the right house for us. The Sisters had often besought St Joseph that they might have a house by his Day; and, although they had no idea it could be done so quickly, their desire was fulfilled. Everyone urged me to conclude the bargain: and so it was done; for the licentiate met a notary at the door, which seemed providential, and came in with him and said we must settle it, and brought in a witness; and having locked the door of the room, that nobody might know—for that was what he was afraid of—the purchase was effected in all legal security, on the Eve of St Joseph, as I have said, through the energy and intelligence of this kind friend.

Nobody thought it would be sold so cheap: and so when the news began to get abroad, purchasers began to come forward saying that the ecclesiastic who made the bargain had sold it below its value, and that the sale must be set aside because it was a great fraud. The good ecclesiastic had much to bear. It was at once reported to the owners of the house; who were, as I said, a gentleman of considerable position and his wife. But they were so delighted at their house being made into a convent that they gave their approval—though indeed they had no choice. Immediately on the day after, the deeds were executed, and the third part of the price was paid, exactly as the ecclesiastic asked: for in some points of the contract they pressed us unduly, but for his sake we accepted it all.

It may seem to be going out of my way to spend so much time in narrating the purchase of a house: but really the thing seemed nothing less than a miracle to those who considered it carefully: both the low price, and also that so many members

of Religious Orders who had seen it had been blinded so that
they did not take it. Those who afterwards saw it were
amazed, as if it had not been all the time in Burgos, and
blamed them and called them foolish. There was a convent of
nuns engaged in seeking a house, and two more: one which
had only lately been founded, and one which had come into
the city from outside because their house had been burned
down. And there was another wealthy person seeking to
found a monastery, who had seen this house a little before,
and had set it on one side. All these were now bitterly
repenting it. The talk in the city was such that we saw
clearly how wise the good licentiate had been in keeping it
secret and hastening it on: for we may truly say that, under
God, it was he who gave us the house. A good head for
business is worth much. His is first rate; and God gave him
the good will: and so the work was accomplished by means of
him.

He spent over a month in helping us and making plans
for fitting up the house conveniently and cheaply. It seemed
indeed that our Lord must have reserved this house for
Himself; for it all seemed almost to have been made on
purpose for us. Indeed, directly I saw it, all just as if it had
been made for us, it seemed like a dream that it should be
done so quickly. Well did our Lord repay us for what we had
been through, by bringing us into a paradise—for with its
garden, its views, and its water it seems no less. May He be
blessed for ever! Amen.

The Archbishop heard of it immediately, and was delighted
that all had turned out so well, and put it down to his own
obstinacy—and quite rightly. I wrote to him that it gave me
great pleasure to hear that it was to his satisfaction, and
I would make haste in fitting up the house, so that I might at

last gain his gracious permission. At the same time that I thus wrote, I made haste to get into the house; because I was warned that otherwise we should be detained where we were until all sorts of papers were signed. And so, although the tenant was still there, and it took a little time to get him out, we went into a part of it. I was told at once that the Archbishop was very indignant at this. I appeased him as best I might: and being a good man, even if he is angry, it soon passes off. He was angry too, when he heard that we had got gratings and a turn; for he thought it meant that I meant to found, whether or no. I wrote to him saying I did not, but that in a house of enclosed nuns there were always these things: and that I had not even ventured to put up a cross, lest it might have that appearance: which was the truth. With all the goodwill which he shewed, there was no making him willing to grant the licence.

He came to see the house, and was 'much pleased with it, and was very gracious to us, not so gracious, however, as to give us the licence. But he did give us more hope, saying there had to be some papers or other signed between us and Catalina de Tolosa. There were great fears that he would not give it at all: but Doctor Manso, the other friend of the Father Provincial whom I have mentioned, being very intimate with the Archbishop, watched for opportunities of reminding him and persuading him; for it grieved him to see us living as we were living. For even in this house, although there was a chapel which had never been used by the owners for anything but saying mass, the Archbishop would not let us have mass said in the house; on festivals and Sundays we had to go out to hear it at a church which luckily was close at hand. Yet it was about a month, more or less, from the time when we went to the house, to the time when the foundation was made. All the learned men said that there was no valid obstacle. The Archbishop is very learned, and knew this too: so there seems to have been no reason for it but that our Lord wished us to suffer. I, however, did not mind so much; but there was one nun who shook with misery when she found herself in the street[1].

We went through not a little in drawing up the deeds; for at one time they were satisfied with sureties, and at another they required the money; and many other such vexatiousnesses. This was not so much the fault of the Archbishop as of a Vicar-general, who fought hard against us; so that if God had not opportunely sent him on a journey, so that his office devolved on another, I think we should never have got through. Oh, what Catalina de Tolosa suffered no words can say! She bore it all with marvellous patience, and never wearied of providing for us. She gave us all the furniture we required for setting up house, beds and many other things, for she had plenty in her house; and even if she went without something in her own house, there was no question of allowing us to go without. Some other women who have founded convents for us have given us much more money; but there is not one to whom it has cost a tenth part of the trouble she had: and if she had had no children, she would have given us all she had to give. But she so earnestly desired to see the thing accomplished that she thought nothing of all she did.

I, when I saw such long delays, wrote to the Bishop of

[1] Not finding any better means of worrying St Theresa, he stipulated that she must get the Nuncio's leave before she had mass said in the Chapel. The Jesuits had had the Blessed Sacrament reserved for fourteen years in the house which St Theresa first occupied ; and yet he would not allow her to have mass said there.

Palencia, begging him to write again to the Archbishop: for
he was much put out with him; because he felt all that the
Archbishop did against us, as though done to himself. (And
what astonished us was that the Archbishop never seemed to
think he was doing us the least injury.) I begged him to
write again asking him to give his consent, now that we had
a house and what he required was done. He sent me, open,
such a letter to the Archbishop that if I had forwarded it, all
would have been lost for us. So Doctor Manso, who was my
confessor and adviser, would not let it go. For, although it
was exceedingly courteous, it conveyed certain truths which,
considering the Archbishop's temper, were enough to offend
him; and so indeed he had been already by certain messages
the Bishop had sent him. And they were great friends.
And to me he said that, as through the death of our Lord
those had been made friends who were not so before, so now
through me these two had been made enemies. I answered
that by this he might see what sort of a person I was. I had,
as I thought, taken special care that they should not fall out.
I again entreated the Bishop, pleading the best arguments I
could, that he would write another very friendly letter, setting
before the Archbishop the service he would be doing to God.
He did what I asked, which was no light matter. But more
because he saw that it would be to God's service, and it was
doing me a kindness—for he has been uniformly kind to me.
Finally, he did violence to himself, and he wrote to me saying
that all he had done for the Order was nothing to compare
with this letter. In short, the letter was such that, together
with Doctor Manso's insistence, it made the Archbishop give
the licence, and he sent it by the good Hernando de Matanza,
who came with no little rejoicing. That day the Sisters had
been much sadder than ever, and there had been no consoling

the good Catalina de Tolosa, and I myself, who had never
been hopeless, had been so the night before. It seemed that
our Lord was pleased to give us greater affliction just when He
was going to send us joy. Blessed be His Name for ever and
praised, world without end! Amen.

The Archbishop gave leave to Doctor Manso to say mass
next day, and to reserve the Blessed Sacrament. He said the
first mass, and the High Mass was sung by the Father Prior
of St Paul's, of the Order of St Dominic, to which, and to the
Company of Jesus, our Order has always been greatly in-
debted. He, the Father Prior, sang it, with great magnificence
of musicians, who came of their own accord. All our friends
were rejoicing, and so was almost the whole city, for everyone
pitied our plight: and they so strongly condemned the
Archbishop's conduct that sometimes I minded what I
heard said of him more than what I myself was suffering.
The joy of the good Catalina de Tolosa and of the Sisters was
so great as to move my devotion, and I said to God, "O Lord,
what other aim have these Thy handmaidens save that of
serving Thee and being enclosed for Thy sake in a cloister
whence they are never more to go out!"

No one who has not experienced it could believe the
fulness of satisfaction we feel in these foundations when at
length we find ourselves enclosed where no secular person may
enter; for however dearly we may love them, it does not
prevent us from being delighted to find ourselves alone. It
seems to me like as when a number of fishes are taken out of
the river in a net, which cannot live unless they are put back
into the water. So it is with souls which are used to living
within the flowing waters of their Spouse: when they are
drawn out thence and find themselves in the net of
worldly affairs, they really do cease to live until they find

themselves back again. This I see always in all these Sisters; this I know by experience: that nuns who find in themselves any desire to go out among seculars, or to have much converse with them, may well fear that they have not found that living water of which our Lord spoke to the woman of Samaria; and that the Spouse has hidden Himself from them, seeing that they are not content to dwell with Him. I fear this arises from two causes: either that they have taken upon themselves this estate not for His sake alone; or that since they took it, they have not recognised the greatness of the favour which God has done them in choosing them for Himself, and freeing them from subjection to a human being, who often wears out their life, and pray God he may not destroy their soul too! O Thou, Very Man and Very God, Who art my Spouse, is this a favour which can be lightly esteemed! Let us praise Him, my daughters, for having granted it to us; and let us never be weary of praising so great a King and Lord, Who, for a light endurance of hardship surrounded with a thousand joys and lasting but a day, has prepared for us a kingdom without end. Be He blessed for ever! Amen. Amen.

Some time after the house was founded, the Father Provincial and I came to think that in the endowment which Catalina de Tolosa had given the house there were certain drawbacks; for there might be some law-suit, and some annoyance might come upon her: and we felt we would rather trust to God than let there remain any chance of her being in any way troubled. So for this and for certain other reasons, all we nuns, with the Father Provincial's sanction, renounced before a notary the property which she had given us, and returned her all the papers. This was done with great secrecy, that the Archbishop might not hear of it; for he would have thought it an injury done him: whereas the injury really is to the house. For when it is known that a house is dependent on alms there is no fear, for everyone helps it: but there is an apparent risk when a house is thought to be endowed; and it may be left for a time without anything to eat.

So Catalina de Tolosa took means to ensure our support after her death. Two daughters of hers who were to be professed that year in our Convent at Palencia, had signed a deed to renounce their property in her favour when they should be professed. She caused them to revoke this, and to renounce it in favour of the Convent at Burgos. And another daughter, who desired to take the habit here[1], left to this house what she inherited from both father and mother. This came to as much as the endowment; the only drawback being that the convent does not come into possession at once. But I have always held that the Sisters will never be in want; because our Lord, Who moves people to give alms to the other convents which live by alms, will stir up people to do so here, or give other means of maintenance.

However, as in no other house had such an arrangement been made, I sometimes besought Him that, as the foundation had been His will, so He would order affairs to the relief of its necessities; and I did not like to go away until I saw whether anyone would enter it as a nun[2]. But one day when I was thinking about this after my Communion, our Lord said to me, Why dost thou doubt? This is already done with; thou mayest safely depart: giving me to understand that their needs would be supplied. For it was said in such a way that I never troubled myself again any more than if I had been

---

[1] [At Burgos. Tr.]   [2] [*i.e.*, bringing a dowry. Tr.]

leaving them amply endowed: but I at once arranged to be going; for I felt I was no longer doing anything here, except enjoying myself in this house which I so much like; while elsewhere, although with more difficulty, I might be doing more good.

The Archbishop and the Bishop of Palencia remained very good friends; for the Archbishop soon shewed himself very gracious towards us, and gave the habit to Catalina de Tolosa's daughter, and to another nun who presently entered the convent. And up to the present time certain people have not failed to take care of us, nor will our Lord let His brides suffer, if they serve Him as they are in duty bound. May His Majesty, of His great mercy and goodness, grant them the grace to do this!

JESUS.

I have thought it good to set down here how it is that the nuns of St Joseph's at Avila, our first convent, whose foundation is narrated elsewhere and not in this book, having been founded under the Bishop's jurisdiction, afterwards passed under that of the Order.

When it was founded, the Bishop was Don Alvaro de Mendoza, who is now Bishop of Palencia. All the time he was at Avila, the nuns were very well cared for. And when the convent was placed under his jurisdiction, I understood from our Lord that it was fitting so to place it. And so it has since proved: because in all the disagreements within the Order, we received great help from him; and on many other occasions too this was quite clear. And he never allowed Visitations of the convent to be made by a secular priest;

nor did the nuns do anything beyond what I asked of him. Thus it went on for seventeen years more or less, so far as I remember, nor did I meditate any change of jurisdiction.

At the end of this time, the Bishopric of Palencia was given to the Bishop of Avila. At that time I was staying at the convent at Toledo: and our Lord said to me that it would be a good thing that the nuns of St Joseph's should come under the jurisdiction of the Order; and that I must bring this to pass, because otherwise the house would fall into laxity. As I had formerly understood that it was better for it to be under the Bishop, there seemed to be a contradiction, and I did not know what to do. I told my confessor, the present Bishop of Osma, a most learned man. He said that this did not matter; but that one thing must have been needful in the past, and another thing now. He saw that it would be better for that convent to be united with the others, and not to stand alone. And what he said has already been very clearly shewn to be true, in many ways.

He made me go to Avila to arrange for it. I found the Bishop of a very different opinion, and he would by no means agree to it. But, when I told him certain reasons why harm might come to the nuns, he, having a great affection for them, thought it over carefully: and having a very sound judgement, and God helping him, he thought out other reasons more weighty than what I had given him, and resolved to do it. Although some secular priests went to try to dissuade him, they did not prevail.

The votes of the nuns were necessary for this change: some very much disliked it; but, as they loved me well, they yielded to my reasonings: to this, especially; that now the Bishop to whom the Order owed so much, and whom I loved, was gone, they would not again have me with them otherwise. This came home to them forcibly. Thus was concluded a matter so important that, as they and everyone else now see, the house would have gone to ruin if it had not been carried out. Oh, blessed be our Lord Who with so great solicitude considers all that concerns His handmaidens! Blessed be He for evermore! Amen.

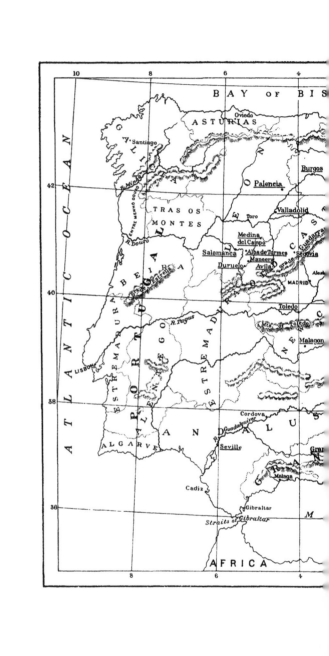

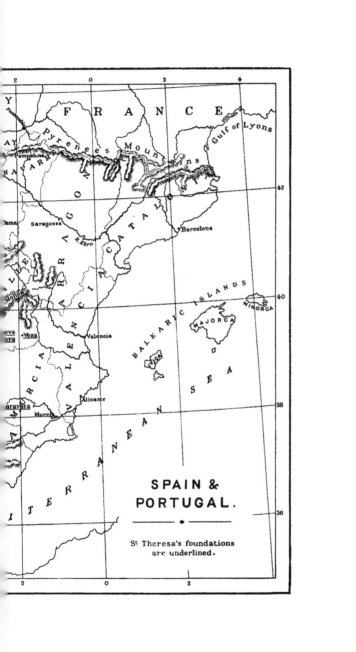

SPAIN &
PORTUGAL.

St Theresa's foundations
are underlined.

INDEX

www.ingramcontent.com/pod-product-compliance
Ingram Content Group UK Ltd.
Pitfield, Milton Keynes, MK11 3LW, UK
UKHW042142280225
455719UK00001B/39

9 781107 655454